Happy Gardenii

Peter Pratt

June 1st, 2018

Veterans Gardening Guide

Promoting Allergy-Friendly Planting

GARDENING TIPS GEARED FOR THE NOVICE TO EXPERIENCED GARDENER

Tellwell Talent
www.tellwell.ca

ISBN
978-1-77370-342-8 (Paperback)
978-1-77370-344-2 (eBook)

Veterans Gardening Guide

Promoting Allergy-Friendly Planting

GARDENING TIPS GEARED FOR THE NOVICE TO EXPERIENCED GARDENER

PETER PRAKKE

I shall pass through this world but once. Any good, therefore, that I can do or any kindness that I can show to any human being, let me do it now. Let me not defer or neglect it, for I shall not pass this way again.

Stephen Grellet, Quaker missionary

1773 — 1855

TABLE OF CONTENTS

FOREWORD

Very few authors in the world of gardening books, if any, were in part inspired by memories of the Great Britain and Canadian Armies liberating their countries. Horticulturist Peter Prakke was born and educated in the village of Eibergen, in the eastern part of Holland, and subsequently under German occupation in World War II. During the battle to liberate the village, two British soldiers died, and their graves are in the village cemetery.

With the passing of time, Peter has never forgotten the sacrifice made by the soldiers and has created this book as a tribute to them and all veterans representing their country during peacekeeping, war and conflicts. Peter's commitment to honouring the brave men and women is also evident in him developing the Bravery Park™ initiative.

This definitive guide to indoor and outdoor gardening enables the reader to create his or her safe and healthy island of beauty in whatever space that is available to them. It is a beautiful book full of his experience and knowledge of a lifetime in all aspects of horticulture.

Experienced gardeners, or budding gardeners new to the world of plants, will discover a new world in this book for those with allergies, asthma and Chronic Obstructive Pulmonary Disease (COPD). Yes, it is all about liberation. No one should be forgotten. The sacrifices made by the veterans are so that all, especially the most vulnerable, can enjoy the beautiful world around us.

I highly recommend this book with full confidence that everyone who uses the information will inspire others to do the same. I know that God says we must account for our deeds and for what we've done with the allotment he's given us. There you have it; get reading and get gardening.

Nigel Clarke
Founder of Queux Plant Centre, Guernsey, UK

INTRODUCTION

The *Veterans Gardening Guide* was written to honour our brave and courageous veterans who are at home, in the hospital, in a revalidation centre or special veterans' care centre. These men and women have earned our respect for their sacrifice and should be taken care of in a manner they deserve.

Nature inspires and is a "healer" to all of us. Caring for a garden plot, container garden or a few houseplants can give us a peaceful moment from a stressful day. Why? Plants have a natural cycle that is comforting. Plants are stimulating because they change through growth and blossoming periods. Plants can alter the environment that surrounds us by cleaning the air.

I invite and encourage family, friends, and care facility staff to assist in the horticultural experience. I share my experiences to provide practical gardening information and benefits to work with indoor or outdoor plants.

The *Veterans Gardening Guide* promotes landscapes of allergy-friendly plantings to ease the discomfort of individuals with allergies, asthma and other respiratory challenges.

Special thanks to Janice Johnston, my collaborator and co-writer of this project, in the editing, researching, and writing of this guide. For years she has help me with many of my gardening articles and editorials. Janice shares in my love of gardening, and that makes her my special kindred spirit.

Without the encouragement of my wife, Catharina; son, Jan; daughter-in-law, Joyce; and daughter, Carina, I would be completely lost in undertaking this project. Their unwavering support has been a blessing as I navigate the exciting world of authorship.

My dear friend and colleague, Thomas Ogren, author of the book *The Allergy-Fighting Garden*, has supplied me with a tremendous amount of information about allergy-friendly gardening, and has encouraged me to continue spreading the message.

Thanks to my long-time friend J. Paul Lamarche for providing gardening information.

Thanks to Kelly Davy, Allan Dennis and Peter Wynnyczuk for their time to review this guide and provide valuable comments.

This project has been a labour of love, and I hope that you are inspired to get your hands dirty. One who gardens honours their ancestors.

Peter Prakke

ONE
ALLERGIES AND ASTHMA INFORMATION

Plant Smart and Stay Healthy

A runny or stuffy nose, red eyes, sneezing or wheezing caused by allergies are a fact of life for millions of allergy sufferers. Individuals with asthma are also susceptible to breathing problems caused by plants. What we plant in the garden has a direct effect on our health and the health of those near us.

Male and female plants of separate-sexed species behave differently.

Female plants produce fruit and seeds, and male plants produce pollen.

Male plants don't produce pollen year-round.

This last statement may be true, but we are seeing the allergy season getting longer based on an extended growing season.

Many towns, cities and property owners don't want the fruit to dirty their sidewalks. They resort to planting pollen-producing male cultivars, such as maple or willow trees.

A pollen-producing male tree in your yard will easily expose you to ten times more pollen than a similar tree growing down the neighbourhood block. This can be compared to second-hand smoke.

It's possible to inhale a trace of smoke from a person smoking a block away from you, but it's hardly the same as someone smoking right next to you. It's the same with plants. If your garden is full of allergenic plants, then you will have a higher exposure. Remember, the greater the exposure to pollen, the greater the incidence of pollen-triggered allergy and asthma.

If we continue planting male clonal, native and non-native, pollen-producing shrubs and trees, the rates of allergies and asthma will continue to rise. The fact is that 8.3% of all Canadians are asthmatic. Of all school-aged children, 8% have asthma. Each year, emergency departments are seeing a stark increase in the number of children admitted during the pollen season. Pollen levels in the city and urban areas are high and increasing due to global warming and the interaction with air pollution. The perfect solution is to limit the number of male plantings and focus our attention on female plants that trap pollen, clean the air of particles and shed no pollen.

According to Thomas Ogren, horticulturist, pollen isn't always that easy to see, nor is it only bright yellow. It can be white, grey, green, brown, red and even purple.

Unfortunately, even if you diligently plant an "allergy-friendly" garden, many of the wind-borne pollens that might affect you can travel to your yard from other neighbouring gardens, nearby parks or even from afar. At best, you will learn from reading this gardening guide about which plants to avoid in your garden if you are susceptible to allergies or asthma. You will come to know the worst pollen offenders.

Peak pollen times will depend on the plant, the weather and your location.

I am frequently asked by amateur gardeners and gardening professionals if it's possible to plant for allergies and asthma. Yes, and it's quite easy. Let's take a look with ten tips to remember as we plan our gardens:

1. **Avoid planting any male shrubs or trees**. **These are sold as** *fruitless* **or** *seedless* **varieties**, but they are classified as males and produce large amounts of allergenic pollen.

2. **Plant female shrubs and trees**. Although female species may be messier than males, they produce no pollen, and trap or remove pollen and particulates from the air.

3. **Plant disease-resistant varieties.** Disease-resistant plants won't become infected as much, and the air around them will be healthier.

4. **Use only shrubs and trees adapted to your climate zone.** Often native plants are the healthiest choices, but native plants can also cause allergies.

5. **Don't plant too many of the same varieties**. Diversity is good. Use a wide selection of asthma- and allergy-friendly plants.

6. **Attracting birds to your garden is a big plus because they eat many insects**. Insect dander causes allergies, and birds consume an incredible number of aphids, scale, whiteflies and other pests.

7. **Know the exact cultivar name of the shrub or tree before you purchase it**. Plants that are clearly tagged with the correct cultivar and Latin scientific name will help you determine the allergen ranking.

8. **Use pollen-free selections whenever possible. Double chrysanthemums usually have no pollen.** Almost all of the erect tuberous begonias have female flowers, making them pollen-free.

9. **If you must have some high-allergy potential plants in your garden, because "you like them so much," plant downwind and as far away from the house as possible**.

10. **If you have a tree or hedge that has high-allergy potential and you don't want to remove it, consider keeping it sheared so that it will produce fewer flowers.** For example, the boxwood has allergenic flowers, but if given a yearly hard prune, it will rarely bloom.

> **Just a Thought...**
>
> *Take time to smell the roses, as they say, but remember the beauty of the garden may also cause you to reach for a box of tissues.*

Allergy Ranked Plants (OPALS)

OPALS® is an abbreviation of Ogren Plant Allergy Scale, founded by Thomas Ogren and developed based on the following criteria:

What do well-known plants that create allergies have in common?

What do plants that are well-known to NOT cause allergies have in common?

With these two questions, it was possible to build two opposing sets of medical and botanical-allergy information.

There are now well over 130 criteria used to develop OPALS rankings. 1 = low and 10 = high in allergens for plants.

Low-allergy rankings are considered to be 1 through 3 on the allergy scale. Mid-range rankings are 4 through 6, and high rankings are 7 through 10. Plants with rankings of 9 or 10 have an extremely high potential to cause allergic reactions.

OPALS Allergy Ranking	Explanation Note: Each individual ranking will have a different allergy reaction.
1 to 3	Very low potential to cause allergies. For example, the red sunset maple (*Acer rubrum*) is 1 on the OPALS ranking, meaning the least allergenic.
4 to 6	Moderate potential to cause allergies, exacerbated by overuse of the same plant throughout a garden. Most pine trees (*Pinus spp.*) are ranked at 4 to 5 as they will cause some allergies.
7 to 8	High potential to cause allergies; advised to plant as little as possible. The sycamore (*Platanus spp.*) has an OPALS ranking of 8 and can cause quite a bit of allergy problems.
9 to 10	Extremely high potential to cause allergies; should be replaced with less allergenic species. The worst on the OPALS ranking can often cause both hay fever and asthma. They may also trigger skin rashes. 'Autumn Spire,' a male cultivar of the red maples, has far more potential for allergy and is ranked at 9.

OPALS Allergy Index Scale excerpt taken from *The Allergy-Fighting Garden* by author Thomas Leo Ogren with guidelines updated July 2017.

Depending on the plant cultivar and/or species, the OPALS ranking may result in a given range. For example, sunflowers (*Helianthus*) are ranked 1 to 6.

According to Thomas Ogren, **a plant need not necessarily be female to be allergy-free, and a good OPALS ranking is always an indication of low potential to cause allergy or asthma. If you can purchase a plant that has an actual OPALS ranking (1 to 10) tag on it, then that is something you can trust.**

The United States Department of Agriculture and the American Lung Association use the scale to make improved landscaping decisions. Other organizations are sure to follow and endorse the cause.

Pollen dispersal rates have been measured since 1972 by Gilbert Raynor, a New York meteorologist. Many pollen grains travel a far distance, but research often shows that 99% of a tree's pollen is dispersed and sticks within 15 metres (50 feet) of the tree. This means the closer one is to the pollinating shrub or tree, the greater the allergy exposure.

Plants with Potential Risk and Allergy Ranking

The following plants can be found in our business institutions, gardens, homes and parks, and are available for sale in local garden centres/nurseries. They can cause skin irritation and eye sensitivity or be poisonous if ingested. The allergy ranking is based on OPALS for allergy/asthma sufferers.

Common Name (Cultivar)	Botanical/Scientific Name	Skin	Eye	Poisonous If Ingested	OPALS Ranking
Aloe	*Aloe vera*			X	1
Amaryllis	*Amaryllidinae*			X	3
American elder	*Sambucus canadensis*			X	4
Angel wings	*Caladium bicolor*			X	4
Angel's trumpet	*Brugmansia x candida*			X	2 – 4, varies
Arrowhead vine	*Syngonium podophyllum*	X	X	X	2
Autumn crocus	*Colchicum autumnale*			X	3
Belladonna lily	*Amaryllis belladonna*			X	2
Black locust, tree	*Robinia pseudoacacia*			X	5
Calla lily	*Zantedeschia*			X	4
Castor bean plant	*Ricinus communis*			X	10

Common Name (Cultivar)	Botanical/Scientific Name	Skin	Eye	Poisonous If Ingested	OPALS Ranking
Chenille plant	*Acalypha hispida*	X	X		m = 7, f = 1
Chinese evergreen	*Aglaonema araceae*	X	X	X	5
Christmas rose	*Helleborus niger*	X		X	4
Chrysanthemum	*Chrysanthemum*	X			4 – doubles, 6 – singles
Comfrey	*Symphytum spp.*	X			3
Common rue (herb)	*Ruta*	X			4
Coral berry	*Symphoricarpos orbiculatus*			X	3
Daffodil	*Narcissus*	X		X	4
Devil's ivy	*Epipremnum aureum*	X	X	X	2
Dumb cane	*Dieffenbachia*	X	X	X	m = 7, f = 1
English laurel	*Prunus laurocerasus*			X	6
False hellebore	*Veratrum viride*			X	8
Flamingo flower	*Anthurium scherzeranum*	X	X	X	2
Flowering tobacco	*Nicotiana*			X	3
Four o'clock flower	*Mirabilis jalapa*	X		X	3
Foxglove	*Digitalis purpurea*			X	2
Glory lily	*Gloriosa superba*			X	3
Hyacinth	*Hyacinthus orientalis*	X			3
Japanese wisteria	*Wisteria floribunda*			X	4

Common Name (Cultivar)	Botanical/Scientific Name	Skin	Eye	Poisonous If Ingested	OPALS Ranking
Leyland cypress	*Cupressocyparis leylandii*	X			8
Lily of the valley	*Convallaria majalis*			X	4
Lungwort	*Pulmonaria spp.*	X			2
Lupine	*Lupinus perennis*			X	3
Monkshood	*Aconitum napellus*	X		X	4
Morning glory	*Ipomoea purpurea*			X	4
Mountain laurel	*Kalmia latifolia*			X	8
Ornamental pepper	*Capsium annum*	X	X	X	1
Passion flower	*Passiflora caerulea*			X	3
Peace lily	*Spathiphyllum spp.*	X	X	X	2
Peruvian lily	*Alstroemeria*	X			4
Poison ivy	*Toxicodendron radican*	X		X	8 – 10, varies
Primula	*Primula obconica*	X			3 – 6, varies
Privet	*Ligustrum*			X	9
Solomon's seal	*Polygonatum biflorum*			X	2
Split-leaf philodendron	*Monstera deliciosa*	X	X	X	4
Spurge	*Euphorbia spp.*	X	X	X	m = 10, f = 1
St. John's wort	*Hypericum perforatum*			X	5
Star of Bethlehem	*Ornithogalum arabicum*	X		X	3

Common Name (Cultivar)	Botanical/Scientific Name	Skin	Eye	Poisonous If Ingested	OPALS Ranking
Tall larkspur	*Delphinium exaltatum*			X	3
Taro	*Colocasia esculenta*	X	X	X	2
Thornapple	*Datura stramonium*	X		X	2
Tulip	*Tulipa*	X			1 – doubles, 3 – singles
Weeping fig	*Ficus benjamina*	X			2 – 3, varies
Wintergreen	*Gaultheria*			X	m = 5, f = 1
Yew	*Taxus*			X	m = 10, f = 1

Legend:

m = male; f = female plants

Doubles = double-flowering varieties; Singles = single-flowering varieties

The OPALS ranking: 1 represents a female, allergenic-pollen-free plant (an allergy-friendly plant); a rating of 10 represents a predominantly male, allergenic, airborne pollen-intensive plant. Avoid high allergen plants.

Indoor Plants with Potential Risk and Allergy Ranking

The following indoor plants can be found in our classrooms, homes, hospitals, and medical and home care facilities, and are available for sale in local garden centres/nurseries. They can cause skin irritation and eye sensitivity or be poisonous if ingested.

Common Name (Cultivar)	Botanical/ Scientific Name	Allergen	Reaction	OPALS Ranking
Dumb cane	*Dieffenbachia*	Sap/juice	Skin rash	m = 7, f = 1
Fig tree	*Ficus carica*	Chemical allergens	Skin rash	2 – 3, varies
Flannel bush	*Fremontodendron*	Irritant hairs	Itching	6
Poinsettia	*Euphorbia pulcherrima*	Milky sap	Skin rash	9
Pride of Madeira	*Echium fastuosum*	Irritant hairs	Itching	5
Rue	*Ruta*	Sap	Blistering	4
Split-leaf philodendron	*Monstera deliclose*	Sap	Blistering	4

Legend:

m = male; f = female

According to OPALS ranking: 1 = low and 10 = high, very allergenic

Trees with Potential Risk and Allergy Ranking

The following trees can be found in our forests, city landscapes, gardens and parks, and are available for sale in local garden centres/nurseries. They can cause skin irritation and eye sensitivity or be poisonous if ingested. The allergy ranking is based on OPALS for persons with allergies/asthma.

Common Name (Cultivar)	Botanical/Scientific Name	OPALS Ranking
Alder	*Alnus spp.*	9
Beech	*Fagus spp.*	6
Birch	*Betula spp.*	9
Black walnut	*Juglans nigra*	8 – 9, varies
Buckhorn	*Rhamnus*	m = 9, f = 1
Catalpa	*Catalpa spp.*	6
Eastern cottonwood	*Populus deltoides*	m = 8, f = 1
Eastern red cedar	*Juniperus virginiana*	m =10, f = 1
Elm	*Ulmus spp.*	5 – 9, varies
False cypress	*Chamaecyparis spp.*	8
Golden chain tree	*Laburnum anagyroides*	7
Hornbeam (Ironwood)	*Carpinus spp.*	7
Horse chestnut	*Aesculus hippocastanum*	6 – 7, varies
Katsura tree	*Cercidiphyllum japonicum*	m = 6, f = 1
Kentucky coffee tree	*Gymnocladus dioicus*	m = 8, f = 1
Linden (Basswood)	*Tilia spp.*	6
Magnolia, deciduous	*Magnolia spp.*	4 – 6, varies
Maidenhair tree	*Ginkgo biloba*	m = 7, f = 2
Maple	*Acer spp.*	1 – 10, varies

Common Name (Cultivar)	Botanical/Scientific Name	OPALS Ranking
Maple – Silver	*Acer saccharinum*	m = 9, f = 1
Maple – Sugar	*Acer saccharum*	7
Mountain laurel	*Kalmia latifolia*	8
Oak	*Quercus spp.*	8
Poplar	*Populus spp.*	m = 8, f = 1
Privet	*Ligustrum vulgare*	m = 9
Pussy willow	*Salix discolor*	m = 10, f = 1
Red oak (Northern)	*Quercus rubra*	8
Russian olive	*Elaeagnus angustifolia*	9
Smoke tree (shrub or tree)	*Cotinus coggygria*	m = 8, f = 2
Sweet gum tree	*Liquidambar spp.*	6
Sycamore (London plane tree)	*Platanus acerifolia*	8
Thornless honey locust	*Gleditsia triacanthos var. inermis*	m = 7, f = 1
White birch	*Betula papyrifera*	9
White cedar	*Thuja occidentalis*	8
White fringetree	*Chionanthus virginicus*	m = 8, f = 1
White mulberry (Common)	*Morus alba*	m = 10, f = 1

Legend:

m = male; f = female

According to OPALS ranking: 1 = low and 10 = high, very allergenic

Allergy and Toxicity in the Garden

Pay special attention when selecting plants for the garden, especially if you have young children or grand-children. There are plants that are toxic to people and animals. If ingested, they may cause minor or serious illness or death if timely treatment is not received. Depending on the severity, individuals can experience symptoms of respiratory difficulties, burning pain, stomach upset and throat swelling.

The juice, sap or thorns (skin puncture) from some plants may cause a skin rash or irritation. In this case, wash the affected area of the skin with soap and water as soon as possible after contact.

Call the Poison Control Centre or your doctor if any symptoms appear following contact with the plants.

If you are unsure of a plant's toxicity, take a sample to your local garden centre/nursery for identification.

The following chart illustrates the toxicity level of flowers/vines. This is not to be considered an inclusive list.

Common Name (Cultivar)	Botanical/Scientific Name	Toxicity Level	OPALS Ranking
Arum	*Arum*	Toxic (all parts)	4
Aster	*Symphyotrichum spp.*	Toxic (all parts)	2 – doubles, 4 – singles
Baby's breath	*Gypsophila paniculata*	Toxic (all parts)	6
Blanket flower	*Gaillardia spp.*	Toxic (all parts)	6
Bleeding heart	*Dicentra spectabilis*	Toxic (all parts)	4
Bloodroot	*Sanguinaria canadensis*	Toxic (all parts)	3
Bougainvillea	*Bougainvillea spp.*	Toxic (thorns)	1
Bracken fern	*Pteridium aquilinum*	Toxic (leaves)	5
Bugbane (Snakeroot)	*Cimicifuga racemose*	Toxic (all parts)	3
Cactus	*Cactus spp.*	Toxic (thorns and sap)	1
Chinese wisteria	*Wisteria sinensis*	Toxic (all parts)	4
Clematis	*Clematis*	Toxic (all parts)	5
Columbine	*Aquilegia spp.*	Toxic (all parts)	1

Common Name (Cultivar)	Botanical/Scientific Name	Toxicity Level	OPALS Ranking
Corn cockle	*Agrostemma githago*	Toxic (all parts)	4
Creeping buttercup	*Ranunculus repens*	Toxic (all parts)	4
Daylily	*Hemerocallis*	Toxic (all parts; especially toxic to cats)	6
Delphinium	*Delphinium spp.*	Toxic (all parts)	3
Flowering tobacco	*Nicotiana*	Toxic (leaves and flowers)	3
Jasmine	*Trachelospermum jasminoides*	Toxic (all parts)	7
Matrimony vine	*Lycium barbarum*	Toxic (all parts)	5
Meadow rue (Giant)	*Thalictrum rochebruneanum*	Toxic (all parts)	m = 9, f = 1
Poinsettia	*Euphorbia pulcherrima*	Toxic (sap)	m = 10, f = 1
Scotch broom	*Cytisus scoparius*	Toxic (all parts)	5
Sweet box	*Sarcococca*	Toxic (all parts)	5
Windflower (Japanese anemone)	*Anemone x hybrida*	Toxic (all parts)	3

Legend:

m = male; f = female

Doubles = double-flowering varieties; Singles = single-flowering varieties

According to OPALS ranking: 1 = low and 10 = high, very allergenic

The following chart illustrates the toxicity level of shrubs and trees. This is not to be considered an inclusive list.

Common Name (Cultivar)	Botanical/Scientific Name	Toxicity Level	OPALS Ranking
American elder, shrub	*Sambucus canadensis*	Low toxicity	4
Amur privet, shrub	*Ligustrum amurense*	Highly toxic	9
Black elderberry, shrub	*Sambucus nigra*	Poisonous (unripe fruit and leaves)	5
Bog rosemary, shrub	*Andromeda spp.*	Highly toxic	2
Boxwood, shrub	*Buxus spp.*	Highly poisonous (all parts, but especially the leaves)	7
Buckthorn, shrub	*Rhamnus spp.*	Low toxicity	m = 9, f = 1
Buffalo berry, shrub	*Shepherdia canadensis*	Non-toxic	m = 6, f = 1
Burning bush, shrub	*Euonymus alata*	Poisonous (all parts)	1 – 7, varies
Canadian yew, shrub	*Taxus canadensis*	Highly toxic	m = 10, f = 1
Chokecherry, shrub	*Prunus virginiana*	Toxic	5
Inkberry holly, shrub	*Ilex glabra*	Poisonous (fruit)	m = 7, f = 1
Mountain holly, shrub	*Ilex mucronata*	Poisonous (fruit)	m = 7, f = 1
Mountain laurel, shrub	*Kalmia latifolia*	Highly toxic	8
Pussy willow	*Salix discolor*	Toxic	10
Red mulberry, shrub	*Morus rubra*	Low toxicity	m = 8, f = 1
Rhododendron, shrub	*Rhododendron spp.*	Highly toxic	4
Scarlet leucothoe, shrub	*Leucothoe spp.*	Extremely poisonous	4
Somerset daphne, shrub	*Daphne x burkwoodii*	Highly toxic	5
Snowberry, shrub	*Symphoricarpos albus*	Highly toxic	3
Winterberry, shrub	*Ilex verticillata*	Poisonous (fruit)	m = 7, f = 1

Common Name (Cultivar)	Botanical/Scientific Name	Toxicity Level	OPALS Ranking
American beech, tree	*Fagus grandifolia*	Bark and leaves poisonous	6
Black locust, tree	*Robinia pseudoacacia*	Poisonous (all parts)	5
Black walnut, tree	*Juglans nigra*	Fatal (nuts)	8 – 9, varies
Burr oak, tree	*Quercus macrocarpa*	Low toxicity	8
Butternut, tree	*Juglans cinerea*	Fatal (nuts)	8 – 9, varies
Fragrant sumac, tree	*Rhus aromatic*	Poisonous	m = 10, f = 1
Golden chain tree	*Laburnum anagyroides*	Highly toxic	7
Horse chestnut, tree	*Aesculus hippocastanum*	Poisonous (seeds)	6 – 7, varies
Kentucky coffee, tree	*Gymnocladus diocius*	Poisonous (seeds – female)	m = 8, f = 1
Ohio buckeye, tree	*Aesculus glabra*	Poisonous (seeds)	6 – 7, varies
Pin oak, tree	*Quercus palustris*	Low toxicity	8
Shagbark hickory, tree	*Carya ovata*	Fatal (nuts)	8 – 10, varies
Shellbark hickory, tree	*Carya laciniosa*	Fatal (nuts)	8 – 10, varies

Legend:

m = male; f = female

According to OPALS ranking: 1 = low and 10 = high, very allergenic

Plants with Higher OPALS Ranking

The next few charts have been compiled with plants that can be found in many of our landscapes. The plants were given OPALS rankings from 6 to 10 because of their levels of pollen. The higher the OPALS ranking, the more of a pollen offender it is. We should be cognizant to limit the number or avoid these plants when planning our gardens for allergy and asthma sufferers.

PERENNIALS

The following are favourite perennials in the garden that present problems for people with allergies and asthma. As cut flowers are brought inside, the fragrant flowers may be even more irritating due to the confinement of the indoor space. The silver mound in the chart bears larger flowers and doesn't release as much pollen as the smaller-flowering species.

Common Name (Cultivar)	Botanical/Scientific Name	OPALS Ranking
Baby's breath	*Gypsophila paniculata*	6
Blanket flower	*Gaillardia spp.*	6
Daylily	*Hemerocallis*	6
Dusty miller	*Senecio cineraria*	4 – 10, varies
Japanese spurge	*Pachysandra terminalis*	6
Leopard's bane	*Doronicum cordatum*	8
Love-lies-bleeding	*Amaranthus caudatus*	6
Shasta daisy	*Leucanthemum x superbum*	4 – doubles, 6 – singles
Silver mound	*Artemisia schmidtiana*	7 – 9, varies
Sunflower	*Helianthus annuus* 'Sunny Smile' and 'Teddy Bear'	6

Legend:

Doubles = double-flowering varieties; Singles = single-flowering varieties

According to OPALS ranking: 1 = low and 10 = high, very allergenic

CLIMBERS AND WALL PLANTS

Climbers and wall plants are a versatile group used to give visual interest to a fence, wall, trellis, arch or pergola. For individuals sensitive to pollen, some climbing plants emit a strong scent or release pollen in the air. Here are a few plants that you may encounter in the garden that can bring on allergy symptoms.

Common Name (Cultivar)	Botanical/Scientific Name	OPALS Ranking
Climbing hydrangea	*Hydrangea anomala petiolaris*	6
English ivy	*Hedera helix* 'Baltica'	7
Persian ivy	*Hedera colchica*	8

Legend:
According to OPALS ranking: 1 = low and 10 = high, very allergenic

GRASSES (INCLUDING ORNAMENTAL GRASSES)

Many people are allergic to the pollen that comes from grass. Grass tends to start growing in early spring, and by late spring and early summer, pollen is released in the air. The grass pollen can bring on symptoms of a runny or stuffy nose, itchy eyes and a cough. You may be allergic to only one type of grass or many, as there are thousands of grass types (including ornamental grasses). The following types of grass can be found in green spaces, park settings, parkways and neighbourhood yards, and have high OPALS rankings.

Common Name (Cultivar)	Botanical/Scientific Name	OPALS Ranking
Bentgrass	*Agrostis spp.*	9
Bermuda grass	*Cynodon dactylon*	10
Big bluestem grass	*Andropogon gerardii*	6
Blue fescue	*Festuca glauca*	6
Buffalo grass	*Bouteloua dactyloides*	7
Cordgrass	*Spartina spp.*	7
Crown grass	*Paspalum quadrifarium*	9

Common Name (Cultivar)	Botanical/Scientific Name	OPALS Ranking
Feather reed grass	*Calamagrostis x acutiflora*	9
Fountain grass	*Pennisetum setaceum*	8
Gamma grass	*Tripsacum dactyloides*	6 – 9, varies
Johnson grass	*Sorghum halepense*	6 – 10, varies
Kentucky bluegrass	*Poa pratensis*	m = 9, f = 1
Orchard grass	*Dactylis glomerata*	10
Perennial ryegrass	*Lolium perenne*	9
Sweet vernal	*Anthoxanthum odoratum*	10
Timothy grass	*Phleum pratense*	9
Velvet grass	*Holcus spp.*	8

Legend:

m = male; f = female

According to OPALS ranking: 1 = low and 10 = high, very allergenic

FLOWERING SHRUBS

Each month you can be treated to different flowering shrubs blooming in your garden. In general, we tend to overlook the important segments of education of different non-allergenic plant varieties and overall health for continuous flowering plants. In this chart, I am including some common flowering shrubs.

Blooming Month	Common Name (Cultivar)	Botanical/Scientific Name	OPALS Ranking
March	Winter hazel	*Corylopsis glabrescens*	7
	Dappled willow	*Salix integra*	m = 10, f = 1
April	Kumson forsythia	*Forsythia koreana*	6
May	Oak leaf hydrangea	*Hydrangea quercifolia*	6
May – June	Common lilac	*Syringa vulgaris*	5 – 6, varies

Blooming Month	Common Name (Cultivar)	Botanical/Scientific Name	OPALS Ranking
June – July	Common privet (European privet)	*Ligustrum vulgare*	9
June – August	Oleander	*Nerium oleander*	6
August	Smoke bush/tree	*Cotinus coggygria*	m = 8, f = 2

Legend:

m = male; f = female

According to OPALS ranking: 1 = low and 10 = high, very allergenic

PALMS AND PALM EQUIVALENT PLANTS

Depending on where you live, having a palm tree can transform your garden into a tropical oasis. Being relatively low-maintenance makes them a favourite with some gardeners. Although aesthetically pleasing, some palms have a high OPALS ranking. The chart lists a few palms that you may be familiar with seeing at your local garden centre/nursery.

Common Name (Cultivar)	Botanical/Scientific Name	OPALS Ranking
Alexander palm	*Ptychosperma elegans*	7
Carpentaria palm	*Carpentaria acuminate*	6
Coconut palm	*Cocos nucifera*	7
Cocos palm	*Syagrus romanzoffiana*	6
Fishtail palm	*Caryota mitis*	9
Macarthur palm	*Ptychosperma macarturii*	7
Royal palm	*Roystonea regia*	7

Legend:

m = male; f = female

According to OPALS ranking: 1 = low and 10 = high, very allergenic

TREES

We seem to think of allergy season as early spring and fall, and not the winter months. But some trees start to release pollen as early as January. Where we live plays a role in when our allergies begin to manifest themselves. Wind-pollinated trees can have a large health effect on the population at large. Thankfully, not all tree species cause allergies. Here are a few common trees with high OPALS rankings that we may find in our landscapes.

Common Name (Cultivar)	Botanical/Scientific Name	OPALS Ranking
Almond tree	*Prunus dulcis*	10
American	*Fagus grandiflora*	6
Basswood	*Tilia americana*	6
Bitternut hickory	*Carya cordiormis*	8 – 10, varies
Black ash	*Fraxinus nigra*	m = 9, f = 1
Black walnut	*Juglans nigra*	8 – 9, varies
Bur oak	*Quercus macrocarpa*	8
California black oak	*Quercus kelloggii*	8
European ash	*Fraxinus excelsior*	m = 7, f = 1
Green ash	*Fraxinus pensylvanica*	m = 7, f = 1
Holly (shrub/tree)	*Ilex spp.*	m = 7, f = 1
Ironwood	*Ostrya virginiana*	6
Norway maple	*Acer platanoides*	8
Pin oak	*Quercus palustris*	8 – 9, varies
River birch	*Betula nigra*	9
Singleleaf ash	*Fraxinus anomala*	6

Common Name (Cultivar)	Botanical/Scientific Name	OPALS Ranking
Western red cedar	*Thuja plicata*	8
White ash	*Fraxinus americana*	m = 7, f = 1

Legend:

m = male; f = female

According to OPALS ranking: 1 = low and 10 = high, very allergenic

WEEDS

Weeds usually release pollen in the late summer and fall. They produce a great deal of powdery, easy to inhale pollen that can trigger allergic reactions. It's best to eliminate weeds from the garden early before they reach maturity and flower. If allergies prevent you from being in the garden during certain periods, it may be wise to hire a yard care service. As you can see from this list of common weeds, ragweed is by far the worst offender.

Common Name (Cultivar)	Botanical/Scientific Name	OPALS Ranking
Alfalfa	*Medicago sativa*	8
Lamb's quarters	*Chenopodium album*	9 – 10, varies
Mugwort (Common wormwood)	*Artemisia vulgaris*	7 – 9, varies
Common nettle (Stinging)	*Urtica spp.*	m = 9, f = 5
Giant hogweed	*Heracleum mantegazzianum*	10
Pigweed	*Amaranthus spp.*	6
Ragweed	*Ambrosia artemisiifolia*	10
Silver sagebrush (Sagewort)	*Artemisia ludoviciana*	7 – 9, varies
Sorrel (Dock)	*Rumex spp.*	8

Legend:

m = male; f = female

According to OPALS ranking: 1 = low and 10 = high, very allergenic

Allergy-Friendly Gardening Q&A

I have prepared this question-and-answer section to assist in understanding the correlation of what you plant and your neighbourhood gardens and park surroundings in relation to allergies and asthma.

Q. Why are male trees so prevalent in public landscaping, and what role do they play in allergic reactions?

A. Male trees produce no seeds or seed pods or fruit. This makes them litter-free and low-maintenance. This sounds ideal when comparing to female trees that have flowers, seed pods, fruit and seeds that drop and make a mess of porches, roadways and sidewalks. In some cities, male trees now make up more than 85% of all the planted trees, and it's the same for shrubs. Unfortunately, the impact of all these male shrubs and trees is an abundance of allergenic pollen!

For dioecious species (that is, separate-sexed species) the pollen from the males must sometimes travel a considerable distance to reach the females. As such, the males of these species produce huge amounts of pollen grains, which are very small, light and buoyant. This kind of pollen is the most allergenic, and everyone nearby is constantly overexposed to allergenic pollen "proximity pollinosis." The result is an ever-increasing number of people with allergies and asthma.

The worst landscaping, from an allergy point of view, is found in urban areas, especially schoolyards. The most common shade trees planted are allergenic or produce high amounts of pollen. Childhood asthma is now the number one chronic childhood disease in Canada and the United States.

Q. What plants do you recommend for an allergy-free home garden, and why?

A. I strongly recommend the use of any female plants. The benefits are multiple and wide-ranging. Most importantly, female plants have flowers that carry a negative electrical charge. Airborne pollen has a positive charge. This is where a mutual attraction comes into play: female plants trap pollen, lots of it, and the plants are in effect one of nature's finest air cleaners.

As a side benefit, flowers on female plants produce much more nectar than flowers on male plants, and this attracts bees, butterflies and hummingbirds. Female plants also produce fruit and seeds that feed numerous bird species. These birds also eat large amounts of insects, leaving the whole garden much cleaner and healthier. As you look for specific plant options, I always recommend using the OPALS guidelines. You don't want any plant (male or female) with a ranking above 5 or 6 in your gardens, parks or schoolyards if you're concerned about allergies.

Q. What plants are particularly problematic for those with allergies and asthma?

A. The worst for urban landscapes are willow (*Salix spp.*), poplar (*Populus spp.*), birch (*Betula spp.*), aspen (*Populus spp.*), cottonwood (*Populus spp.*), ash (*Fraxinus spp.*), cedar (*Thuja spp.*), mulberry (*Morus spp.*), juniper (*Juniperus*), yew (*Taxus spp.*), red maple (*Acer rubrum*), silver maple (*Acer saccharinum*), box elder (*Acer negundo*), fern/yew pine (*Podocarpus spp.*), holly (*Ilex spp.*) and sedges (*Carex*) ornamental grasses.

In addition, there are some monoecious selected trees that are also quite allergenic and greatly overused. Monoecious flowered means both male and female flowers are produced on the same plant. These include olive (*Olea spp.*), gumtree (*Eucalyptus spp.*), oak (*Quercus spp.*), sycamore (*Platanus spp.*), Australian willow (*Acacia spp.*) and cypress (*Cypress spp.*).

Q. What might surprise people about the connection between city planning and allergies?

A. In general, town or city planning has only made allergies worse. Typically, the more recently planted the landscape, the more allergenic, but this is changing! In some cities, planners are starting to pay attention to the impact they can have on combatting allergies. In New Zealand, the cities of Auckland and Christchurch are now using OPALS and planting allergy-friendly trees. In other cities, like Albuquerque, New Mexico, they now have a pollen control ordinance. It's illegal to plant or sell male shrubs and trees of many species. Las Vegas, Nevada, and Tucson, Arizona, have banned the planting of olive and male mulberry trees.

The female Katsura tree (OPALS ranking of 1) makes an ideal addition to the garden.

We need to get our local governments involved to develop urban greenspaces that are friendly for all of us, including those with allergies and asthma. In the meantime, millions of extremely allergenic, male clonal shrubs and trees are being sold and planted across Canada and the United States. Education is the key, and those with allergies and asthma need to help to spread the word.

Q. Is there really a positive solution? Can we enjoy the many benefits of trees without increasingly severe allergenic side effects?

A. Certainly! The answer lies in the **balance** of male versus female plants. Municipalities, homeowners, property owners and landscapers need to stop planting male trees in urban areas and start planting larger numbers of female trees of the same species. Once we restore the balance of nature, with greater bio-diversity, we are likely to see our urban allergy/asthma rates decline. We should embrace the simple, easy-to-use OPALS guidelines. By pursuing some easy-to-implement suggestions, we can ensure cities and towns are not only greener but have cleaner air to foster the health of future generations. The recommendation of planting female trees over male trees will not cure all pollen allergies or asthma, but taking this important step could reduce many of the seasonal triggers and help reduce symptoms to make drug therapies more effective.

TWO
GARDENING 101

Latin in the Garden

Throughout this guide, you will notice that I have included the Latin, otherwise known as the botanical/scientific name, to identify plants. Why? Well, when you are searching for a flower, shrub or tree, it's advantageous to know the botanical name. Scientific Latin plant names are used universally as a means to specifically classify or identify plants.

Unlike a plant's common name, of which there may be several, the Latin name is unique to each plant. It also helps to describe both the "genus" and "species" of plants to better categorize them. In the mid-1700s, Swedish naturalist Carl Linnaeus grouped plants based on similarities, such as leaves, flowers and fruit, to form a binomial (two name) system of nomenclature. From there, he named the plants accordingly. The Latin plant name — the genus — is listed first and is always capitalized. The species follows the genus name in lowercase, and the entire Latin plant name is italicized or underlined. For example, Botanical/Scientific name: *Acer rubrum*; Common name: red maple. Where a cultivar is listed, the exact name of the cultivar will be enclosed in single quotation marks. For example, purple coneflower — *Echinacea purpurea* 'Magnus.'

You may also see other parts of a botanical/scientific name such as: sp (species), spp (multiple species), var (botanical variety), and ssp (subspecies).

The use of Latin plant names may be confusing to the home gardener, but think of it as another helpful tool in describing a specific type of plant and its characteristics.

For quick reference, I have included a botanical nomenclature guide containing some of the most common meanings of Latin plant names.

Colour	
albus - candida	White
argentea	Silver
atropurpurea	Reddish purple
aurantica	Orange
aureus - chrysantha	Gold
azureum	Sky blue
azureus - caerulea	Blue
cinerea	Smoky grey
coccinea	Dark red
coelestina	Pale blue
eosea	Pink
flava - citrina, crocea	Yellow
glaucous	Hazy grey
lutea	Golden yellow
nigra	Black
nivea	Snowy white
purpurea	Purple
ruber - cardinalis, rubra	Red
sanguinea	Dark red
violaceus - amethystina	Violet

Growth Habit	
angustifolia	Narrow leaved
arborea	Treelike
compacta	Compact
cordifolia	Heart-shaped leaves
divaricata	Spreading
elatus alta, elata, excelsa	Tall
fastigata	Erect
flore pleno	Double flowers
foetida	Strong scent
fragrans, odorata	Fragrant
giganteum	Giant
maculatatus, meleagris	Spotted
microphylla	Small leaved
nanus - nana	Dwarf
parvus - pumilla	Small
pendula	Weeping
procumbens	Trailing
reptans	Creeping
rotundifolia	Round leaved
sempervirens	Evergreen

Growth Habit	
tormentosa	Hairy
viscaria	Sticky

Common Root Words	
anthos	Flower
brevi	Short
flora	Flower
folius	Foliage
grandi	Large
hetero	Diverse
laevis	Smooth
lepto	Slender

Common Root Words	
macro	Large
mega	Big
micro	Small
mono	Single
phyllos	Leaf/Foliage
platy	Flat/Broad
poly	Many

Heighten the Five Senses in the Garden

To understand and intensify our personal connection with our gardens, we need to use plantings to engage the five senses of sight, smell, sound, taste and touch. The beauty of a garden is a gift to us; let's make the best of them to heighten our sensory experiences.

SIGHT Decorative stems, bark and berries captivate our eyes with their vivid colours.

Cornus alba or red osier has a distinctive shiny red bark. Twigs have white pith.

Viburnum lentago or nannyberry produces white flowers in June, followed by blue/black fruit.

Malus makamik or flowering crabapple tree is covered in rose-red blossoms and dark red fruit, with bronze foliage.

SMELL Fragrance and aroma can be heightened in the garden by using not only flowers, but also foliage. Try planting geraniums (scented with fragrances of fruit, flowers, spices and even chocolate) or *Helichrysum* (used as an essential oil for its smell of burnt sugar and ham).

SOUND Different plants, ornamental grasses and bamboo shoots create a musical score in our gardens. Just hearing foliage sway and rustle in the breeze has a calming "Zen" effect.

TASTE Nothing beats picking fresh berries (blueberries, raspberries, strawberries) from the garden to savour and awaken our taste buds. Edible flowers (most common are nasturtium, pansy and impatiens) can be used in salads and cooking. **You need to remember** that not every flower is edible, and some can make you very sick. Most herb flowers have a taste that's similar to a leaf and can be much spicier. Use flowers sparingly in your recipes. Herbs and vegetables provide our bodies with important vitamins and nutrients.

TOUCH You can plant wonderfully textured foliage, such as *Stachys byzantine* or lamb's ears in the mint family, with its fuzzy, soft grey leaves and purple flowers.

Acanthus, also called bear's breeches, looks like a thistle and offers sturdy spires of white, blue or pink blossoms. It makes a striking cut flower.

Asarum, usually called wild ginger, has red flowers, big leaves and a pleasing scent. It's a useful plant to have as a ground cover for shady gardens. The plant requires ample moist and rich soil.

Limonium latifolium or statice has abundant small flowers, with blooms in the summer. It makes for good, everlasting dry flowers.

Identify Your Soil

Stop! Can you identify the composition of your garden soil? Is it clay, loam, sand or silt? Knowing this will help you identify if there are any weaknesses that may hinder your garden from thriving. Some soils are naturally fertile and need little to no altering, while others need some special care.

Here's an easy 30-minute do-it-yourself soil test that will show you the soil type in your garden or the soil composition you have purchased this year.

Fill a Mason jar about 1/3 full with the soil. Add water until the jar is almost full, then 15 millilitres (1 tablespoon) of liquid dishwasher detergent. Why use dishwasher detergent? Well, it helps you see the "lines" between the different soil structures. Screw the lid on tightly, and shake well until all the clumps of soil have dissolved. Now set the jar on a windowsill and watch as the large particles — sand — begin to sink to the bottom. Mark the level of sand on the side of the jar. Leave the jar undisturbed for several hours until the finer (silt) particles settle onto the sand. You will see the layers are slightly different colours, indicating various types of particles. After five hours or so, mark the silt level. Leave the jar overnight. The next layer above the silt will be clay. On top of the clay will be a thin layer of organic matter. Some of this organic matter may still be floating in the water.

The jar content should be murky and full of floating organic sediments. If not, this indicates you should add organic matter to your garden soil, such as sheep/cow manure or compost. This will improve the soil's fertility and structure.

TEST RESULTS

Soil is considered *clay* when it contains 40% or more clay particles. It drains slowly and is difficult to work with. Clay soil sometimes clings together in big clumps when it's worked. It compacts easily, but in its favour, it usually has a high nutrient content and the capacity to hold high amounts of nutrients. The problem is that these nutrients are not readily available to your plants. With the addition of organic matter (compost or manure) and soil life, these nutrients are released and available for plant uptake. You can improve your clay soil by mixing in a high-quality compost and coarse sand.

Your soil test result should contain 40% sand, 40% silt, 20% clay. This is also called *loam* soil. Loam is an ideal soil when mixed with organic matter. A loamy garden is what every gardener really should want to maintain. It holds moisture well and is fertile in order to produce great plants.

Soil is considered *sand* when the sand layer is 85% or more of the soil profile. Sandy soils dry quickly, have a low nutrient content and leach nutrients rapidly. Organic matter will decompose much faster in sandy soils and must be added more often.

Silt soils contain 40% or more of silt. Silt has smaller grain particles than sand. They can't be seen, but you can feel them if you rub the particles between your fingertips. Silt is mixed with sand or clay. It drains well but often needs extra organic matter.

To keep your plants happy and healthy, get out those gardening gloves and get digging. Changing the composition of your soil is just one way to ensure your garden blooms and prospers for years to come!

Organic Garden Solutions

A pesticide ban is in effect in many areas, and "green" solutions are on the shelf in your local garden centre/nursery. **Read** the label of the product for application use, and **follow** the proper safety precautions (eye protection, rubber gloves, etc.) when handling.

You should take steps to reduce the risk of pesticides from being **touched, inhaled or eaten** by anyone. Store in a safe area to avoid accidental contact. Make sure the product is properly labelled for quick identification. "Green" products still require the same care as pesticides. If you have pets or small children, keep them away from treated areas while using the pesticide/herbicide.

Pesticide/ Herbicide Name (Ingredient)	Purpose	Application	Safety Risk
Acetic acid (Horticultural vinegar)	Effective for annual broad-leaf weeds (dandelions). In general, it won't kill roots of perennial weeds, but worth a try.	Liquid spray. Since vinegar herbicide works best in full sun, it's recommended that you apply on sunny, warm days with no chance of rain.	Environmentally safe. Read the label for proper safety precautions.
Bacillus thurengiensis kurstaki (Btk)	To kill the insect larvae of budworm, caterpillars, gypsy moth, spruce beetle, etc.	Purchase at your local garden centre/nursery. Dust infected plants per recommended instructions.	Even though Btk has an excellent safety record, as a precaution, take the following steps to minimize exposure: • Remain indoors for at least 30 minutes after the spray application. It's a good idea to keep family pets inside. • If you come in contact with the wet spray, wash the affected skin with soap and water. If wet materials should get into the eyes, flush them with water for 15 minutes.

Pesticide/ Herbicide Name (Ingredient)	Purpose	Application	Safety Risk
Boric acid	Insect control of ants, cockroaches and other crawling insects. This is a stomach poison (dry powder or liquid).	Powder form. For best results apply at night and leave until morning. Clean all areas where the powder was applied with a wet rag or vacuum.	Although boric acid is non-toxic to humans, it's highly toxic to insects. Be careful not to inhale when applying it.
Capsaicin	Used as a repellent against squirrels, around bird feeders or mixed with bird feed.	This is the active ingredient in hot peppers (cayenne). Sprinkle capsaicin-based granules on or around areas.	Capsaicin is very irritating to the eyes and skin, and causes swelling in lung tissue. You may be exposed if you are applying capsaicin and you breathe it in or get it on your skin. Safety precautions are necessary.
Corn gluten meal	Inhibit the germination of annual weeds (crabgrass in lawns).	Apply in open spaces of the lawn in the spring. Read and follow the instructions.	Don't inhale the dust.
Dried blood meal	Animal repellent, such as rabbits and deer.	Before applying blood meal, wet the plants with water and liquid detergent.	Wash the plant leaves before eating.
Iron phosphate	Slugs and snails stop eating when consumed.	Compound (granular) of phosphorus and oxygen. Check the label for instructions.	Keep children and pets out of the applied area.

Pesticide/ Herbicide Name (Ingredient)	Purpose	Application	Safety Risk
Mineral oil	This is to control the "scale" insects, such as aphids and white flies that lay their eggs on the plants.	Mix mineral oil with 1/3 liquid detergent in the spray bottle.	Keep away from children.
Permethrin	Affects insects that touch or eat it.	Insecticide derived from the flowers of the chrysanthemum. Apply by following instructions on the label.	Cats are sensitive to this product.
Silicon dioxide (Diatomaceous earth)	This product is used against ants, caterpillars, earwigs, potato beetle and slugs. It damages the skeleton, and if eaten, it damages the digestive system.	Made from ground skeletons of fossilized animals. Apply according to the instructions.	Safe insecticide

Worms in the Garden

Long, ugly, squishy and dirt-covered are just some of the colourful adjectives to describe a worm. Before you go and dig them up from your garden soil or squish them with your shoe, know that worms provide a significant component in soil construction and recycling of organic waste. Worms turn refuse into nutrient-rich soil that benefits plant growth.

Seeing a worm crawl around in your yard may make you marvel how this species has existed for thousands of years. Worms can live up to ten years, depending on their species and environmental conditions.

Worms don't have legs but are covered by prickly hairs that help them to move. There are over 34,000 different types of worms. An interesting fact about worms is that they are a thousand times stronger than a human being, relatively speaking. When you dig in the garden or lawn and cut a worm in half, only half will die. The pink part (thicker section) will recuperate.

The worm is a hermaphrodite; that means they don't need another worm to reproduce. In the burrow, they lay their eggs to be hatched.

Why do we use worm castings as fertilizer? Worms eat organic waste, such as minerals and soil. They **don't** eat living plants. It's known that worms eat their weight DAILY and excrete the castings, which improves the soil.

Worms don't like the light, and that's why they crawl deep in the soil to survive hot summers or cold winters.

> ### Just a Thought...
>
> *Be nice to worms, as they are helpful in the garden!*

THREE
ATTRACT BIRDS TO YOUR GARDEN

Birds in the Garden

The more birds in your yard, the fewer insects will pester you, especially while dining al fresco. Feed the birds in the winter, and they will take care of your insects in your garden during spring, summer and fall. There are four different ways that birds eat insects in your yard:

1. There are birds that feed in flight, such as flycatchers, mockingbirds, purple martins and swallows. These birds eat aphids, beetles, cabbageworm moths, gypsy moths, horseflies, houseflies, leafhoppers and mosquitoes.

2. Birds that clean the bark on shrubs or trees are woodpeckers, warblers, wrens and chickadees. They eat bark borers, bark lice, codling moths and plant lice.

3. Birds that clean the leaves of the plants are blackbirds, crows, orioles, purple finches and warblers. These birds eat aphids, gypsy moth larvae, leaf miner, potato beetles and tent caterpillars.

4. Birds that are ground eaters (cleaners) include blackbirds, bluebirds, cardinals, sparrows, starlings and warblers. These birds eat ants, chinch bugs, cutworms, grasshoppers, June bugs, root maggots, rootworms and white grubs.

Attract Hummingbirds to Your Garden

Many of us are fascinated with the sight of hummingbirds. Could it be their small size (2 – 20 grams) with long narrow bills, or the intensely coloured feathers, or their resiliency? The wing beat of up to 45 times per second makes it the most versatile bird known. They are truly a marvel to behold.

Hummingbirds have learned that trumpet-shaped, red flowers often have more nectar, and also that the dispersal of pollen has taken place (insect pollination). Each day, a hummingbird must consume approximately half of its weight in sugar. The average hummingbird feeds 5 – 8 times per hour. Don't be surprised to see a hummingbird visit up to 1,000 flower blossoms a day. In addition to nectar, these birds also eat many small insects and spiders, and may also sip tree sap or juice from the fruit.

For allergy/asthma sufferers, I have added an OPALS ranking list of plants to attract hummingbirds.

Blooming Time	Common Name (Cultivar)	Botanical/Scientific Name	OPALS Ranking
Jul – Sep	Bee balm	*Monarda didyma*	3
Jun – Sep	Bush honeysuckle (Northern)	*Diervilla lonicera*	4
Aug – Sep	Butterfly weed	*Asclepias tuberosa*	3
Jul – Sep	Cardinal flower	*Lobelia cardinalis*	m = 4, f = 1
Jun – Jul	Columbine	*Aquilegia spp.*	1
Jun – Sep	Coral bells	*Heuchera sanguinea*	1
May – Jun	Foxglove	*Digitalis purpurea*	2
May – Aug	Fuchsia	*Fuchsia spp.*	3
Jul – Oct	Godetia (Farewell to Spring)	*Clarkia amoena*	2
Aug – Sep	Hollyhocks	*Alcea rosea*	2 – 3, varies
Jun – Oct	Impatiens, red	*Impatiens spp.*	1
Jun – Sep	Nasturtium	*Tropaeolum*	3
May – Sep	Petunia, red	*Petunia x hybrida*	2
Jun – Oct	Scarlet larkspur	*Delphinium cardinale*	3
Jun – Aug	Sweet William	*Dianthus barbatus*	1 – 3, varies
Jul – Sep	Trumpet creeper	*Campsis radicans*	5 (Vine)
Aug – Oct	Yarrow	*Achilea millefolium*	4

Legend:

m = male; f = female plants

According to OPALS ranking: 1 = low and 10 = high, very allergenic

Gardening Tip...

If hummingbirds are not native or no migratory flight paths run through your area, it's very unlikely that you will see any of these winged wonders in your garden.

Bird-Friendly Plants

By creating a bird sanctuary in your garden or care facility, you will be rewarded with the beauty of birds and their songs. Consider planting "food" for the birds, such as pine trees for robins, sparrows and warblers. Your plantings will offer a full buffet of food options in the form of fruit, insects, leaves, nectar, nuts, sap and seeds.

Shrubs and trees provide the birds with the added benefit of shelter from the elements and foes. Conifers, such as fir, hemlock, pine and spruce, make excellent nesting sites for many birds. When selecting trees, pick species that are compatible with your climate, light conditions and soil type.

Common Name (Cultivar)	Botanical/Scientific Name	Offering	OPALS Ranking
Allegheny serviceberry, shrub	Amelanchier laevis	White flowers and black fruit	3
American elderberry, shrub	Sambucus canadensis	Edible black fruit	4
Arrowwood, shrub	Viburnum dentatum	Creamy white flowers and black berries	3 – 5, varies
Beautyberry, shrub	Callicarpa dichotoma	Tightly clustered berries	3
Butterfly bush, shrub	Buddleia davidii	Conical spikes, fragrant flowers	3
European cranberry bush, shrub	Viburnum opulus	Bell-shaped white flowers and fruit	3 – 5, varies
Flowering dogwood, shrub	Cornus spp.	Insects, buds and fruit for birds to eat	5
Honeysuckle, shrub	Lonicera spp.	White or pink flowers and red berries	5 – 6, varies
Nannyberry, shrub	Viburnum lentago	Very interesting fruit	3 – 5, varies
Oregon grape, shrub	Mahonia aquifolium	Yellow flowers mature to blue/black fruit	2
Snowberry, shrub	Symphoricarpos albus	Winter interest and fruit	3

Common Name (Cultivar)	Botanical/Scientific Name	Offering	OPALS Ranking
Trumpet vine, shrub	*Campsis radicans*	Orange-red trumpet flowers	5
Chokecherry, tree	*Prunus virginiana*	Berries not for human consumption, but the birds like them	5
Maples (*female species*) tree	*Acer spp.*	Birds and small mammals devour the seeds within the winged samaras of maples	1

Legend:

According to OPALS ranking: 1 = low and 10 = high, very allergenic

Feed the Birds in the Winter

When the snow swirls and the temperatures drop, we need to think about looking after our feathered neighbours. Most birds that stay in cold regions need some help, as insects are scarce in freezing weather.

I get many questions about choosing a seed blend to feed wild birds in the winter. What do birds like to eat, and what don't they eat? Research continues, but it boils down to this: birds are like kids; there are some foods they enjoy and some foods they avoid. Smell and taste are not major criteria for them in choosing one food over another. The experts tell us that birds select seeds based on colour, texture and weight.

Birds are warm-blooded, and the maintenance of their body temperature depends on the amount of food they ingest. On wintery days, you may see a bird fluff up its feathers, which creates air pockets to keep warm. Birds need energy-rich food, such as seeds, insects and suet, to deal with temperature drops and winter storms. Providing food for birds is very helpful to their continued existence.

Throwing out bread (fresh or stale) chunks provides no nutritional value for birds. Table scraps may not be safe or healthy for our winged friends, and you may find rodents are more attracted to what you put out.

Water is a welcome gift for birds as they can become dehydrated in the winter. There are bird baths available for sale that provide water in winter with heating elements built into the bowl. A word of caution: not all bird baths (such as concrete basins) are suitable for winter as the material may crack with expansion and contraction.

Black seeds and white seeds are preferred. For example, black sunflower seeds, niger seeds (thistle seeds), white millet and the list goes on. It's interesting to note that birds love red fruit and berries but tend not to like red seeds.

What is it that makes a red seed undesirable?

Tannin. Tannin is also known as tannic acid and is used in tanning shoe leather. It's also the thing that gives tea its reddish-brown colour. Tannin is bitter; birds don't like bitter seeds and tend to discard them from the bird feeder. That's why so much waste is found on the ground during spring clean-up.

What are the red seeds with tannin?

Red millet and milo. Both are the colour of tea. It should be noted that milo or cafir doesn't have tannin.

Why would manufacturers put red seeds into a bird mix? The deciding factor is price. As a filler, red seeds cost less.

Are there other foods/seeds that the colourful backyard birds don't care for?

Yes! Whole grains like barley, canola seed, flax seed, oats, rye and wheat.

Bird seed can be bought commercially for your convenience, or you can make your own blend to add to your bird feeder. Ingredients can be found in a grocery store bulk bin or most bird/nature stores selling individual seed types in bulk.

Here are some additional tips for a successful winter bird feeding season:

1. Offer fatty food as birds need to burn more calories in the winter to stay warm. I have included a recipe for suet cake that is a favourite of woodpeckers and other insect-eating birds.

2. Situate the bird feeder out of prevailing cold winds. It's best near a shrub or tree to provide a perching spot for the bird to view the feeding area for safe refuge from predators.

3. Keep your bird feeders full as birds need to replenish calories lost during long, cold winter nights.

4. Keep the bird feeder clean as they can get a little incrusted. When cleaning, use some hot water and let dry before refilling.

Winter Homemade Treats for Birds

Making your own treat for birds is a fun and economical way to help the birds in the winter. Ask your children or grandchildren to help.

HOLIDAY PUDDING

Mix the following ingredients in a shallow pan. Allow to harden before setting outdoors for your feathered friends.

- 2 cups rolled oats or any uncooked dry cereal
- 2 tablespoons butter
- 2 cups wild bird seed
- 1.5 cups melted fat
- 4 cups breadcrumbs

SUET CAKE

Suet is a superb food source for the birds that will visit your backyard this winter. Suet is a high energy, pure fat substance that provides birds the calories they need to keep their bodies warm and energy levels up.

To make your own suet cake for our feathered friends during the winter, gather the following ingredients:

- 4 cups bird seed
- 2 cups cornmeal or oats
- 2 cups bacon fat or lard
- 1 cup peanut butter
- 1 tablespoon sugar

In a saucepan on the stove at medium heat, melt the bacon fat or lard. In a bowl, combine the dry ingredients. Mix in the melted bacon fat or lard. Form into a ball, and place into an onion bag. Place into your freezer until needed. **Or** spread the mixture out on a cookie tray. Freeze, and cut into desirable size for your squirrel feeder.

WILD BIRD BACON BALL

Don't throw away bacon grease after cooking. When the fat is partially hardened, add about 1/4 pound of wild bird seed mixture and mould into a ball.

Cookies have gone to the birds! Try this recipe with young children or your grandchildren as a fun winter snow day activity. For this crunchy cookie that birds will love, you will need:

2 cups bird seed	Spoon
2 cups melted coconut oil	Baking sheet
Large cookie cutters	Wax paper or parchment
Straws cut into 2-inch pieces	String (jute, baker's twine or ribbon)
Large bowl	

Mix equal parts bird seed and melted coconut oil (adult help might be needed for this step). Set large cookie cutters on a wax-paper-lined tray and press the seed mixture into each cutter. Be sure to overfill the cookie cutter a bit with seed mixture as you will want the seeds to be nice and tight. Gently insert a straw piece to make a hole for ribbon or twine. Refrigerate overnight. In the morning gently pull the straw out of the seed cookie, then slowly ease the seed cookie out of the cookie cutter. Add ribbon or twine and hang from an outdoor tree.

Just a Thought...

Feeding the birds in winter will attract them back to your garden in the spring to feed on "undesirable" insect visitors.

Bird Nest Houses

When you are purchasing a birdhouse, the most important thing to know is that each bird type has different requirements. Knowing this, it makes sense to check the birdhouse specification as to the inside area, the entrance hole size and the height of the hole from the floor. These are very important considerations in attracting birds to one's backyard.

Use this size of entrance hole guide when deciding what bird you would like to attract.

Chickadee	2.8 centimetres (1 1/8 inches)
Flycatcher	4 centimetres (1 9/16 inches)
Purple marlin	6 centimetres (2 1/4 inches)
Titmouse and house wren	3 centimetres (1 1/4 inches)
Warbler	3.5 centimetres (1 3/8 inches)

The location of your birdhouse is important. Don't use screws to fasten a birdhouse to a tree. Birdhouses secured this way will injure the tree, as the sap stream will be obstructed and the screw will decay the wood around it. You can display your birdhouse using a copper pipe as your pole, the top of a fence post or arbour, plant hook attached to a wall or hanging it from a tree.

There should be easy access for cleaning and monitoring. Birdhouses should be cleaned in early spring of any wasp's nests or other debris. Avoid cleaning during the fall because parasites might enter during the fall or winter. Birdhouses that offer no way to monitor nests or clean out old nests are not considered good bargains.

It's very important where to place the birdhouse.

- In open sunny areas
- Backyards
- Conifer or hardwood trees
- Edge of woods
- Near water
- On trunks of large trees

Check that non-toxic materials have been used to build a structurally stable birdhouse. There should be no danger to the birds if the material is ingested. Select wood over metal when purchasing your birdhouse.

Birds use small twigs, string, wool, thread, cotton yarn or soft cloth strips when building their nests. Spread some of these materials around the base of the birdhouse.

Just a Thought...

Birds have little or no sense of smell! Enjoy the birds, which contribute to the biodiversity in our landscapes.

FOUR
CONTAINER PLANTS

Plant in Containers

Small-scale gardening can complement any space with pops of dazzling colour. Whether you have a green thumb or not, you can transform your apartment balcony, deck, courtyard, porch, windowsill or any other spot with flowers, greenery, herbs and vegetables.

Containers can be moved for greater mobility to suit your needs or to capture a sunny or shady location during the day. Growing plants in containers makes gardening accessible to almost everyone, including those with limited mobility. It's also an ideal way to introduce your hobby to young children. The magic of growing something from seed or plant seedling will give children a sense of accomplishment and wonder. Container gardening is a rather inexpensive hobby with great rewards.

The choice of containers is very broad. The containers can be made of clay, concrete, fiberstone, fiberglass, plastic, terra-cotta, wicker or wood. You can use your imagination in using old bicycle baskets, iron pots, a wheelbarrow, shoes or work boots, and anything you can easily drill drainage holes in the bottom. When choosing the container, make sure that the size of the plant complements the size of the container. For example, planting a beefsteak tomato plant in a small clay pot will hinder the plant's growth. Tomatoes need stakes to support the fruit-laden stems. Fruit need room to expand and ripen to their juicy best.

Don't be afraid to experiment with placing different plants near each other. Don't forget to add your personality to your container garden for unexpected whimsical pieces.

Before you venture to your local garden centre/nursery, take the time to determine where you will be placing your container garden. Does the area get full sun or partial sun/shade? How many containers are you planting? Once you have this information, it's time to check out the wide variety of plants offered at your local garden centre/nursery. Read the plant identification tag or label for information on light conditions (sun to part shade, full sun, shade), bloom time, height and plant spacing.

Pick larger plants for the centre of your container and surround them with smaller flowers and trailing flowers for visual interest. Don't limit your container gardens to just flowers, though. Use the largest containers you can afford for summer vegetables such as squash, eggplant and tomatoes. You don't want to mix too many vegetable varieties in a container as they may compete with each other for nutrients. Smaller clay pots are perfect for growing herbs, which will supply you with nature's best for your cooking.

There are things to remember when container gardening that might not apply to planting directly in a garden plot:

1. Proper drainage is key. To ensure that the soil won't wash through the container's drainage holes, place an old facecloth, towel, or non-scented dryer sheet covering the drainage hole(s). You can secure it in place with a few small stones or pine cones (fallen from pine trees) before adding the soil.

2. Fill the container with good composition soil, such as moistened soilless potting mix. Soilless potting mix tends to weigh less, and you will be able to move your container easily.

3. Take the time to break (split) the plant's solid root ball before planting. You can do this by gently spreading the root ball apart with your hands (about 4 centimetres [1 9/16 inch] into the root ball at several points). As the plant grows, its root system requires space to branch out. You want to give plants room to spread during the growing season so space the plants in the soil with this in mind.

4. After you have finished your planting, "shake or tap" the container to get the air out of the soilless mix. You may need to add more soil mix as the soil settles in the container.

5. Fertilize to give the plants a good start. You can add water with a diluted 15-30-15 water-soluble fertilizer or 20-20-20 at half the suggested rate on the fertilizer's container.

6. Keep your eye on the moisture level of the soil during the growing season as exposure to the elements and sun can quickly dry out the soil. Water — water — water.

> **Gardening Tip...**
>
> *Treat potted plants as if they occupy one planting zone colder, as their roots are not as protected as those deep in the ground.*

Plants for Container Gardening

There's almost an endless array of herbs, plants and vegetables you may plant in a container. Have a theme in mind. For example, try a healing garden, herb garden, tea garden or vegetable garden. Try adding multi-coloured foliage plants to your container for a touch of drama to pull the whole colour scheme together. Gardening experts at your local garden centre/nursery are more than pleased to help you with plant suggestions that complement each other. The only limitation is your imagination.

These drought-tolerant container plants are allergy-friendly. You can make your selection with different plant colours in mind.

Blooming Time	Common Name (Cultivar)	Botanical/Scientific Name	OPALS Ranking
June – October	Alpine calamint (Winter savory)	*Satureja sp.*	1 – 3, varies
July – August	Angelina stonecrop	*Sedum rupestre*	2
July – August	Golden germander	*Teucrium polium*	2
July – August	Hens & chicks	*Sempervivum sp.*	1
June – July	Lupine	*Lupinus perennis*	3
April – June	Rock cress	*Arabis caucasica*	1
June – July	Toadflax (Alpine)	*Linaria alpina*	1

Legend:

According to OPALS ranking: 1 = low and 10 = high, very allergenic

The following vegetable plants work just fine being planted in containers.

Vegetable	Container Pot Size	Plants per Container Pot	Maturity Days = Days until Harvesting
Beans (bush) green	15 cm (6 in.)	3 – 4	50 – 57
Beans (pole) green	15 cm (6 in.) or hanging basket 20 cm (8 in.)	3 – 4	65 – 75
Beans (bush) yellow	15 cm (6 in.)	3 – 4	60 – 70
Beets	15 cm (6 in.)	4 – 5	45 – 55
Carrots	15 cm (6 in.)	8 – 10	60 – 65
Cucumbers	20 cm (8 in.) hanging basket	1 – 2	50 – 70
Celery	15 cm (6 in.)	4 – 5	110 – 120
Eggplants	15 cm (6 in.)	1	60 – 70
Lettuce	15 cm (6 in.)	5 – 7	65 – 85
Peas	20 cm (8 in.) hanging basket	4 – 8	60 – 65
Peppers (green, red, yellow, orange)	20 cm (8 in.)	1	65 – 75
Radishes	15 cm (6 in.)	6 – 8	20 – 30
Spinach	20 cm (8 in.)	3 – 4	40 – 50
Swiss chard	15 cm (6 in.)	3 – 4	55 – 65
Tomatoes (cherry)	15 cm (6 in.)	1	65 – 70
Tomatoes (patio)	20 cm (8 in.)	1	65 – 70
Tomatoes (climbing)	25 cm (10 in.)	1	50 – 60
Tomatoes (large)	30 cm (12 in.)	1	75 – 80
Watermelons	30 cm (12 in.)	1	75 – 95

FIVE
ENVIRONMENTAL INFORMATION

Plant Hardiness Zones for Canada

If you are starting out as a novice gardener or have years of experience, you may have seen a map of different planting zones for Canada and the United States. A **zone** in the field of landscaping and horticulture refers to the overall temperature of an area, marking the annual lows.

The Plant Hardiness Zones map was first released by the United States Department of Agriculture in 1960, based only on minimum winter temperatures. In 1967, Agriculture Canada scientists created a plant hardiness map using Canadian plant survival data with a wider range of climatic variables. The variables included minimum winter temperatures, length of the frost-free period, summer rainfall, maximum temperatures, snow cover, January rainfall and maximum wind speed.

The map is divided into nine major zones with the harshest weather conditions at 0 and the mildest at 8. Subzones (4A or 4B, 5A or 5B, etc.) have subtle local variations in snow cover and are too small to be captured on the map.

The zone map helps you to match a plant to a specific region. When shopping at your local garden centre/nursery, always check the plant identification tag or label for information on best planting zones and hardiness temperatures.

Plant for Environmental Reasons

Many perennials, shrubs and trees are planted for aesthetic reasons. If you have hired the services of a landscape architect/contractor, often they make recommendations based on your instructions to beautify your property. The significance of the environmental value is overlooked. I suggest reconsidering your new landscaping design or "redoing" your property when the opportunity presents itself. When considering any planting, always try to determine the plant's susceptibility to road salt or de-icing compounds used in the winter. Select the plant according to exposure.

The demand for energy for our homes and businesses has never been higher, resulting in costs that stretch our budgets to the limit. Yes, we can do our part by replacing incandescent light bulbs with energy-efficient LED bulbs, and installing programmable thermostats and low-flow shower nozzles, but further savings can be realized with the use of plants on the property. It's impossible to control the wind, rain, temperature and other natural elements, but we can change the climatic conditions surrounding the house or building.

Introducing ornamental grasses to your landscape not only delivers visual interest, but there are many environmental benefits, such as attracting wildlife and preventing soil erosion. Many types are drought tolerant. We may take for granted the green grass in our parks' green spaces and yards, but sod works overtime to provide erosion control, fire retardation, ground water replenishment, noise abatement, oxygen generation, pollution absorption, temperature modification and water purification. Keep in mind those low allergy-ranked grasses!

Planting shrubs, trees and vines, and installing landscape structures strategically around the property, can reduce energy use during summer and winter. This is not only for the energy savings, but a well-planned landscape adds interest, beauty and most of all increases property value.

The summer cooling cost of your house can be reduced by approximately 50% when trees are strategically and fittingly planted. To get the maximum benefits of your trees, plant deciduous trees southwest of your home or building. When prevailing winds are typically from the northwest to southeast, generally planting conifers on the northwest side can reduce winter winds and provide summer shade on your house. By planting trees or hedges near the home to block blistery wind gusts, you can see an average of 9% reduction in heating energy costs during the winter.

The intent of plantings that can shade the roof, exterior of the house and surrounding hard surfaces is to reduce the absorption of heat into these features. Further, this warmed surface can permeate heat into the attic, house or surrounding soils. If the heated hard surface is in contact with the soil or roots, it can lead to soil drying or high soil temperatures, which affect root health. When camping, have you ever taken a hot metal handle frying pan and dipped it into cold water? Depending on how close your hand is to the pan, you can sense a sudden flash of heat up the metal handle. The same applies to hard conductive surfaces such as brick, stone or concrete that absorb and transfer the heat energy to cooler areas.

Avoid planting several trees close together. It might give you more immediate shade, but the canopies will grow together. If one of the trees dies, it will create an unsightly one-sided remaining tree. When you purchase a shrub or tree from a reputable garden centre/nursery, their gardening experts can advise you on the shrubs' or trees' height and growth span, how fast growing, the amount of maintenance required and spacing. As the shrub or tree grows, it can block the air movement around your house. Keep this in mind to avoid heat and humidity concentration. Proper pruning of the shrub or tree can help improve air circulation to offset this.

When the air-conditioner is shaded, count on at least 10% savings on your utility bill.

Vines that are grown on arbours, fences and trellises, if strategically placed and planted, give you privacy and shade. Don't place the arbour or trellis too close to the house because there should be air movement between the house and the structure. Furthermore, if the structure is too close to the house, the home's exterior and interior heat up rather than the desired effect of cooling down in the blazing summer sun.

Evergreen (female) shrubs planted on the north and west sides of your house serve as an effective barrier of winter winds. Evergreen and shrubs on the south and west sides keep the summer winds under control.

Awnings over decks and windows can reduce the southern heat by 60% or more. Always look for light colours that reflect, instead of dark colours that absorb the sun's rays. The initial expenditure of a stationary or retractable awning might be pricey, but the return may pay high dividends in future energy savings.

Slatted wood structures or wooden arbours can be useful when attached to the house or in the landscape by shading the house or leisure area or as a privacy fence. Garden structures block the wind/sun and provide a privacy barrier from the neighbours.

The percentage savings listed above are just a guide, and it's best to look at where your house is located and the prevailing weather conditions.

Just a Thought...

Consider the effect of your actions on the many generations yet to come.

Plant with Natural Controls

No garden is exempt from disease and pests. Overnight attacks can leave your plants battle weary. Before you reach for your spray bottle of toxic chemicals, know there's an easier way. You can be proactive in your approach to protecting your plants from predators with natural controls. We can use plants that will help deter these invaders to our gardens.

The ratio of planting with natural controls depends on the size of your garden and what is being grown. Integrate the "plant protectors" amongst your flowers and vegetables by spacing about every 1 metre (3 feet) if possible.

Pest Invader	Common Name (Cultivar)	Botanical/Scientific Name	OPALS Ranking
Apple aphid	Nasturtium	*Tropaeolum*	3
Carrot fly	Rosemary	*Rosmarinus officinalis*	3 – 5, varies
	Sage	*Sage (Salvia)*	1 – 4, varies
	Coriander	*Coriandrum*	3
Chinch bug	Soya beans	*Glycine max*	Not ranked
Cutworm	Tansy	*Tanacetum*	5
Japanese beetle	Borage	*Borago officinalis*	3
	Garlic	*Allium sativum*	2
	Tansy	*Tanacetum*	5
	Rue	*Ruta*	4
Leaf hopper	Painted daisy	*Anthemis*	5
Rose chafer	Geranium	*Geranium*	3
	Petunia	*Petunia*	2
	Rue	*Ruta*	4
Slug	Masterwort	*Astrantia*	3
Striped pumpkin beetle	Nasturtium	*Tropaeolum*	3

Pest Invader	Common Name (Cultivar)	Botanical/Scientific Name	OPALS Ranking
Tomato hornworm	Basil	*Ocimum*	2
	Borage	*Borago officinalis*	3
White fly	Chamomile	*Chamaemelum nobile*	5
	Marigold	*Tagetes*	3 – 6, varies
	Nasturtium	*Tropaeolum*	3

Legend:

According to OPALS ranking: 1 = low and 10 = high, very allergenic

> **Gardening Tip...**
>
> *Put potato peelings and some water in your blender. Strain through an old stocking or cheesecloth and use the water for watering your geraniums. The liquid mixture makes the leaves shiny green and healthy looking.*

Our Garden Friends

There are many "garden friends" to keep our garden "clean." The next time you see a caterpillar, slug or snail, think about the balance of nature. These are your garden friends, and future generations can learn from this.

✓ Moles, skunks and toads depend almost entirely on insects for their food.

✓ Lady beetles — bugs for you and me — eat aphids, corn borer lavae, mealybugs, spider mites and whiteflies.

✓ Chickadees eat huge amounts of cankerworms each day.

✓ Warblers, such a colourful bird, can eat as many as 10,000 tree lice a day.

✓ Sparrows bring about 2,000 insect larvae to their young daily.

✓ Cardinals, herring gulls, robins and starlings consume large quantities of insects.

- ✓ Toads can eat about 10,000 insects, such as caterpillars, cutworms, grubs, gypsy moths, mosquitoes and slugs, in a 3-month span.

- ✓ Moles feed on Japanese beetle grubs and consume 200 sawfly cocoons daily.

- ✓ Spiders can eat over 2,000 caterpillar cocoons a year.

Try to keep your garden healthy by using techniques that guard against infestation such as crop rotation, composting and proper pruning. Learn to control plants that control other insects. It's a worthwhile experience.

Air Pollution and Pollen Allergy

Many have asked me if there's a connection between air pollution and pollen allergy, and how it works. Yes, there's a connection. Particles of inorganic air pollution stick to individual pollen grain and cause them stress. In turn, this often causes a small rupture of the outside (extine) of the pollen grain and thus exposes the inside (entine) of the pollen grain. The extine is allergenic, but the entine is exceedingly more allergenic, and so the urban pollen is becoming much more allergenic than it was in the past.

This also explains why allergy rates are now far worse in urban areas than in rural ones, according to Thomas Ogren (*Allergy-Fighting Garden*). There's also a somewhat similar phenomenon at work with air pollution and pollen grains. When the air pollution gets bad enough to cause acid rain, during a rain storm, umpteen pollen grains will explode. This does several things:

First, the entine is now exposed and more allergenic.

Since the individual grains explode into even more tiny particles, the results are that these are then small enough to be inhaled much deeper into the lungs, which makes them perfectly capable of triggering asthma.

Second, because these organic pollen particulates are now so small, they are almost no longer identifiable when trapped on air-monitoring devices. They are often mistakenly described as dust particles. This can lead to a miscount of the actual amount of pollen in the air, resulting in it being described at lower levels.

Based on my research and years of experience, any city or town with a polluting industry and/or congested vehicular traffic patterns ought to be especially concerned about limiting the amount of allergenic pollen in their area. The cities print brochures with all the health information and benefits of trees but gloss over allergies as though it's not important for them to make any urban planning changes.

Water Conservation in the Garden

Being conscious about saving water in the garden is just as important as in our homes. Collecting rainwater, mulching and planting drought-tolerant plants can help reduce your water consumption. It's important to save water in the garden for two main reasons. First, to save money if you are on a water meter, and second, restrictions are placed on households when water reservoir levels are low.

Mulching flowerbeds and around the base of shrubs and trees will help prevent moisture from evaporating during dry spells. Natural mulches include bark chips, compost and pine needles. You can improve the soil composition to retain moisture by adding organic matter.

When watering your lawn, the best time is early morning 5 – 7 a.m., or if that's not possible later evening 7 – 9 p.m. Be aware of the placement of the sprinkler in order to not let water run onto the street. For the size of lawns that most average households have, I suggest 15 minutes ON and 30 minutes OFF. It gives the water time to percolate into the root zone. The lawn needs only 3 centimetres (1 3/16 inch) of water/rain per week!

Water in the cool of the morning when you will lose less water to evaporation in the heat of the day for your annuals, perennials, shrubs and trees.

Filling a watering can to water your flower beds, hanging baskets and container gardens may be labour intensive, but it's precise watering.

You can collect rainwater from your roof with a strategically placed rain barrel for use in your garden. All you need is a capture system (roof gutter and downspout), a storage system (rain barrel) and a delivery system (garden hose). Plants thrive with rainwater because it's naturally soft and free of chlorine and other harsh chemicals. Just a half inch of rain falling on a 1,000-square-foot roof (catchment area) will yield approximately 300 gallons of water. A debris screen and a well-fit lid are necessary to protect children and prevent mosquitoes from breeding in the water. Remember that your foundation must be able to support the rain barrel when it's full and heavy.

These simple tips will help you reduce your water consumption and ultimately do something good for the planet.

> **Gardening Tip...**
>
> *Your roof catchment area is equal to the total square metres (feet) of your house plus the extension of your eaves.*

Backyard Composting

Composting garden and household kitchen waste is not only an important environmental initiative to reduce greenhouse gases, but it offers tremendous benefit to improve your garden soil. Microorganisms in compost help break down organic matter into plant-available nutrients. Plants will grow stronger! When we add compost to soil, the amount of moisture the soil retains increases, which in turn requires less water. We also know that compost improves soil structure and will clean up and repair contaminated soil. Compost also helps break up clay soils. It's an easy and inexpensive solution to help the environment and your garden.

Weather conditions play a significant role in the composting process. When the compost waste becomes moist by rain (open compost pile) or by physically adding water into the bin, a chain reaction starts. The damp (residue) is invaded by microorganisms like actinomycetes, algae, bacteria and fungi, which decompose the

waste. Eelworms and protozoa devour the bacteria and algae. Earthworms pull pieces into their burrows, and the microbes get into action, which forms the rich plant food called humus. Earthworms do a fantastic job of mixing organic and inorganic materials.

All you need is a container with a lid and a little soil or organic material. Add water to get you started. There are many different sizes and shapes of compost bins available. Choose or build the compost bin that suits your needs.

The position of your compost bin should be accessible from all sides. It should receive partial sunlight, to heat the waste matter. When choosing where to locate your compost bin, consider your next-door neighbours and prevailing wind direction to avoid compost odours drifting in their backyards. Depending on the size of your backyard, locating your compost bin to a far back corner near the garden shed or away from the house is ideal. Composting can be a smelly process because you're breaking down food and yard waste. If your compost pile does start to create an odour, you can add lime or calcium to neutralize the offending scent. If your compost smells like ammonia, try adding carbon-rich elements, such as dried leaves, peat moss, straw or wood chips.

What can you include in the compost bin?

- ✓ Coffee grounds, eggshells, fallen leaves, fresh grass clippings, fruit and vegetable scraps, tea leaves and weeds
- ✓ Finely clipped bushes, sawdust (clean), wood ashes and wood chips
- ✓ A layer of soil will help to mask any odour.

DON'T include bones, dairy products, disease or infested plants, oils and fats, meat and meat by-products, pet waste and whole eggs.

NOTE

1. The particle size you place into the bin is very important. The smaller the pieces, the faster the breakdown of the material.

2. The heat of the compost bin should be between 54° – 71°C (130° – 160°F) to kill all weed seeds. Otherwise, when you transfer the compost to your garden beds, the weed seeds will start sprouting new weeds in your garden.

3. Check the moisture/dry ratio regularly. If dry, add water to improve the bacterial process. If wet, place newspaper or shredded paper scraps into the bin.

4. To accelerate the composting, add high nitrogen lawn fertilizer (NO weed and feed), sparingly.

5. In case you have placed pine needles with the waste you might add one cup of lime to promote the breakdown of the needles.

HOW TO COMPOST

For kitchen waste, keep a container with a lid under the sink. The container can be a stainless steel compost pail with air filter, a small plastic compost bin or an old ice cream pail. Chop up any large chunks before you add them to the compost container. When the container is full, transfer the waste to your outdoor compost bin.

Composting materials will decompose at different rates, but they will all break down eventually. If you want to speed up the composting process, chop the larger material into smaller pieces. If adding grass clippings and leaves, which are excellent for composting, they should be sprinkled into the bin with other materials and dug in to mix within the pile.

Add compost materials in layers, alternating moist and dry. Moist ingredients are such things as food scraps, tea bags, etc. Dry materials are leaves, shredded paper, straw, sawdust and wood ashes.

Keep the compost moist by watering occasionally, or let the rain do the job.

Every few weeks you will need to give the pile a quick turn with a pitchfork or shovel. This process will aerate the pile. Oxygen is required for the composting process to work, and turning the matter adds the needed oxygen.

Once your compost pile is established, you can add new materials by mixing them in, rather than adding them in layers. Mixing or turning the matter is key to aerating the composting materials and helps to speed the process to completion.

All compostable materials are either carbon- or nitrogen-based to varying degrees. Garden professionals know the secret to a healthy compost pile is to maintain a working balance between these two elements. Carbon-rich matter is produced with branches, stems, dried leaves, peels, bits of wood, coffee filters, eggshells, straw, wood ash, etc. Nitrogen is produced from food scraps, green leaves and lawn clippings. A healthy compost pile should have much more carbon than nitrogen.

HOW TO KNOW WHEN YOUR COMPOST PILE IS READY

Compost matures in its own time, so patience is an important virtue for gardeners. It can take a few months to a year to be ready to apply in your garden beds. Warm conditions help the composting process to work much faster in the summer than in the winter. Compost piles made in the fall often mature the following summer. Mid-summer compost, made from garden and kitchen waste, is finished within a few weeks due to more microorganisms being very active in warm temperatures.

When compost is ready to use, it will have a crumbly texture, a dark brown colour and a rich, earthy smell. Mature compost doesn't contain slimy things. Garden refuse and ordinary kitchen scraps shouldn't be recognizable. You may see the occasional woody stem or autumn leaf.

You can save large plastic bags from purchased potting soil for storing ready compost until you are prepared to add it to your garden. This will free up space in your compost bin to add more waste material.

Fire-Resistant Plants

If you are in areas with a high fire risk, such as near forests, bush areas or dense bushland environments, mountains or prairies in Western Canada or the United States, choose plants that are fire-resistant.

A fire-safe landscape uses fire-resistant plants that are strategically planted to resist the spread of fire to your home. There are no "fire-proof" plants. You will want to select high-moisture plants that grow close to the ground and have a low sap or resin content. Fire-resistant plants are ideal in California because they are often drought tolerant. You can also check your local garden centre/nursery or landscape architect/contractor for advice on fire-resistant plants that are suitable for your area.

Creating a fire-resistant barrier around your home involves far more work than just picking out the right plants. An important fire protection tool is keeping them maintained and pruned. Keep low-growing plants within 9 metres (30 feet) of the home. Remove dead and dying vegetation, and keep plants properly spaced. The closer the plants are to the house, the more care that is required.

Here's a list of suitable fire-resistant perennial plants.

Blooming Time	Common Name (Cultivar)	Botanical/Scientific Name	OPALS Ranking
Mid – late summer	Angelina stonecrop	*Sedum rupestre*	2
June	Beardtongue	*Penstemon digitalis*	2
May – June	Columbine	*Aquilegia spp.*	1
Early – late summer	Coral bells	*Heuchera sanguinea*	1
June – August	Coreopsis	*Coreopsis*	3 – 5, varies
Summer – fall	Geranium	*Geranium*	3
Summer	Lamb's ear	*Stachys spp.*	3
June – August	Lavender	*Lavandula*	5
Late summer	Red-hot poker	*Kniphofia uvaria*	4
June – September	Salvia	*Salvia*	1 – 4, varies
July – August	Sweet William	*Dianthus barbatus*	1 – 3, varies
May – June	Thrift	*Armeria*	1

Blooming Time	Common Name (Cultivar)	Botanical/Scientific Name	OPALS Ranking
June – August	Yarrow	*Achilea millefolium*	4

Here's a selection of suitable fire-resistant perennial shrubs.

Common Name (Cultivar)	Botanical/Scientific Name	OPALS Ranking
Cotoneaster	*Cotoneaster spp.*	5
Fragrant sumac	*Rhus aromatica*	f = 1, m = 10
Honeysuckle	*Lonicera spp.*	5 – 6, varies
Lilac	*Syringa spp.*	5 – 6, varies
Rose	*Rosa spp.*	Low allergy rating; fragrant

Drought-Tolerant Perennials

Drought-tolerant landscapes will grow or thrive with minimal water and rainfall. In drought areas that result in mandatory water rationing, this type of garden is preferable.

Most drought-tolerant plants are what are considered "native" plants to a particular region. To reduce water requirements of drought-tolerant perennials, begin with good drainage and location/exposure. The design of this type of garden or container garden expresses your care for our environment.

Common Name (Cultivar)	Botanical/Scientific Name	Exposure	OPALS Ranking
Angelina stonecrop	*Sedum rupestre*	Sun	2
Barrenwort	*Epimedium*	Sun	1

Common Name (Cultivar)	Botanical/Scientific Name	Exposure	OPALS Ranking
Blue false indigo	*Baptisia australis*	Sun	2
Bugleweed	*Ajuga reptans*	Sun	1
Candytuff	*Iberis sempervirens*	Sun	2
Carpathian bellflower	*Campanula carpatica*	Sun/Part Shade	1
China pink (Dianthus)	*Dianthus chinensis*	Sun	1 – 3, varies
Cranesbill	*Geranium spp.*	Sun	3
Creeping lamium	*Lamium maculatum*	Sun/Part Shade	f = 1, m = 6
English lavender	*Lavandula angustifolia*	Sun	5
Flax	*Linum*	Sun	4
Lamb's ears	*Stachys spp.*	Sun	3
Lily-turf	*Liriope muscari*	Sun	3
Peony	*Paeonia spp.*	Sun	1 – full doubles, 3 – singles
Poppy	*Papaver oreophilum*	Sun	3
Purple coneflower	*Echinacea purpurea*	Sun	5
Rock rose	*Helianthemum*	Sun	3
Sea holly	*Eryngium planum*	Sun	4
Sea lavender	*Limonium*	Sun	3
Silver sage	*Salvia argentea*	Sun	1 – 4, varies
St. John's wort	*Hypericum perforatum*	Sun/Part Shade	5
Thrift	*Armeria*	Sun	1
Thyme	*Thymus*	Sun	3
Tickseed	*Coreopsis grandiflora*	Sun	3 – 5, varies

Common Name (Cultivar)	Botanical/Scientific Name	Exposure	OPALS Ranking
Yarrow	*Achilea millefolium*	Sun	4

Gardening and UV Index

Gardeners are especially susceptible to ultraviolet (UV) radiation from the sun while working in the garden. Often, we lose track of time as we immerse ourselves in the joys of gardening. The amount of damage from UV exposure depends on the strength of the light levels, the length of exposure and whether the skin is protected.

Check the UV Index to find out the intensity of the sun's UV rays when planning your daily outdoor activities. The greater the UV Index, the stronger the UV rays and the more you should be protected. You can obtain the daily UV Index by checking the local weather forecast or weather network from your computer.

If you will be out in the sun for more than 15 minutes, especially between 10 a.m. and 4 p.m., when the intensity of UV rays is the highest, protect yourself. Keep in mind that cloudy skies don't protect you from UV radiation.

SAFETY TIPS

- Cover up. Wear tightly-woven clothing that blocks out light.

- Generously apply broad spectrum sunscreen at least 15 minutes before you go out; a sunscreen with a sun protection factor (SPF) of 30 or more should be applied every two hours. You want to block both UVA and UVB rays to guard against skin cancer.

- Use a lip balm with an SPF of 30 or higher.

- Wear a hat. A wide brim hat (not a baseball cap) is ideal because it protects the ears, eyes, forehead, neck, nose and scalp.

- Wear UV-absorbent shades. Sunglasses should block out 99% to 100% of UVA and UVB radiation.

✓ Limit exposure. Stay in the shade or indoors near midday when the sun is the strongest on low or moderate days. Try to avoid sun exposure between 10 a.m. and 4 p.m. on days registering high, very high, and extreme on the UV Index scale.

✓ Stay hydrated. Drink plenty of water.

UV INDEX SCALE

0 to 2:	Low danger from the sun's UV rays for the average person.
3 to 5:	Moderate risk of harm from unprotected sun exposure.
6 to 7:	High risk of harm from unprotected sun exposure. Protection against eye and skin damage is needed.
8 to 10:	Very high risk of harm from unprotected sun exposure. Take extra precautions because unprotected eyes and skin will be damaged and can burn quickly.
11 or more:	Extreme risk of harm from unprotected sun exposure. Take all precautions because unprotected eyes and skin can burn in minutes.

There are many steps people can take to minimize their risk of overexposure to the sun's ultraviolet radiation, a primary cause of skin cancer. The importance of following the recommended protective steps for various UV Index levels is more important than ever. The ozone layer shield that protects the earth from harmful UV radiation is depleted, and we all need to adopt sun protection habits.

Just a Thought...

Don't think you can stay in the sun longer because you are wearing high-SPF products. Most people only apply 25% to 50% of the recommended amount of sunscreen, according to the American Academy of Dermatology. Because of this, exposure to UVA and UVB rays is greater.

SIX
FLOWERING GARDEN PLANTS

Perennials for the Garden

To obtain the best display of blooms with varying bloom times, make a garden plan. This can be your winter project when your garden is at rest, and you have time to research your wants, especially if you intend to have a pollinator/biodiverse garden. Do you want a formal or rustic garden, English cottage garden, relaxed or spiritual garden, etc.?

Keep in mind how your garden will look from inside and outside of your house and select a pleasing colour scheme that can be enjoyed from different angles. The garden plan should list plants that are suitable for your growing conditions. Consider including in your plan the soil conditions, how much daily sun exposure the area receives, trees nearby that may impede the area with root systems, fences or other structures, etc.

Wherever you live, you can follow a convenient rule for planting perennials. Plant perennials in the spring to be rewarded with yearly blooms in summer right into the fall. During early fall, plant perennials that bloom in spring. The blooming times and colour will be based on the climatic conditions in your area. When choosing various height perennials, look for length of the blooming season and combine with low ground cover or annuals for visual interest. Allergy/asthma sufferers should check for low-allergen perennials.

Here are some other helpful tips when planning a perennial garden:

1. If you're not sure what to plant, let the gardening experts at your local garden centre/nursery assist you. Staff can advise on plant suggestions to match your soil conditions, quantities of perennials you will need for the plot size, and growth habit(s) of the perennial.

2. Check the plant identification tag or label to make the right choice regarding your planting zone, desired bloom time, colour scheme, light conditions (sun to part shade, full sun, shade), plant height and spacing.

3. Fragrance in the garden is very important. Think about prevailing winds when planting fragrant annuals, perennials, shrubs or trees. Fragrance stimulates the senses and can reduce stress but has a detrimental effect for allergy/asthma sufferers.

Here are some other helpful tips for planting a perennial garden:

1. The best time to plant is during a cloudy day or later in the day when the heat of the sun is less prevalent. There's less chance of the plant's root system drying out during planting.

2. Situate the plant in the garden with the correct spacing for its mature size. So many times, I see plants jammed together because the gardener didn't consider the plant's growth pattern.

3. When digging a hole for plant placement, ensure the hole is no deeper than the height of the root ball and a few centimetres/inches wider than the container.

4. To remove the plant from the pot, invert the container with one hand splayed over the soil and cradle the stem(s). If the plant doesn't easily slide out, lay the container on the ground and roll it, pressing firmly down with your hands.

5. You will want to free some of the root ball (about 4 centimetres [1 1/2 inches] into the root ball at several points) to allow the roots to spread; otherwise you may stunt the plant's growth. You can do this by gently spreading the root ball apart with your hands, or use a clean, sharp knife, spade or scissors.

6. Set the plant into the hole, spreading the loosened roots. You may need to adjust the depth of the hole so that the plant's crown is at the right level. Adding compost or composted manure to the planting hole or surrounding area will help to improve water, nutrient holding capacity and drainage. If you have clay soil, the addition of very coarse sand will help to break up clay particles and improve drainage.

7. Backfill the hole halfway and firmly pack the soil with your hands. Water to settle the soil with a 15-30-15 water-soluble fertilizer or 20-20-20 mix according to label instructions. When the water solution is absorbed, finish backfilling the hole with more soil. Water from the garden hose or rain barrel.

8. Exposure to the sun and other weather elements can quickly dry out the soil. Don't forget to water your plants through the growing season.

SMALL HEIGHT PERENNIALS

The following perennials are typically less than 30 centimetres (ground loving to 1 foot) in height.

Blooming Time	Common Name (Cultivar)	Botanical/Scientific Name	OPALS Ranking
June – August	Angelina stonecrop	*Sedum rupestre*	2
April – May	Basket-of-gold	*Aurinia saxatilis*	3
June – September	Bellflower	*Campanula* 'Kent Belle'	1
April – June	Candytuff	*Iberis sempervirens*	2
May – June	China pink (Dianthus)	*Dianthus chinensis*	1 – 3, varies
April – July	Cinquefoil	*Potentilla spp.*	3
May – September	Cranesbill	*Geranium spp.*	3
April – May	Creeping phlox	*Phlox subulata*	3
April – June	Forget-me-not	*Myosotis spp.*	2
June – July	Golden stonecrop	*Sedum acre* 'Aureum'	2
June – August	Mother-of-thyme	*Thymus serpyllum* 'Magic Carpet'	3
May – June	Periwinkle	*Vinca minor*	2
April – June	Primrose	*Primula spp.*	3 – 6, varies
May – June	Pussy toes	*Antennaria spp.*	f = 1, m = 5
April – June	Rockcress	*Aubretia deltoidea*	2
May – June	Sea pink (Thrift)	*Armeria maritima*	1
June – July	Tufted violet	*Viola cornuta*	1
April – July	Wall cress	*Arabis caucasica*	1

Legend:

m = male; f = female plants

According to OPALS ranking: 1 = low and 10 = high, very allergenic

The following perennials are typically 30 – 90 centimetres (1 – 3 feet) in height.

Blooming Time	Common Name (Cultivar)	Botanical/Scientific Name	OPALS Ranking
June – July	Bachelor's button	*Centaurea montana*	3
June – August	Balloon flower	*Platycodon grandiflorus*	2
June – July	Bearded iris	*Iris germanica*	1 – 4, varies
April – June	Bergenia	*Bergenia cordifolia*	2
June – July	Bleeding heart	*Dicentra spectabilis*	4
July – August	Blue bomb speedwell	*Veronica spicata* 'Blue Bomb'	2
June – August	Butterfly weed	*Asclepias tuberosa*	3
May – June	Columbine	*Aquilegia spp.*	1
May – July	Coral bells	*Heuchera sanguinea*	1
July – September	Garden phlox	*Phlox paniculata*	3
May – August	Geum	*Geum spp.*	2
May – June	Globe flower	*Trollius spp.*	3
August – October	Michaelmas daisy	*Aster* 'Celeste'	2 – doubles, 4 – singles
June – October	Orange coneflower	*Rudbeckia fulgida*	5
May – July	Poppy	*Papaver*	3
June – September	Red valerian	*Centranthus ruber*	2
June – July	Speedwell	*Veronica incana*	2
June – August	St. John's wort	*Hypericum perforatum*	5
May – August	Sweet William	*Dianthus barbatus*	1 – 3, varies
May – July	Sweet William catchfly	*Silene armeria*	1 – 5, varies

Blooming Time	Common Name (Cultivar)	Botanical/Scientific Name	OPALS Ranking
June – August	Wood sage (Salvia)	*Salvia x sylvestris*	1 – 4, varies
June – August	Yellow sundrops	*Oenthera fruiticosa*	3

Legend:

Doubles = double-flowering varieties; Singles = single-flowering varieties

According to OPALS ranking: 1 = low and 10 = high, very allergenic

TALL HEIGHT PERENNIALS

The following perennials are typically 90 centimetres (3 feet) or taller in height.

Blooming Time	Common Name (Cultivar)	Botanical/Scientific Name	OPALS Ranking
April – June	Beadtongue	*Penstemon digitalis*	2
July – August	Blazing star	*Liatris spicata*	4
August – September	Bugbane	*Actaea matsumurae*	3
July – September	Cardinal flower	*Lobelia splendens*	f = 1, m = 4
June – August	False spirea	*Astilbe arendsii*	4
April – June	Foxglove	*Digitalis purpurea*	2
May – June	Garden peony	*Paeonia lactiflora spp.*	1 – full doubles, 3 – singles
June – September	Globe thistle	*Echinops ritro*	5
July – September	Hibiscus (Rose mallow)	*Hibiscus moscheutos*	3
July – August	Hollyhock	*Alcea rosea*	2 – 3, varies
June – July	Larkspur	*Delphinium exaltatum*	3
May – July	Lupine	*Lupinus perennis*	3

Blooming Time	Common Name (Cultivar)	Botanical/Scientific Name	OPALS Ranking
August – October	Michaelmas daisy	*Aster* 'Celeste'	2 – doubles, 4 – singles
July – August	Monkshood	*Aconitum napellus*	4
May – June	Peony	*Paeonia spp.*	1 – full doubles, 3 – singles
July – September	Purple coneflower	*Echinacea purpurea*	5
August – September	Red-hot poker	*Kniphofia uvaria*	4
June – September	Russian sage	*Perovskia atriplicifolia*	1
June – August	Scarlet bee balm	*Monarda didyma* 'Gardenview Scarlet'	3

Legend:

m = male; f = female plants

Doubles = double-flowering varieties; Singles = single-flowering varieties

According to OPALS ranking: 1 = low and 10 = high, very allergenic

Gardening Tip...

To give the illusion that your garden is larger than it is, strategically place framed mirrors on a garden fence.

Seasonal Flowering Plant Chart

This chart will assist you to design your continuous-flowering garden and/or the container growing plants, depending on the environmental conditions in your area (zone). Emphasis has been placed on allergy-friendly gardening for everyone's enjoyment.

| Common Name | Botanical/Scientific Name | Blooming Season | | | OPALS Ranking |
		Spring	Summer	Fall	
Astilbe	*Astilbe arendsii*		X	X	4
Black-eyed Susan vine	*Thunbergia alata*		X	X	2
Bleeding heart	*Dicentra spectabilis*	X	X	X	4
Blue flax	*Linum perenne*	X	X		4
Bridal wreath	*Spiraea spp.*		X	X	5
Butterfly weed	*Asclepias tuberosa*		X	X	3
California poppy	*Eschscholzia californica*	X			3
Candytuft	*Iberis sempervirens*	X	X		2
Carnation	*Dianthus caryophyllus*	X			1 – 3, varies
Catnip	*Nepeta cataria*	X	X	X	2
China pink (Dianthus)	*Dianthus chinensis*	X	X	X	1 – 3, varies
Clematis	*Clematis spp.*	X	X	X	5
Columbine	*Aquilegia spp.*	X			1
Coral bells	*Heuchera sanguinea*	X	X		1
Daffodil	*Narcissus*	X			4
English lavender	*Lavandula angustifolia*		X		5
Evening primrose	*Oenothera spp.*		X	X	3

| Common Name | Botanical/Scientific Name | Blooming Season | | | OPALS Ranking |
		Spring	Summer	Fall	
Fleabane	*Erigeron spp.*	X	X		4
Floss flower	*Ageratum houstonianum*		X	X	2
Flowering tobacco	*Nicotiana*		X	X	3
Forget-me-not	*Myosotis*	X			2
Foxglove	*Digitalis purpurea*	X	X		2
French marigold	*Tagetes patula*	X	X	X	3 – 6, varies
Gazania	*Gazania rigens*		X	X	4
Geranium (Zonal)	*Pelargonium x hortorum*		X	X	3
Globe amaranth	*Gomphrena globosa*		X	X	4
Hellebores	*Helleborus spp.*	X			4
Hollyhock	*Alcea rosea*	X	X	X	2 – 3, varies
Honeysuckle	*Lonicera spp.*		X	X	5 – 6, varies
Impatiens	*Impatiens spp.*		X	X	1
Lantana	*Lantana camara*		X	X	2 – 6, varies
Larkspur	*Delphinium exaltatum*	X	X		3
Lily	*Lilium hybrids*		X		4
Lindheimer's beeblossom (Gaura)	*Gaura lindheimeri*		X	X	2
Love-in-a mist	*Nigella damascena*		X	X	3

| Common Name | Botanical/Scientific Name | Blooming Season | | | OPALS Ranking |
		Spring	Summer	Fall	
Mandevilla	Mandevilla x amabilis		X	X	4
Money plant	Lunaria annua	X	X		4
Morning glory	Ipomoea purpurea	X	X	X	4
Moss rose	Portulaca grandiflora		X	X	2
Mullein	Verbascum spp.		X	X	2 – 5, varies
Nasturtium	Tropaeolum		X	X	3
Oriental poppy	Papaver orientale	X	X		3
Pansy	Viola spp.	X	X	X	1
Peony	Paeonia hybrids	X	X		1 – full doubles, 3 – singles
Petunia	Petunia	X	X	X	2
Pincushion flower	Scabiosa columbaria	X	X	X	3
Poppy	Papaver oreophilum	X			3
Rock rose	Helianthemum	X	X		3
Scarlet bee balm	Monarda didyma	X	X		3
Scarlet runner bean	Phaseolus coccineus		X	X	4
Shasta daisy	Leucanthemum x superbum	X	X		4 – doubles, 6 – singles
Snapdragon	Antirrhinum majus	X	X	X	1
Soapwort	Saponaria spp.	X	X		3

| Common Name | Botanical/Scientific Name | Blooming Season | | | OPALS Ranking |
		Spring	Summer	Fall	
Spiderwort	*Tradescantia spp.*	X	X		4
Spotted dead nettle	*Lamium maculatum*	X	X		f = 1, m = 6
Strawflower	*Helichrysum bracteatum*		X	X	4
Sweet alyssum	*Lobularia maritima*		X	X	5
Sweet marjoram	*Origanum majorana*		X		3
Sweet William (Dianthus)	*Dianthus barbatus*	X	X	X	1 – 3, varies
Tulip	*Tulipa*	X			1 – doubles, 3 – singles
Verbena	*Verbena x hybrida*		X	X	3
Vinca	*Catharanthus roseus*		X	X	1
Wax begonia	*Begonia semperflorens*		X	X	4
Wood sage (Salvia)	*Salvia x sylvestris*	X	X		1 – 4, varies
Yarrow	*Achillea millefolium*		X	X	4
Zinnia	*Zinnia elegans*		X	X	3

Legend:

m = male; f = female

Doubles = double-flowering varieties; Singles = single-flowering varieties

According to OPALS ranking: 1 = low and 10 = high, very allergenic

Just a Thought...

Gardening awakens our creativity. Share your gift and inspire others in their garden.

Everlasting Flowers

When you see arrangements of everlasting flowers, the question quite often is: Why can't I have some of those in my garden? Everlasting flowers are species that naturally retain their colour and shape after they have been air-dried. I have chosen several varieties that you can grow from seed, or you can purchase established plants for your garden to use and display next fall.

Some growers of everlasting flowers use a "weed barrier" (weed barrier cloth or fabric) or equal weed control method. Of course, you can use any of the well-known mulches.

Fertilizing with water-soluble fertilizer makes no difference because it's permeable, which means it allows liquids to pass through it.

Each plant variety has its optimum harvest time to best retain colour and form. You will learn this from experience, either too early or possibly too late. As well, the colour may darken or the cutting may be misshapen when they dry. Don't harvest plants for drying in the morning… wait until the dew has dried.

Before drying, carefully remove the foliage from the stems, unless you are drying it specifically for its foliage. There are four popular ways of drying flowers: air drying, glycerine, moist drying and desiccant.

Air drying is the simplest method, with flowers picked just as they are fully in bloom. Strip off the leaves and hang the plant by its stem in a cool, dark and airy place until fully dry.

Glycerine is helpful in giving grasses a lovely sheen or to retain the plant's suppleness. Dilute one part glycerine in two parts boiling water. Mix well and stand the plant in a jar containing 5 – 7 centimetres (2 – 3 inches) of the mixture. Set aside for 4 to 5 days until the plant changes colour.

Moist drying occurs when flowers are fully mature, then cut, with foliage removed. Stand the plant in a jar containing 5 centimetres (2 inches) of water. The plant will dry naturally. If the petals show signs of withering once the water evaporates, then add a little more water.

Desiccant method is useful for fleshy flowers (chrysanthemum, dahlia) that don't dry easily by any other method. Use a cardboard shoe box or similar and cover the bottom with 2 centimetres (3/4 inch) of silica gel or similar (desiccant). Place the cut flowers on this and work the desiccant carefully in among the petals until they are fully covered and only the stems show.

Seal the lid on the box with tape and place in a warm, dry place until fully dry. The drying time depends on the size and texture of the flowers, but it usually takes around two weeks. Lift the flowers out of the box with extreme care. Brush off any lingering desiccant with a soft brush.

Here are just a few plants you can try in your garden that work well as everlasting flowers.

Common Name (Cultivar)	Botanical/ Scientific Name	Drying Method	OPALS Ranking
Celosia (Cockscomb)	*Celosia argentea*	Desiccant. Most of the celosia is the crested variety used in everlasting arrangements. To dry the flowers, pick when the leaves are dry and the flowers are only half open.	4 – 5, varies
Chrysanthemum	*Chrysanthemum*	Desiccant. Flowers to be dried should be picked just before they are at the peak of maturity. Place the flowers face up on top of the silica. When fully dry, the plant material will be very brittle, so care should be taken.	4 – doubles, 6 – singles
Cornflower (Bachelor's button)	*Centaurea cyanus*	Air drying. Seed direct outdoors after last frost. This one is also good as a cut flower. Preference is full sun. Sow successively for cut flowers during the growing season. The seeds can also be seeded during the fall, before freeze-up.	3
Dahlia	*Dahlia*	Desiccant. Place the flowers face up on top of the silica. When fully dry, the plant material will be very brittle, so care should be taken.	2 – doubles, 5 – singles

Common Name (Cultivar)	Botanical/ Scientific Name	Drying Method	OPALS Ranking
Globe amaranth	*Gomphrena globosa*	Air drying or glycerine or moisture. Just before the first frost, cut the whole plant off at ground level and hang to dry. Globe amaranth resemble clover blooms and will flower from July – September.	4
Hydrangea	*Hydrangea*	Moisture or air drying. Hydrangeas are one of those flowers that almost dry themselves. Once dry, they can look gorgeous for years. The biggest challenge in drying hydrangeas is timing when to cut the blossoms. If you cut them in peak bloom, they will have too much moisture and won't dry quickly enough to retain their beauty. The perfect time is towards the end of the season when the larger petals are just starting to fade or change colour.	3 – 6, varies
Lavender	*Lavandula*	Dried seed head (air drying). Leave the seed heads on the plant until fully ripe, cut stems, and hang to dry in bunches.	5
Sedum (Stonecrop)	*Sedum alboroseum*	Moisture or air drying. You need to pick the plant before the blooms are completely open. Store in a cool, dark place for about a week. They will dry faster in a warm place, but they will lose more of their colour this way.	2

Common Name (Cultivar)	Botanical/ Scientific Name	Drying Method	OPALS Ranking
Strawflower	*Helichrysum bracteatum*	Air drying. The strawflower plant comes in yellow, orange, red, pink, burgundy, white or purple, and the colour will remain vivid after drying. Select strawflowers to be dried before the yellow centre of the flower opens and is visible. As the strawflower begins to dry, it will continue to open. Cut the selected strawflower with at least 25 cm (10 in.) of stem remaining on each flower head. It's better to band together small clusters of no more than a dozen flower heads at one time to improve air circulation and retain flower shape. Wrap with string or a rubber band. Hang the clusters upside down in a cool, dry and shaded place that receives good air circulation. They should dry and be ready to use in two or three weeks.	4

Legend:

Doubles = double-flowering varieties; Singles = single-flowering varieties

According to OPALS ranking: 1 = low and 10 = high, very allergenic

Your Cut Flower Garden

While you are browsing through the seed rack at your favourite store or garden centre, or intend to purchase plant seedlings, consider planting for a cutting garden. You can bring your garden indoors with fresh blooms displayed in vintage vases or other decorative containers. Keep in mind that some annual and perennial flowers are more useful for this purpose than others. Flowers with long stems fit well in floral arrangements, but the key is not to forget the contrast added by shorter ornamental flowers.

Tall, spike snapdragons for the vertical element and annual baby's breath (*Gypsophila*) are wonderful filler plants. Take note that baby's breath does have a higher OPALS ranking of 6. Working with a colour scheme looks good in your landscape but also later in your cut flower arrangement. Try and achieve a harmonious colour scheme that matches your personality. Your colour palette can be bold and playful, or restrained and softly demure, all by the choice you make with your plant selection.

Most annuals and perennials do well in a sunny, well-drained location with good air circulation. Arrange the annuals and perennials as a grouping in your landscape, a border along your driveway or your vegetable garden. Create visual interest with progressive plant heights by placing the low growing annuals or perennials in front with taller plants in the back.

As the cutting garden grows and you reap the harvest of your hard work, keep in mind these helpful tips:

1. Cut only the partially opened or newly opened flowers, and remove the older flowers from the plant.

2. Harvest the flowers early in the morning after the dew has dried or just before sunset.

3. Cut the stems with a sharp knife and keep the cuttings in a shady place to protect them from the heat of direct sunlight as you work.

4. Place the cut flowers in water as soon as possible so that they don't dry out.

Here are some suggestions for your annual cutting garden.

Common Name (Cultivar)	Botanical/Scientific Name	OPALS Ranking
Cornflower (Bachelor's button)	*Centaurea cyanus*	3
Cosmos	*Cosmos bipinnatus*	5
Dahlia	*Dahlia hybrid*	2 – doubles, 5 – singles

Common Name (Cultivar)	Botanical/Scientific Name	OPALS Ranking
Gerbera daisy (Transvaal)	*Gerbera jamesonii*	5
Marigold	*Tagetes*	3 – 6, varies
Rocket larkspur	*Delphinium ajacis*	3
Snapdragon	*Antirrhinum majus*	1
Star scabious	*Scabiosa stellata*	3
Strawflower	*Helichrysum bracteatum*	4
Sweet pea	*Lathyrus odoratus*	3

Legend:

Doubles = double-flowering varieties; Singles = single-flowering varieties

According to OPALS ranking: 1 = low and 10 = high, very allergenic

Evening Flowering Garden

We all deserve to relax at the end of the day with a cold beverage, with our feet up while on the balcony, deck or porch. There are night-bloomer plants that can calm us with intoxicating scents that tempt us outdoors. The evening scented garden is your "stress-reducing" site to be savoured with family and friends.

Water features in the garden are extremely soothing with the moonlight reflecting on the water's surface. If you don't want the expense or upkeep of a pond or water feature, add some candles and twinkle lights. It's the next best mood lighting solution.

Natural fragrance is preferred, but not for asthma/allergy suffers. Take the time to read plant identification tags and labels, and check the OPALS ranking to limit fragrances that may trigger an unpleasant reaction.

Common Name (Cultivar)	Botanical/Scientific Name	OPALS Ranking
Angel's trumpet	*Datura innoxia*	2
China pink (Dianthus)	*Dianthus chinensis*	1 – 3, varies
Columbine (Fragrant)	*Aquilegia spp.*	1

Common Name (Cultivar)	Botanical/Scientific Name	OPALS Ranking
Devil's trumpet	*Datura wrightii*	2
Evening primrose	*Oenothera spp.*	3
Evening scented stock	*Matthiola incana*	5
Flowering tobacco	*Nicotiana*	3
Four o'clock flower	*Mirabilis jalapa*	3
Gladiolus (Night)	*Gladiolus tristis*	3
Lily	*Lilium hybrids*	4
Moonflower	*Ipomoea alba*	4
Phlox	*Phlox spp.*	3

Legend:

According to OPALS ranking: 1 = low and 10 = high, very allergenic

Memorial Garden – A Living Tribute

When a loved one passes, it can offer some comfort by honouring them in the garden. There are no rules when creating a memorial garden. It can be a small or grand tribute to remind you of the time you spent with your loved one. For five years, my neighbour planted a rose bush to honour her mother every Mother's Day. Roses were her mother's favourite flower, and the family home had numerous rose beds lovingly tended.

What your memorial garden will look like will depend on the kind of dedicated space you have. Even a small space like an apartment balcony can offer you an opportunity to grow a single potted plant. You can move the plant indoors to over-winter when the weather turns.

A memorial tribute in the garden can help keep your mind focused on something beautiful and provide a peaceful place to retreat for reflection. You may want a quiet area where you can mediate or find inspiration and hope. Incorporate outdoor lighting to the area with candles, lanterns or solar lights so that you can visit the garden any time of the day.

Personalize the space by considering their personality traits, special interests and accomplishments. Incorporate special plants that they loved, such as hydrangea, rose or a lilac bush. Other ways you can memorialize a loved one in the garden may include adding a garden angel, bird feeder, concrete statue, engraved rock, sundial, water feature or wind chime. There are many symbolic details you can add to the garden.

Plants with favourite fragrances or colours will evoke fond memories. Perhaps the scent of lavender, lilacs or roses reminds you of the loved one. If red was the person's favourite colour, you can add a mixed bed of red geraniums, impatiens, poppies and verbena. Select plants that are the most meaningful for you or your loved one.

Many cities offer a program to dedicate a commemorative bench or tree in local parks for individuals to establish a living legacy. Through these programs, you may purchase a plaque with a desired inscription. During your visits to the park, you or other visitors can spend time sitting in a comfortable spot. Check with your local city or town officials to see if they have a commemorative program.

What form your memorial tribute takes is all about making it personal and relevant. Involve your family and friends in the planning, planting and caring for the garden to also help them with the healing process. By memorializing a loved one, you introduce future generations to a relative they never met. In Chapter 21 – Honouring Veterans, I discuss how you can honour a soldier with a Bravery Park.

Just a Thought...

"What a lovely thing a rose is!" — Sir Arthur Conan Doyle, author and physician

Climbers and Wall Plants

Growing climbers and wall plants have most of the same qualities of shrubs and trees: colours of leaves, fruit and flowers. The advantages of climbers and wall plants are that they cover unbecoming walls or fences, provide privacy and enhance archways, trellises or pergolas.

There are three different kinds of climbers and wall plants:

1. **SELF-CLINGING** These plants don't need support once they're established. They're true climbers that attach themselves to masonry and wooden surfaces by means of holdfasts (aerial roots). The fear that these plants damage the mortar of brick houses is generally unfounded. The exception is with older brick houses that used different mortar, compared to what builders use today.

Common Name (Cultivar)	Botanical/ Scientific Name	Description	OPALS Ranking
American bittersweet	*Celastrus scandens*	Fast growing vine with good fall showing. Flowers are yellow-white with yellow-orange-red fruit. Spring leaves are dark and glossy green but change to green-yellow during the fall. Height is 8 m (26 ft.).	f = 1, m = 6

Common Name (Cultivar)	Botanical/ Scientific Name	Description	OPALS Ranking
Boston ivy	*Parthenocissus tricuspidata* 'Veitchii'	This is one of the flattest growing vines and will adhere to brick walls and fences. The "tendril" vines have adhesive discs at their tips. Grows well in any available soil, but it's recommended to add compost or composted manure at time of planting. It will grow in sun, reflecting the heat of the south-facing wall, and can be grown on an east or west wall or fence.	4
Fiveleaf akebia	*Akebia quinata*	Hardy climber with small red-purple flowers. Clusters of five finger-like leaves in blue-green. Height 10 m (32 ft.). Partial to full sun.	4
Silver lace vine	*Polygonum aubertii*	This fast-growing vine requires little care. Grows in sun and light shade. Bright green leaves from July – October. The lacy vine has tiny creamy flowers in late summer. Prune to control the shape.	4 – 6, varies
Trumpet vine	*Campsis radicans*	Vigourous deciduous vine with dark green leaves. Has showy trumpet-shaped flowers that bloom in shades of red, orange or yellow. Prune during the month of February at 15 cm (6 in.) from soil level. The height of growth can be 3 m (10 ft.). This vine prefers full sun.	5

Common Name (Cultivar)	Botanical/ Scientific Name	Description	OPALS Ranking
Virginia creeper	*Parthenocissus quinquefolia*	Green leaves during the spring and summer change to bright red and orange in fall. Grows 20 m tall (65 ft.) and needs pruning in summer to curtail growth.	4

Legend:

m = male; f = female

According to OPALS ranking: 1 = low and 10 = high, very allergenic

2. **TWINING** These plants are capable of climbing to a greater or lesser height above the ground by twining the stems around a support, such as an arbour, fence, trellis or wall.

Common Name (Cultivar)	Botanical/ Scientific Name	Description	OPALS Ranking
Clematis	*Clematis spp.*	Many different varieties and colours are available. Showy, cup-shaped flowers from spring until fall. At planting time and every year thereafter apply a handful of garden lime, if preferable. The roots must be kept cool and moist; cover with bark mulch.	5
Dutchman's pipe	*Aristolochia macrophylla*	This vine is used as a dense screen. The large mid-green leaves can be 75 cm (30 in.) long. Mid-June it produces yellowish-brown pipe-shaped unique flowers that look like Dutchman's pipes. Plants need winter protection and grow well in well-drained soil. Plant in sun or shade.	3

Common Name (Cultivar)	Botanical/ Scientific Name	Description	OPALS Ranking
Fiveleaf akebia	*Akebia quinata*	Hardy climber with small red-purple flowers. Cluster of five finger like leaves in blue-green. Height 10 m (32 ft.). Partial to full sun.	4
Japanese wisteria	*Wisteria floribunda*	A strong growing vine with large leaves and a long chain of fragrant flowers during May and June, and seed pots in fall. Prune back in February.	4
Porcelain vine	*Ampelopsis brevipedunculata*	Small greenish flowers with variegated leaves produce lilac-blue berries that birds and squirrels relish. When choosing a supporting structure, keep in mind that the vine can grow 6 m (19 ft.) long and become quite heavy. They prefer a moist, well-drained soil but once established will tolerate drought. Grows in sun or shade.	2
Trumpet honeysuckle	*Lonicera sempervirens*	From spring until fall, this vine produces large fragrant flowers that attract hummingbirds. Grows well in rich garden soil but likes its roots in the shade. Recommended to prune in early spring. The vine has a twining stem and berries attractive to birds.	5 – 6, varies

Legend:

According to OPALS ranking: 1 = low and 10 = high, very allergenic

3. **HOOKED THORNS** The most familiar is the climbing rose with hooked thorns that claws its way up on a trellis or supporting wall. The plants need to be gently tied for support.

Common Name (Cultivar)	Botanical/ Scientific Name	Description	OPALS Ranking
Bougainvillea	*Bougainvillea spp.*	This is a tropical, shrub like vine that bursts with colourful flowers every year if it's planted in the right climate. It's commonly seen with red or purple flowers. Known for its colourful flower leaves (bracts), but its thorny stems make it an excellent species to consider for making a fence more secure. Requires excellent drainage in a relatively hot and dry climate. Can be used in colder zones as container plants.	1
Climbing rose	*Rosa spp.*	Hook-shaped rose thorns help some climbing roses grasp rough surfaces. From 0.9 m – 6 m (3 – 20 ft.). Plant in part sun. Loose anchoring to a support (arbour, fence, trellis or wall) will encourage young plants to climb. They develop either large single flowers or clustered blooms in shades of white, red, pink, orange or blue.	2 – 6, varies

Legend:
According to OPALS ranking: 1 = low and 10 = high, very allergenic

Plants for Dense Shade

Is there something that will grow in really shaded areas? This is a common question asked at garden centres/nurseries. A garden surrounded by shade trees can present a bit of a challenge for gardeners. There are shade-tolerant plants that have enticing flowers and foliage that will thrive without direct sunlight. You can use a layered, well-edited selection of plants for specific shade conditions to create a dramatic garden with delightful colours and textures.

Follow these guidelines to determine if you have a full sun, part shade (part sun) or shade garden:

Full Sun – 6 or more hours of bright, direct sun a day

Part Shade/Part Sun – gets 4 – 6 hours of direct sun a day

Shade – 4 hours or less of direct sunlight

Before planting in a shady area, dig and turn the soil before adding compost or other organic matter for soil preparation. Shaded areas are typically dry due to tree and other root systems competing for water. Plants growing in shade need to be regularly watered (2.5 centimetres [1 inch] per week if it doesn't rain). Don't overly saturate the area, as this will encourage diseases and plant rot. You can remove low tree branches to encourage more air circulation around the plants as another means of avoiding disease.

Fertilizer should be applied less frequently in shade areas, every 6 – 8 weeks, compared to garden beds in full sun. You can use a soluble fertilizer such as Miracle Gro™ if that is your preference. Here are some suggested shade-loving plants.

Common Name (Cultivar)	Botanical/Scientific Name	Type	OPALS Ranking
Bearberry	*Arctostaphylos uva-ursi*	Ground cover	2
Periwinkle	*Vinca minor*	Ground cover	2
Snow-on-the-mountain	*Aegopodium podagraria*	Ground cover	3
Hosta	*Hosta spp.*	Perennial	1
Carolina allspice	*Calycanthus floridus*	Shrub	3
Chokecherry	*Prunus virginiana*	Shrub	5

Common Name (Cultivar)	Botanical/Scientific Name	Type	OPALS Ranking
Emerald gaiety euonymus	*Euonymus fortunei*	Shrub	1 – 7 (All male plants would be allergenic)
Firethorn	*Pyracantha spp.*	Shrub	5
Fiveleaf aralia	*Acanthopanax sieboldianus*	Shrub	5
Flowering dogwood	*Cornus florida*	Shrub	5
Fringetree	*Chionanthus spp.*	Shrub	f = 1, m = 8
Gray dogwood	*Cornus racemosa*	Shrub	5
Japanese pieris	*Pieris japonica*	Shrub	3
Japanese yew	*Taxus cuspidata*	Shrub	f = 1, m = 10
Judd viburnum	*Viburnum x juddii*	Shrub	3 – 5, varies
Oregon grape	*Mahonia aquifolium*	Shrub	2
Red osier dogwood	*Cornus sericea*	Shrub	5
Serviceberry	*Amelanchier spp.*	Shrub	3
Snowberry	*Symphoricarpos albus*	Shrub	3
Sweet pepperbush (Summersweet)	*Clethra alnifolia*	Shrub	4

Legend:

m = male; f = female plants

According to OPALS ranking: 1 = low and 10 = high, very allergenic

Ground Covers for Low-Maintenance

Ground covers have a special place in each landscape. They grow in harmony with plants you already have or intend to use. They cut down on maintenance practices like weeding. In areas that are sloping, they reduce soil erosion. Ground covers can be as simple as gravel and mulch. To add beauty and interest, look to include plants with varying blooming times, colour combinations and height.

Ground covers can replace grass in many situations, especially in drought areas or where water usage is expensive. Use low-growers near walkways or at the front of the house if you want a greener look.

When you are purchasing a ground cover, think about the following factors:

1. Does it flower at the same time when the other plants surrounding it are just a green leaf?
2. Are the plant's berries and fruit edible for birds?
3. Are the plant's berries and fruit poisonous for small children if ingested?
4. Is it an evergreen, or will it drop its leaves when the cold weather starts?
5. Is there visual interest with the plant's unusual texture, colour or foliage?
6. Will this plant tolerate dry or wet conditions?
7. Is this ground cover allergy-friendly (OPALS 1 – 4 scale ONLY)?
8. Is this ground cover a fast or slow grower, and will it tolerate the sun or shade location?

Keep these pointers in mind as you walk through the garden centre/nursery to select plant material. Sometimes visiting other gardens in your neighbourhood or area can provide you with inspiration. A great resource is a botanical garden within your town or city.

The following chart provides an interesting blend of ground covers for your garden.

Common Name (Cultivar)	Botanical/Scientific Name	Description	OPALS Ranking
Ajuga (Bugleweed)	*Ajuga reptans*	Height: 15 cm (6 in.); sun or shade; leaves form a tight mat; purple foliage looks attractive	1
Hosta (Plantain lily)	*Hosta*	Height: 45 cm (18 in.); shade; many varieties and very hardy plant	1
Lily of the valley	*Convallaria majalis*	Height: 25 cm (10 in.); sun or shade; fragrant white blooms in spring, dark foliage	4
Periwinkle	*Vinca minor*	Height: 10 – 15 cm (4 – 6 in.); sun or shade; easy to grow, fast growing, different colour blooms	2
Purple leaf wintercreeper	*Euonymus fortunei* 'Coloratus'	Height: 30 cm (11 in.); sun; bold fall colour and dense cover	1 – 7, varies
Snow-on-the-mountain	*Aegopodium podagraria*	Height: 30 cm (12 in.); light shade; fast spreader, variegated leaves	3
Virginia creeper	*Parthenocissus quinquefolia*	Height: 25 – 30 cm (10 – 12 in.); sun or light shade; fast grower, good fall colour, hardy	4

Legend:
According to OPALS ranking: 1 = low and 10 = high, very allergenic

Guide for Dividing Perennials

After a successful blooming season, your garden bed may start to look like it's bursting at the seams with some plants taking over. Fall is the optimal time to evaluate your perennial beds and determine what plants need to be thinned. As years go by, perennial plants may start to show their age. Dividing the plants will give them a much-needed boost for health and longevity. Also, it's the perfect opportunity to move plants to other garden spots to flourish or to share plants with your family and friends.

Look for foliage that has started to turn colour or has started to droop after the first frost. This signals that the perennial is heading into its dormancy stage. As a general rule, I suggest moving spring and early summer flowering perennials in the fall and any late summer through fall bloomers in the spring.

Before you divide your perennials, it's helpful to first cut back most of the foliage. It will be easier to dig around the plant. Place your shovel into the ground around the outside of the plant and gently work to loosen the patch of soil. You want to get as much of the root ball as possible to keep the plant healthy. Carefully lift the plant from the hole, keeping excess soil around the roots. If any of the roots are soft and rotted, cut them out. You only want healthy roots. Once you have the perennial clump, you can start to divide the plant.

The most effective way to divide large, heavy perennials, such as daylilies, hostas and peonies, is to use a garden fork or a sharp spade. You want clean cuts to avoid damaging the plant or its roots. In a pinch, you can use a clean, sharp knife to carefully cut through the clump. Smaller plants can be divided successfully with a sharp spade.

After dividing perennials, you need to replant immediately so that the roots don't dry out. Replant the plant clump at the same soil depth before the division. You can add compost or manure in the hole to help rejuvenate the soil around the plant. After replanting, you will need to give the plant a good deep watering to settle the soil around the roots. You may wish to add a layer of mulch, keeping it away from the crown of the plant, for winter protection.

Most perennials benefit from being divided every few years. Use this chart to help you keep your plants healthy and your gardens from becoming overcrowded.

Common Name (Cultivar)	Botanical/Scientific Name	Season to Divide	How Often?
Aster	*Symphyotrichum spp.*	Spring	Every year or two
Astilbe	*Astilbe*	Early Spring or Fall	Every 3 – 4 years
Autumn joy sedum	*Sedum telephium*	Spring	Only divide to increase plant volume
Bearded iris	*Iris*	After flowering up to September	Every 2 – 3 years
Bee balm	*Monarda didyma*	Spring or Fall	Every 3 years
Bellflower	*Campanula*	Spring or early Fall	Every 3 – 4 years
Bergenia	*Bergenia spp.*	Spring	Every 3 – 4 years
Black-eyed Susan	*Rudbeckia hirta*	Early Spring or Fall	Every 3 – 4 years
Bleeding heart	*Dicentra spectabilis*	Early Spring	Every 3 – 5 years
Canna	*Canna*	Spring	Every 3 or 4 years
Chrysanthemum	*Chrysanthemum*	Spring	Every year or two
Coral bells	*Heuchera sanguinea*	Spring	Every 3 – 5 years
Cranesbill	*Geranium spp.*	Spring or Fall	Every 2 to 4 years
Garden peony	*Paeonia lactiflora spp.*	Fall	Wait up to 3 years
Hosta	*Hosta*	Early Spring or Fall	Every 4 – 7 years
Larkspur	*Delphinium exaltatum*	Early Spring	Every 2 – 3 years
Lily of the valley	*Convallaria majalis*	Early Spring	Every year divide for plant increase
Ornamental grasses		Spring for most grasses	Every 3 – 4 years
Ostrich fern	*Matteuccia*	Spring	Every 2 – 3 years

Common Name (Cultivar)	Botanical/Scientific Name	Season to Divide	How Often?
Pansy	*Viola spp.*	Early Spring	Every 3 – 4 years
Prairie coneflower	*Ratibida*	Spring	Every 3 – 4 years
Purple coneflower	*Echinacea purpurea*	Spring or Fall	Every 4 years
Red-hot poker	*Kniphofia uvaria*	Spring or Fall	Only to divide to increase plant volume
Sneezeweed	*Helenium*	Early Spring	Every 2 – 3 years
Spiderwort	*Tradescantia spp.*	Spring	Every 2 – 3 years
Tickseed	*Coreopsis grandiflora*	Spring or Fall	Every 1 – 2 years
Wormwood	*Artemisia*	Spring and Fall	Every 3 – 4 years
Yarrow	*Achillea millefolium*	Fall	Every 2 or 3 years

Legend:

According to OPALS ranking: 1 = low and 10 = high, very allergenic

Pollenless Sunflowers

How can you not smile when you see sunflowers blowing in the breeze? From reds, yellows, whites and bi-coloured, there are sunflowers for every taste. Did you know that sunflowers were the subject of a series of still life oil paintings by Dutch painter Vincent van Gogh? Perhaps he was as intrigued as I am by the large, dramatic heads and petals. Not only is the sunflower a widely recognized beauty, it's also known as an important source of food (seed and oil).

Sunflowers are related to ragweeds, and cross-allergenic reactions with other plants can occur. The good news is there are now some sunflowers for sale in local garden centres/nurseries that are pollen-free, making them nonallergenic.

Sunflowers come in a wide assortment of sizes that will fit in any garden. Depending on the cultivar, choose a site that will receive full sun and some protection from the wind. The ideal time for planting is when the soil has warmed, around the last frost date in your area. You have options of sowing seeds indoors or outdoors or planting established seedlings. If you decide to sow seeds directly in the garden soil, place at least 2.5 centimetres (1 inch) deep and 15 centimetres (6 inches) apart. Always check the seed package instructions for the chosen sunflower variety.

While not all varieties require staking, you may want to increase their stability and strength with some well-placed stakes. Bamboo canes are relatively inexpensive and natural looking, and serve the purpose well. You can use waxed garden string to loosely fix your sunflower to the stake. Sunflowers don't like to be too constricted, and if so, the stem will remain thin and weak.

You will want to give them enough room to grow, so that tall sunflowers won't shade other plants once they mature. A layer of organic mulch will conserve moisture and keep down weeds. Sunflowers are drought-resistant but will grow healthier if you water regularly during the initial growth period.

Birds do like going after the seeds. You can cover the flower with mesh bags, cheesecloth or another breathable material until the threat lessens. Both the honey- and bumble-bee are the primary pollinators of sunflowers.

Besides accommodating the allergy/asthma sufferers and the cut flower trade, these pollenless sunflowers in the garden are ideal for flower arrangements without the "pollen" mess and asthma triggers.

Common Name (Cultivar)	Botanical/Scientific Name	Description	OPALS Ranking
Cherry rose	Helianthus annuus	Red flowers, seedless and allergenic pollen free. Height: 1.5 m (5 ft.)	1
Dorado	Helianthus annuus	Brilliant yellow flowers, allergenic pollen free and seedless. Height: 1.5 m (5 ft.)	1
Fantasia	Helianthus annuus	Blend of all sunflower colours, allergenic pollen free and seedless. Height: 1.5 m (5 ft.)	1
Lemon aura	Helianthus annuus	Early blooming, light yellow and long-lasting. Height: 1.2 m (4 ft.)	1

Common Name (Cultivar)	Botanical/Scientific Name	Description	OPALS Ranking
Monet's pallete	*Helianthus annuus*	Excellent mix of colours, allergenic pollen free and seedless. Height: 2 m (6.5 ft.)	1
Strawberry blonde	*Helianthus annuus*	Flowers have burgundy, sometimes pink, petals with lemony tips and dark centres. Height: 1.5 – 1.8 m (5 – 6 ft.)	1
Sunrich series (Sunrich orange, Sunrich lemon, Sunrich gold and Sunrich orange summer)	*Helianthus annuus spp.*	All plants are pollenless and can be used for cut flowers. Heights range from 1.2 – 1.5 m (4 – 5 ft.)	1
Zebulon	*Helianthus annuus*	Amazing geometrical pattern in the bright green centre. Single stem, early flowering and perfect as a cut flower. Height: 0.9 – 1.5 m (3 – 5 ft.)	1

Legend:

According to OPALS ranking: 1 = low and 10 = high, very allergenic

Just a Thought...

Sunflower seeds are a good source of magnesium that your bones need to stay strong.

Spring Bulbs Are Blooming All Over

To me, the sure sign of spring renewal is the bursts of colour popping up in the garden after a long winter. I marvel that the bulbs I planted reward me with their tenacious spirits year after year. Whether you have a small or large garden plot, or are creating a container garden, there are spring or summer flowering bulbs for every growing condition.

There are bulb choices that will attract butterflies and hummingbirds and are happy in containers. They can make perfect cut flowers, are sun or shade loving, and are easy to grow. At one time, gardeners tended just to plant tulips, crocuses and daffodils, but that has changed with a wide selection that has endless possibilities for colour, texture and blooms. Let's look at finding the right flower bulb for your garden.

Here's a selection of fall-planted bulbs for spring flowering.

Common Name (Cultivar)	Botanical/Scientific Name	OPALS Ranking
Allium	*Allium giganteum*	2
Anemone	*Anemone blanda*	3
Daffodil	*Narcissus*	4
Dutch crocus	*Crocus vernus*	2
Four o'clock flower	*Mirabilis jalapa*	3
Freesia	*Freesia*	3
Fritillaria	*Fritillaria imperialis*	2
Gladiolus	*Gladiolus spp.*	3
Hyacinth	*Hyacinthus orientalis*	3
Muscari	*Muscari armeniacum*	2
Siberian squil	*Scilla siberica*	3

Common Name (Cultivar)	Botanical/Scientific Name	OPALS Ranking
Virginia bluebells	*Mertensia virginica*	1
Tulip	*Tulipa*	1 – doubles, 3 – singles

Legend:

Doubles = double-flowering varieties; Singles = single-flowering varieties

According to OPALS ranking: 1 = low and 10 = high, very allergenic

Try this selection of spring-planted bulbs for summer flowering.

Common Name (Cultivar)	Botanical/Scientific Name	OPALS Ranking
Acidanthera (Abyssinian sword lily)	*Gladiolus callianthus*	3
Bellflower	*Campanula spp.*	1
Caladium	*Caladium bicolor*	4
Calla lily	*Zantedeschia*	4
Canna	*Canna hybrida*	3
Carpet lily	*Lilium spp.*	4
Creeping buttercup	*Ranunculus repens*	4
Cyclamen	*Cyclamen hederifolium*	1
Dahlia	*Dahlia*	2 – doubles, 5 – singles
Dwarf iris	*Iris reticulata*	1 – 4, varies
Elephant's ear	*Alocasia spp.*	1
Gladiolus	*Gladiolus spp.*	3
Lily	*Lilium spp.*	4
Tuberose	*Polianthes tuberosa*	4

Common Name (Cultivar)	Botanical/Scientific Name	OPALS Ranking
Tuberous begonia	*Begonia tuberousa*	2
Wax begonia	*Begonia semperflorens*	4

Legend:

Doubles = double-flowering varieties; Singles = single-flowering varieties

According to OPALS ranking: 1 = low and 10 = high, very allergenic

> **NOTE**
>
> The bulbs that I have included in the charts may be from one species or "family," and there are many bulb varieties available. Always read the instructions on the bulb's package for the ideal plant zone and bloom times (early to late spring).

WHEN AND WHERE TO PLANT

Check the bulb's package for instructions on the best time to plant. Most spring bulbs need to be planted in the fall before the first frost occurs — plan for September or October. In areas with cold winters, bulbs can be planted as long as the soil is workable. If you leave it too late, the roots won't have an opportunity to grow and establish in the soil.

Once the soil temperature has dried and warmed to about 15.5°C (60°F), it's time to plant summer bulbs.

HOW TO PLANT BULBS

Most bulbs prefer a sunny location with well-drained soil. Soggy soil will lead to rot. Check to make sure that after it rains, your garden soil doesn't puddle. If so, either improve the soil's composition or consider planting the bulbs in a raised bed or a container.

Plan where you want the bulbs planted, and consider planting in a loose cluster (within a small oval or circular area) or drifts (grouping masses of one or two same colour bulb varieties in an irregular shape pattern).

When the flowers appear in the spring, they won't be standing in a straight line. Instead, the flowers will blend naturally into the landscape creating an appealing tapestry.

You will want to start by selecting healthy-looking bulbs. This means you want to avoid bulbs that appear withered, spongy or moldy.

Loosen the soil by digging with a trowel or spade to a depth of at least 20 centimetres (8 inches). By adding compost to the loosened dirt, you will help to improve drainage before planting.

Next, use either a trowel, spade or bulb planter to dig a hole to the recommended depth. If the bulb package doesn't state the planting depth, calculate this by measuring the top of the bulb to its base. Then double the bulb size to get the depth needed for planting. If the bulb is 5 centimetres (2 inches) high, dig a hole about 10 – 12 centimetres (4 – 5 inches). The recommended planting depths help to protect the bulbs from frost, animals and physical damage. When planting in a cluster, you will need to provide the bulb's root system, stem and flower bloom enough room to grow without overcrowding.

If a bulb has a pointed end, plant it facing up. If this is not evident, look to see if the bulb has a flat bottom or roots showing. This also indicates how the bulb should be planted and aligned at the bottom of the dug hole. Cover the bulbs with the original soil that was removed to create the hole. Water thoroughly without drenching to settle the soil and close any air pockets around the bulbs. Adding a cover of mulch at soil level will help the soil retain its moisture and acclimate the bulbs to the environmental conditions.

Mark your planting area so that you don't disturb your bulbs by planting other bulbs or plants in the same spot. You can use popsicle sticks for this task or other helpful identification tags.

Daffodils are distasteful to squirrels and chipmunks and, therefore, need no special protection. If you have been plagued with pesky rodents digging up your bulbs, spread a layer of chicken wire over the bulbs just below the soil surface. Or, you can try sprinkling some cayenne or red pepper in the planting hole along with the bulbs.

SPRING CARE

Once your bulbs have finished flowering, let the flower stalks die off naturally. You can tie the stalks and leaves together with string or twine. Try to resist the temptation to cut back while still green. It's not attractive, but the bulb needs time to photosynthesize and create food reserves to nourish next year's flowers.

If your bulbs have spread and made the garden area look overcrowded, you may wish to divide your bulbs. This is done in the dormant period and just after the foliage completely dies back.

STORAGE OF SUMMER-FLOWERING BULBS OVER WINTER

Summer-flowering bulbs tend to be tender perennials. Many gardeners treat these bulbs as annuals and dig up the bulbs in the fall.

For best results, remove the bulbs once the foliage has died. Carefully remove the bulbs so that you don't damage them. Brush off the loose soil by cleaning the tops, roots and old, loose scales. Let the bulb dry naturally for a day or two. Discard any injured or diseased bulbs from the bunch. You will want to store the bulbs in a cool dark place (basement) for replanting every year. Some bulbs, such as begonia, canna and dahlia, like to be stored in dry peat or vermiculite. You can also use a sphagnum moss carton box. Other bulbs, such as gladiolas and crocosmias, do well in a mesh bag. Wash and separate your bulbs before replanting them.

> **Gardening Tip...**
>
> *To complement bulbs purchased from the garden centre/nursery, add some speciality bulbs by selecting from one of the many reputable online merchants. Each year you can find something different from their online catalogues to include in your garden plans with a selection of new and unusual plant varieties.*

SEVEN
HEALTHY VEGETABLE GARDEN

Decreased Risk of Cancer – as Close as Your Garden

You've heard it on TV. You've read about it in magazines. You've probably even done your own research about it on the Internet. It seems that wherever you look, scientists worldwide are finding there's a relationship between eating foods that are high in vitamins A and C and a reduced risk of certain cancers.

With this in mind, the garden begins to look a lot more interesting when you realize just how readily available vitamins A and C can be.

Here's a list of edible plants, along with which vitamin (A or C or both) that they provide to keep our bodies healthy:

Dark green leafy vegetables, such as cabbage (vitamins A and C), kale (vitamins A and C), dandelion greens (vitamins A and C), lettuce, romaine (vitamins A and C) and spinach (vitamin A).

Yellow-orange vegetables, such as carrots (vitamin A), potatoes (vitamin C) and winter squash (vitamin A).

Other vegetables, such as beets (vitamins A and C), cauliflower (vitamin C), endive (vitamin A), green beans (vitamin C), leeks (vitamin A and C), onions (vitamins A and C), red and green peppers (vitamin C), squash (vitamin A), tomatoes (vitamin C) and turnips (vitamin C).

All of the above edible plants can be grown from seed, or you can purchase established plants from your local garden centre/nursery.

1. Plan your garden on a north-south axis to make maximum use of the sun.

2. Minimum amount of sunlight is 6 – 8 hours with protection from prevailing winds.

3. Good soil drainage (add compost to clay soil or sandy soil) and air circulation is a must.

4. Plant tall crops, such as pole beans, on the east side of the garden to minimize their shadow over other crops.

5. Never plant tomatoes or potatoes in the same area two years in a row. It's not the ruin of the garden plot if you do. However, be vigilant. If one of the soil-borne wilt diseases infests your soil, simply excavate the area and replace it with "clean" rich soil from a spot where tomatoes haven't grown.

6. Collect and use rainwater to water your plants, as it's less of a shock to them than cold water.

> **Gardening Tip...**
>
> *Growing tomatoes? Mix a tablespoon of garden lime (or crushed eggshells) with the planting soil at the base of each tomato plant's roots. This will prevent tomatoes from unsightly cracking.*

Companion Vegetable Planting

Since you may not have a huge area to dedicate to a vegetable garden, there's a need to find innovative ways to grow healthy vegetable pairings that won't interfere with each other's root patterns. When we take advantage of companion planting, our garden crops will be enhanced by increased quality and yields. This means you will get more food from smaller garden plots.

Canada's First Nations understand the value of plant combinations. The Three Sisters (*Kionhekwa* in the Iroquois language) are represented by corn, beans and squash. They formed the basis of their farming and cultural traditions. The corn stalks provided a pole for the beans, the beans returned nutrition to the soil and the large squash leaves sheltered the soil from the sun to discourage the growth of weeds. There are online sources if you are interested in learning about the legend related to the Three Sisters.

Just as the First Nations learned, there are many benefits of companion vegetable planting that you can use in your garden.

> **SHELTER** Larger plants can help protect other smaller plants from the wind or too much sun.

> **SUPPORT** Some vegetable plants can be used as a natural support for smaller plants.

> **HELPFUL INSECTS** With our choice of plantings we can attract helpful insects to our vegetable patch, such as bees to spread pollen.

> **IMPROVED SOIL CONDITIONS** Some vegetable plants improve the soil conditions for other surrounding plants by drawing nitrogen from the atmosphere and transferring it to the soil.

> **STOP INSECT INFESTATIONS** There are some plants that emit odours that deter insects. For example, lettuce repels earth flies.

The following is a guideline for companion vegetable planting. It will require some experimentation to find what works best in your garden and zone area.

Vegetable	Plant Companions	Benefits
Beans	Beets, cabbage, carrots, cauliflower, celery, corn, cucumbers, peas, radishes and potatoes	Beans provide nitrogen to garden soil. Corn acts as a natural trellis for beans. Beans get along with most vegetables, but not onions.
Carrots	Beans (bush and pole), garlic, lettuce, onion, peas and tomatoes	Beans provide nitrogen to the soil that is needed by carrots. Tomato plants may stunt the growth of your carrots, but the carrots will still have a good flavour.
Corn	Beans, cucumbers, lettuce, peas, potatoes, pumpkin, squash and zucchini	Beans and peas supply nitrogen.
Lettuce	Beans, beets, carrots, corn, onions, peas and radishes	Mint repels slugs, which feed on lettuce. Keep lettuce away from cabbage. Cabbage will alter the flavour of lettuce.
Onions	Beets, cabbage, carrots, lettuce, radishes, spinach and tomatoes	Onions repel aphids, carrot fly and other pests.
Peas	Beans, cabbage, carrots, celery corn, cucumber, lettuce, parsnip and potatoes	Peas and other legumes, like bean varieties, make good companion plants for many other vegetables, as they increase the availability of nitrogen in the soil.
Potatoes	Beans, cabbage, corn, eggplant, horseradish and parsnips	Horseradish increases disease resistance for plants.
Spinach	Beans, lettuce, peas and strawberries	Shade is provided by the bean and pea plants for spinach.
Tomatoes	Asparagus, basil, broccoli, carrots, celery and peppers	Basil planted within 25 cm (10 in.) will increase the yield of the tomato plant.

Vegetable	Plant Companions	Benefits
Turnip	Peas	Turnip greens protect the roots of peas from excessive sun rays.

Get Growing in a Community Garden

Have you travelled through your neighbourhood lately and spotted a garden patch with individual plots tended by a group of exuberant gardeners? If so, welcome to the joyous sight of community gardening. This gardening practice is not new and dates back through history as a method to provide food during wartime or periods of economic depression.

Community gardening varies widely throughout the world in how it's managed and whether vegetables or flowers are planted. In Europe, "allotment gardens," as they are commonly referred to, are comprised of dozens of plots that are rented by the same family for generations. In North America, community gardens or "victory gardens" contain small plots in a single piece of land that are gardened collectively by a group of neighbours. Inside the fence boundary, there may be a communal garden area where often the garden bounty is shared among "tenants."

Generally, community gardens tend to be operated by local community groups. Local neighbouring residents (tenants) are provided with access to grow fresh, healthy and nutritious vegetables. Since the number of plots is limited in a community garden, residents add their name to a waiting list to become a tenant. Sometimes, a nominal charge for membership is appointed to the successful tenant of the garden plot. An established set of garden rules and regulations must be followed. For example, tenants are required to participate in spring digging, site maintenance and fall cleanup of the garden.

Community gardens promote organic gardening methods and materials, avoiding synthetic fertilizers, pesticides and weed repellents. The gardens help to improve the health of the city's ecosystem by restoring oxygen to the air and reducing air pollution. They also reduce soil erosion and runoff that lessens flooding and saves the city money.

Community gardens create an ideal site for meeting people of diverse backgrounds to nurture friendships and share knowledge and skills. Children and garden novices can learn new skills and discover their connection to food and the earth.

It's not uncommon to find that 50% of residents in the surrounding neighbourhood of a community garden live in rental accommodations. With a community garden, they are provided access to growing land. Community food banks, soup kitchens or other charity groups in need can benefit from the garden's bounty of nutritious produce.

While vacant lots can be magnets for litter and criminal activity, it seems that community gardens can turn such an underutilized piece of land into a thriving neighbourhood asset. Of course, the cleaner space is a benefit, but the best result is a more active community. Vacant lots turned into community gardens give people a safe place to interact with peers and offer an ongoing presence to deter localized crime.

City- or privately-owned vacant land can easily be transformed into community gardens. For example, Vancouver, British Columbia, has over 75 community gardens in city parks, schoolyards and private properties. Many cities in Ontario have established community gardens on the grounds of churches, colleges and schools, city parks and vacant lots. Check with your local government to see if there are any available grants to start a community garden in your neighbourhood. Local churches and neighbourhood associations are another wealth of community partners to approach to get your community garden project off the ground.

Just a Thought...

Gardening involves outdoor activity that has been linked to significant beneficial changes in total cholesterol and blood pressure for optimum health.

EIGHT
HERB GARDEN

Herbs and Our Health Information

Growing a herb garden is not only beneficial for flavouring our food, but research affirms herbs' medicinal powers improve the quality of life. These plants have a long history of treating different ailments. Medicines, as we know them today, were nonexistent for our ancestors. It's interesting to note that recent herbal research shows certain plants are still effective in some of the same ailment treatments. A holistic approach in the treatment for a cold or a sore throat is within reach in your herb garden.

Herbs have been used through time for their unique compositions of antioxidants, essential oils, vitamins and phytosterols to help our bodies fight against germs and toxins and to boost immunity levels. Essential oils derived from herbs have been found to have anti-inflammatory properties that aid individuals with inflammatory health problems.

Caution! Before you rush to your medicine cabinet and throw out your prescriptions, you need to discuss your treatment options with your physician or health care provider.

There are six herb families: aster family (*Compositae*), borage family (*Boraginaceae*), carrot family (*Umbelliferae*), lily family (*Liliaceae*), mint family (*Labitae*) and mustard family (*Cruciferae*).

We'll look at a few common herbs to learn how they can help fuel our bodies.

Common Name (Cultivar)	Botanical/ Scientific Name	General Information	Purpose
Anise	*Pimpinella anisum*	A sweet-smelling annual (attracts butterflies), this plant is drought tolerant and a member of the carrot family. Anise likes full sun and good drained soil, but don't plant with carrots. May plant with lettuce or coriander.	The Greek physician Hippocrates recommended anise for coughs. It was used in a favourite aperitif. The anise herb is therapeutic for the digestive system.

Common Name (Cultivar)	Botanical/ Scientific Name	General Information	Purpose
Basil	*Ocimum basilicum*	This annual likes full sun or partial shade. Borage and opal basil deter the tomato horn worm moth. The taste from your tomato plants improves when you plant with *basil*. The word basil is derived from the Greek word *basileus*, which means king, and was used against scorpion bites.	Instead of an after-dinner mint, have some basil tea, which aids digestion. Basil leaves have chemical compounds that are known for disease-fighting and health-promoting properties.
Bee balm	*Monarda didyma*	This perennial prefers full sun; plant beside garlic to protect from mildew. Hummingbirds and honeybees love this plant for its showy flowers and citrus scent. The plant promotes insect pollination. Cut two or three fresh bee balm leaves and mix with plain yogurt or fresh fruit for dessert.	North American First Nations drank tea (known as "Oswego" tea) from this herb to reduce sore throats.

Common Name (Cultivar)	Botanical/ Scientific Name	General Information	Purpose
Catnip	*Nepeta cataria*	This perennial re-seeds itself easily and is a member of the mint family; grows in partial or full sun. It's advisable to plant catnip in containers to reduce spreading. In the 18th century, catnip was commercially grown and used in the production of sedatives. Catnip is very attractive to deter flea beetles, potato beetles, ants, cabbage and squash bugs.	Catnip grown in containers under the overhang of your house seems to deter cats from using this area as a "kitty litter zone."
Chamomile	*Chamaemelum nobile*	Annual that re-seeds itself and can be grown in full or partial shade. Chamomile is **highly allergenic** and related to ragweed. German chamomile produces more flowers than Roman chamomile. Growing your own plants from cuttings? Chamomile tea is a good fungicide. Spray tea on soil to treat damping off disease, especially for basil, cucumbers and geraniums.	Ancient Egyptians used chamomile for malaria chills and antiseptic properties. It's said that if you plant chamomile next to a sick plant, the plant will recover. Putting chamomile in your compost bin works as an activator.

Common Name (Cultivar)	Botanical/ Scientific Name	General Information	Purpose
Chervil	*Anthriscus cerefolium*	This annual likes semi-shaded areas with slightly moist soil. Chervil is one of the "fine" herbs. The others are chives, parsley and tarragon. Harvest chervil leaves before the flower buds form. When the flowers appear, the leaves lose their aroma.	Chervil can be used with sliced carrots, cheese, corn, eggs, peas and spinach. Use in salads, and it also goes well with corn or potato soup.
Chives	*Allium schoenoprasum*	This perennial grows in clumps and likes moist soil. Chives should be clipped 3 cm (1 1/4 in.) above ground level. Chives are very attractive when in bloom, so you might keep several growing for aesthetics. This herb has a mild onion flavour.	Rich in vitamins A and C, which are cancer "preventers." Chives are known for the control of aphids and carrot flies. Plant some chives under your apple tree to prevent apple scab. Rabbits don't like chives.
Coriander	*Coriandrum sativum*	This herb belongs to the carrot family and is also known as cilantro or Chinese parsley. Coriander grows in part shade or full sun in well-drained soil. If you intend to use the leaves only (Chinese parsley), sow seeds every two weeks to have a continuous supply.	The sweet tasting seed of coriander goes well with pickles, meats and sauces. The seeds add a fresh, spicy flavour to stews and soups.

Common Name (Cultivar)	Botanical/ Scientific Name	General Information	Purpose
Dandelion	*Taraxacum officinale*	Dandelions, because they flower so early in spring, are essential to bees. Goldfinches eat dandelion seeds and line their nest with dandelion fluff. Problems with dandelions in your lawn? Dandelions grow well in slightly acidic soil. Adding garden lime in spring and fall to the grass will eventually sweeten the soil. Grass grows better in sweet soil.	Dandelions are rich in vitamins A and C, and the flowers are an important antioxidant. The Chinese have used this plant for medicinal purposes for centuries. The leaves make a delicious salad.
Dill	*Anethum graveolens*	This annual re-seeds itself. Dill requires full sun and well-drained soil. Companion planting with onions and lettuce.	Dill goes with most dishes but is very tasty in a cucumber salad. This popular herb contains no cholesterol and is very low in calories. Nonetheless, it holds many antioxidants, vitamins like niacin and pyridoxine, and dietary fibers that help in controlling cholesterol levels.

Common Name (Cultivar)	Botanical/ Scientific Name	General Information	Purpose
Garlic	*Allium sativum*	This perennial requires full sun and well-drained soil. Don't let the plant flower as garlic spreads rapidly from seeds. During WWI, army doctors dipped sphagnum moss into garlic juice, which they applied as a disinfectant to wounds.	Garlic has been extensively used for medicinal purposes since biblical times. Noteworthy are the phyto-nutrients, minerals, vitamins and antioxidants for good health promotion. Plant garlic to deter borers, Japanese beetles, moths, and root maggots, and to protect against blights and rust. Plant near rose bushes to control aphids and black spot.
Hyssop	*Hyssopus officinalis*	The perennial is easy to grow and becomes a large bush in the first year. Leave this plant standing in the winter because the birds like it.	Hyssop helps to control cabbage butterflies, as the moths are deterred by the oils of the hyssop. Bees use this plant to make very good honey. Hyssop flowers can be sprinkled over salads.
Lavender	*Lavandula*	This perennial likes full sun and good drainage. During the Middle Ages, lavender was the herb of love.	Lavender is known to repel flies, moths in clothes closets and mosquitoes. Place some in your kitchen or cottage.

Common Name (Cultivar)	Botanical/ Scientific Name	General Information	Purpose
Mint	*Mentha species*	Mint is a perennial and grows best in partial shade. Use containers to confine mint so that it won't spread, as it's an invasive plant. In October dig a clump of mint from the garden and put in a large pot to bring into the house. It will grow all winter in a sunny window.	Mint repels ants, flea beetles and fleas. Mint is very fragrant and the flowers attract bees. The culinary varieties are spearmint and peppermint, and can be used in jellies and sauces. In summer, crush fresh mint leaves and add to iced tea.
Oregano	*Origanum heracleoticum*	Requires full sun and well-drained soil. The ancient Greeks made poultices from the leaves and used them for aching muscles. Golden oregano is suitable for rock gardens and edges of flower beds.	Oregano has a strong flavour and can be used in tomato sauce and stews. For cooking, I prefer to use oregano (*Origanum heracleoticum*), not the vulgare variety. Add 3 – 4 drops of oil of oregano on a tablespoon with orange juice as a daily preventative aid during cold season.
Parsley	*Petroselinum sativum*	There are two types of parsley: curly and flat leaf. Dig a few roots of parsley from the garden and place them in a container in a sunny window for growing indoors during the winter.	This annual has high levels of vitamins A and C content. Parsley tastes good with boiled potatoes and in salads and soups. Parsley helps garlic-lovers keep their breath fresh; it has one of the highest levels of chlorophyll of any herb.

Common Name (Cultivar)	Botanical/ Scientific Name	General Information	Purpose
Rosemary	*Rosmarinus officinalis*	This plant likes a calcium-rich soil. In early September, transplant indoors. It doesn't like to be watered directly so use a spray bottle.	The herb is exceptionally rich in many B-complex groups of vitamins, such as folic acid. Fill a spray bottle with some chamomile and rosemary tea (extracted for 24 hours) to repel mildew. Dried leaves placed in an onion bag will control moths.
Sage (Common)	*Salvia officinalis*	This is a very fragrant annual. It grows in any soil type. Clary sage is one of the oldest English herbs. It has multi-coloured flowers. Plants should be tied up during the winter months in the garden.	Sage herb parts, whether fresh or dried, are rich sources of minerals like calcium, copper, iron, manganese, magnesium, potassium and zinc. The herb contains very good amounts of vitamin A and beta-carotene levels. Sage controls cabbage maggot. Chopped leaves can be added to salads, soups or stews.
Savory	*Satureja hortensis*	Make several plantings because savory can withstand only one cutting.	Dry savory herb has amazingly high levels of minerals and vitamins. This is known as the "bean herb." All dishes containing beans or peas are enhanced with savory. Rub the leaves on insect bites to ease pain and itch.

Common Name (Cultivar)	Botanical/ Scientific Name	General Information	Purpose
Tarragon	*Artemisia dracunculus*	Also called Little Dragon. It grows well in poor soil and full sun. *Artemisia* is a close relative of ragweed (*Ambrosia spp.*). Tarragon is **highly allergenic**.	Fresh tarragon herb is one of the highest antioxidant value food sources among the common herbs. Tarragon is a notably excellent source of minerals like calcium, copper, iron, manganese, magnesium, potassium and zinc.

Plant Selection for a Herb Garden

The herb garden is always welcome because it's practical and healthy, and herbs can be grown in a small area. If you don't have space in your garden, look at growing herbs in containers. You can use various size clay pots to provide an adequate crop that is easily maintainable.

When we buy "fresh" herbs from the grocery or health food store, we don't know when they were packaged. We have no idea how long they have sat on the shelf or if pesticides have been used in the growing process. We take control of these uncertainties when we grow a crop of fresh herbs. We can control when we harvest and use only what we need to maintain freshness and taste.

You don't need to grow all of your herbs found in your kitchen, only the ones that you frequently use. Growing herb plants from seed can be very economical. For the price of one common herb plant from your local garden centre/nursery you can buy a package of seeds. Sharing seeds with family and friends is an ideal solution to keep costs down.

Here's a list of handy herbs to grow for use in your favourite recipes.

Common Name (Cultivar)	Botanical/Scientific Name	Exposure	OPALS Ranking
Basil (Sweet)	*Ocimum basilicum*	Full sun	2
Calendula	*Calendula officinalis*	Full sun/part shade	4
Catmint	*Nepeta racemosa*	Full sun/part shade	2
Catnip	*Nepeta cataria*	Full sun/part shade	2
Chives	*Allium schoenoprasum*	Full sun/part shade	2
Cilantro (Coriander)	*Coriandrum sativum*	Full sun	3
Common sage	*Salvia officinalis*	Sun	1 – 4, varies
Dill	*Anethum graveolens*	Full sun	3
Garlic	*Allium sativum*	Full sun	2
Lavender	*Lavandula*	Full sun/part shade	5
Lemon verbena	*Aloysia citriodora*	Full sun	3
Mint	*Mentha spp.*	Full sun/part shade	3
Oregano	*Origanum vulgare*	Full sun	3
Parsley	*Petroselinum sativum*	Part shade	1
Rosemary	*Rosmarinus spp.*	Sun	3 – 5, varies
Rue	*Ruta graveolens*	Sun	4
Savory (Summer)	*Satureja hortensis*	Full sun	1 – 3, varies
Thyme	*Thymus vulgaris*	Sun	3

Legend:

According to OPALS ranking: 1 = low and 10 = high, very allergenic

Many herbs should be harvested before the flowers open. Herbs must be thoroughly dried before storing. In general, leaves keep their colour when they are dried in the dark. The herbs sage, savory and thyme may be dried in the sun without losing colour.

Unlike garlic, which is sterile and therefore doesn't produce seeds, new plants are grown by planting individual sections of the bulb (cloves). The best time to plant is the fall. The timing of fall planting should be such that the roots have a chance to develop and the tops don't break the surface before winter, which is about three weeks before the ground freezes. In some regions, spring planting is traditional. Ensure the soil is well-drained with plenty of organic matter. Place cloves (keep the papery husk on each clove) 10 centimetres (4 inches) apart and 5 centimetres (2 inches) deep, in an upright position (the wide root side facing down and the pointed end facing up). In the spring, the shoots will emerge through the ground.

HOW TO DRY HERBS

1. Cut healthy stems from your herb plants. Take only what you think you will need.

2. Remove any dry or diseased leaves. Yellowed leaves and leaves spotted by disease are not worth drying. The flavour has already been compromised by the stress of the growing season.

3. Before bringing indoors, gently shake the stems to remove any insects. There are always small insects hidden, and since you won't be thoroughly washing these stems, you want to get rid of as many as you can before hanging the plants.

4. If you picked your herbs while the plants were dry, you should be able to simply shake off any excess soil. But if necessary, rinse with cool water and pat dry with paper towels. Give them plenty of air circulation so that they can dry quickly. Wet herbs will rot.

5. Remove the lower leaves along the bottom inch or so of the stem.

6. To dry leaves, tie 4 – 6 stems in bunches and hang on a drying rack or spread on window screening stapled to a wooden frame. To protect from the dew, never leave the drying herbs outside during the night. The moisture will ruin the herb. Dry in a dark, cool place, such as a basement.

7. Check in about two weeks to see how things are progressing. Keep checking weekly until your herbs are dry and ready to store.

STORING DRIED HERBS

1. Store your dried herbs in air-tight containers, such as zippered plastic bags or small canning or spice jars.

2. Be sure to label and date your containers.

3. Your herbs will retain more flavour if you store the dried leaves whole and crush them when you are ready to use them.

4. Discard any dried herbs that show the slightest sign of mould.

5. Place containers in a cool, dry place away from direct light. You may wish to store your dried herbs in the fridge.

6. Dried herbs are best used within a year. As your herbs lose colour, they are also losing their flavour profile.

Herbs on the Windowsill

A windowsill provides the perfect spot to start a simple indoor herb garden. Regardless if you live in an apartment or a house with plenty of backyard space, almost anyone can grow healthy herbs.

You can start from seed or purchase established plants. If growing herbs from seed, you should first grow in a seed tray or similar container. You can transplant into a pot or window box when the plant has two or more sets of leaves. Always follow the direction on the seed package.

Herbs love the sunlight. Bright sunlight from a south, east or west window is best. Good light quality is important to grow a healthy, strong and richly flavoured plant.

Choose a clay, ceramic or plastic pot or window box with drainage holes. The drainage hole(s) are important to let the extra water drain. Roots that sit in water can't breathe, and when they sit too long in the water, they rot away. Before adding clean gravel or pebbles, place an old cloth, towel or non-scented dryer sheet on the bottom of the pot or window box. Next, add 2 centimetres (3/4 inch) of clean gravel or pebbles. This will keep the moisture in, and the soil won't wash away. The soil should be a soilless mix or potting soil. Garden soil is too dense.

Dig a small hole for each plant, and loosen the roots a little to allow the plant's roots to expand in the new soil. Press the soil firmly around the roots. Water well, but don't saturate.

Keep the herbs healthy by watering when the soil gets dry on the surface. In general, herbs don't like "wet feet." Keep the plants full by pinching off the tips. If planting chives, harvest by pinching back all the way to soil level.

You can grow the following herbs on the windowsill: basil, catnip, chives, curled and plain parsley, garlic chives, lemon balm, oregano, rosemary, and all types of sage and thyme.

WINTERING HERBS INDOORS

At the end of the garden's growing season, there is no reason to discard the herb plants that we would like to bring indoors through the winter. Many herbs will thrive over winter and can be replanted the following spring.

Oregano, rosemary and scented geraniums should be brought indoors. Chives, mint and thyme adapt well from outdoors to growing indoors. Basil, an annual herb, tends to grow weary after a few weeks indoors.

Here are steps to bringing your perennial herb garden indoors for the winter months. The best time to do this is before a frost.

1. Choose the healthiest herb plants from your garden bed. Look for small- to medium-size plants as they will be easier to dig without destroying many roots.

2. Check for any signs of insects and spray with an insecticidal soap before you move the plant inside. An easy insecticide mix is 30 millilitres (2 tablespoons) of dishwashing soap in a litre (quart) of water.

3. If repotting the plant directly from the garden bed, select a container that best fits the size of your plant.

4. Refer to the instructions above for windowsill planting and light conditions.

5. Don't fertilize. Most herbs will grow slowly over the winter months. Cut what you need for cooking and leave some leaves for the plant to survive.

Before you know it, spring is here again and you can replant in the garden once the danger of frost has passed.

> **Gardening Tip...**
>
> *If using reused plastic pots, they should be cleaned with one-part bleach and ten parts water. Rinse well after cleaning. Set aside to dry.*

Small Herb Garden for Cooking

When you only have a small area in the garden to dedicate to herbs, or you want to grow herbs in containers on your deck or balcony, don't despair. Remember you can grow herbs indoors or outdoors. The choice is yours.

Many herbs are chock-full of valuable nutrients that your body needs for maximum health. The most flavourful culinary herbs are harvested from well-tended plants in their leaf-making stage. If your herbs grow too fast to use them fresh, dry or process the extra for later use.

I am including a few herbs for cooking that will elevate your dishes. You can usually substitute 15 millilitres (1 tablespoon) of fresh herbs for 5 millilitres (1 teaspoon) of dried herbs, but always check the recipe for substitution instructions.

Common Name (Cultivar)	Botanical/ Scientific Name	Part Used	Cooking Uses
Basil (annual)	*Ocimum basilicum*	Leaves	Has a strong flavour that has a taste combination like clovers and licorice. Use in pesto, salads, spaghetti sauce or vinaigrettes.
Borage (annual)	*Borago officinalis*	Leaves and flower	The leaves smell and taste like cucumber. The flower has a sweet, honey like taste. Edible decoration in salads.
Dill (annual)	*Anethum graveolens*	Leaves and seeds	Has a light, distinctive flavour. Use in salads, fish and meat recipes, and vegetables.
Chives (perennial)	*Allium schoenoprasum*	Leaves	Related to onions and other bulb vegetables, it has a light onion taste. Use in eggs, fish, salads, vegetables, topping for baked potatoes, soft cheeses or spreads.
Common sage (perennial)	*Salvia officinalis*	Leaves	Has a slightly bitter taste. Use in beef, beef stews, cheeses (cheddar, cream and cottage), eggs, lamb, meat, pasta, pâté, pork, sauces (brown and meat), soups (cream and chowder), stuffing (for fish, meat and poultry) or vegetables.
Fennel (annual)	*Foeniculum vulgare*	Leaves and seeds	This herb is related to celery. Use in dressings and salads.

Common Name (Cultivar)	Botanical/ Scientific Name	Part Used	Cooking Uses
Marjoram (perennial)	*Majorana hortensis*	Leaves	Marjoram is similar to oregano but is milder and sweeter. Use in beans, meats, pork, salads and soups.
Spearmint (perennial)	*Mentha spicata*	Leaves	Has a flavour that is connected to its name; cool to the tongue. Use in jellies, sauces and teas.
Oregano (perennial)	*Origanum vulgare*	Leaves	With a stronger, more pungent aroma and flavour, oregano works well in butters, fish, lamb, pork, sauces (white and tomato), stews, soups, vegetables or vinegars.
Thyme (perennial)	*Thymus vulgaris*	Leaves	Has an intense flavour so use in small amounts when cooking. Use in beef, chowders, fish, games, pâté, poultry, soft cheeses, soups, tomato sauce or vegetables.

Disease Prevention in Herbs

When disease shows up in your herb garden, it's difficult to control. The disease impregnates deep into the leaves or root structure, causing internal injuries before visible symptoms develop. Fungicides and pesticides are only useful for preventing diseases. As the first line of defence, choose the best planting and harvest times, and use resistant varieties and certified plants.

Watering is very important to prevent disease infestation, but weeding and crop rotation of your herbs can prevent disease infestation. If fungicides or pesticides are used, **always** wash the harvested plants with cold water before use.

In the future, plant breeders will develop hardier herbs that will be resistant to the above-mentioned diseases as a result of genetic resistance.

I am including some common diseases that might affect your herb plants. Due to the inexpensive cost of herb plants, you may choose to replace the plant to halt possible cross-contamination with healthy plants.

SOIL-FUNGAL DISEASES

Soil-borne fungal diseases are difficult to control because they are only noticed after the damage has taken place. The most common soil-borne diseases are as follows:

1. **Vascular wilt** is caused by organisms that settle into the water-conducting tissue. Leaves become yellow from the bottom of the plant upwards. You will see this, especially during severe drought conditions. Mint can be affected.

2. **Root rot** is present in every soil. Seed and seedlings are damaged, known as damping-off. For example, damping-off is a frequent problem with parsley when it's seeded too early in a cool, wet spring season.

FOLIAR-FUNGAL DISEASES

Fungi cause the most common disease on herb plants. Fungi can cause blights or leaf spots on nearly every plant you grow. The following are the most common:

1. **Grey mould** establishes itself on ageing (old) flowers and dying plants or yellowed lower leaves. From these places, this fungus attacks the healthy parts (tissue) of the herb.

2. **Rust** is so named for the red to orange powdery spores containing blisters that it produces on infected plants. Mint rust can be found underneath the leaves of the plant or stem.

3. **Powdery mildew** is identified by a large amount of powdery white fungus and occurs on the upper leaf surfaces. This fungus reproduces rapidly during times of high humidity.

4. **Anthracnose** is noticeable as cankers and spots on leaves and stems. The best control is to keep the foliage as dry as possible. Outdoor watering should be done early in the morning so foliage will dry more quickly.

5. **Downy mildew** descends upon ground plants from above. This causes vigourous blighting and a decline of the plant tissue. Downy mildews are also known as "water moulds."

BACTERIAL DISEASES

The bacterial disease is less common, but we can find them in fennel and parsley (soft rot) and bacterial leaf spot on catnip. Bacterial diseases can also affect coriander.

Deter Pests with Herbs

Not only do herbs provide adventurous cooks with seasoning options, but they also work especially well as companion plants in your garden. Herbs multitask by attracting "good" insects and repelling "bad" or "pest" insects. Insects can quickly turn a cabbage to lace, bore holes through peppers or tomatoes, and suck the life out of most plants. Herbs are a perfect solution when you want to control the use of harmful pesticides.

When selecting herbs, you should look for plant options that contain natural pest repellents, such as citronella. How many of these natural pest repellents you will need depends on the size of your garden. The general rule of thumb is to integrate a few of the herb plants among your other plants every 1 metre (3 feet), if possible. You can also plant some of the herbs in containers to place on your deck or porch.

Let's look at a few herbs that will keep pests away from your garden flowers and vegetable crops. These are a viable, economical option for pest control:

- Basil or rosemary will rid your backyard of nasty flies and mosquitoes.
- Chives, coriander or nasturtium flowers will stop aphids appearing on your plants.

- Garlic, rue or tansy will deter the Japanese beetle from attacking your rose garden.

- Lavender will deter flies, moths and ticks.

- Lemongrass contains citronella and will help to repel mosquitoes.

- Lemon balm is a natural bug repellent and contains a compound called citronellai (similar to citronella). You can crush the fresh leaves and rub them directly on the areas of your skin that is most exposed and vulnerable to bug bites.

- Mint will discourage ants and flies.

- Rosemary, marigolds or nasturtium will prevent visits from the bean beetle and carrot fly.

- Sage or rosemary will stop the carrot fly, cabbage moth and slugs from landing in your garden.

Not all insects are bad. As I have mentioned before in this guide, there are many insects that are beneficial to your garden. Some parasitic wasps prey on caterpillars and tomato hornworms that can damage your vegetables. Bees are critical to pollinating vegetable flowers to create the fruit. Ladybugs, ground beetles and hoverflies feed on aphids, mealybugs, mites, scales and other damaging pests.

Just a Thought...

Integrating herbs with your flowers and vegetable plants is a smart gardening decision.

Herb Garden for Bees

Besides the many uses in cooking, drying, teas, dyes for fabrics, fragrances and medicinal purposes, herbs attract bees. We all know that without pollination of our berry bushes, blossoming vegetables and fruit trees, our crops would diminish. You can make a big difference in the declining bee population by creating a bee-friendly garden. Bees are drawn to glorious floral colours as well as sweet smells.

Through improved pollination, we can increase our harvest, and every gardener should plan to grow bee-attractant herbs. In particular, we should grow aromatic herbs. Here are some suggestions to attract bees:

BORAGE The herb's attractive, star-shaped, pink-blue blossoms are in bloom from mid-summer until frost. Borage can also be used for potpourri. This self-seeding annual is also called the bee plant and is often included in pollinator gardens. Other beneficial insects also love the plant's nectar.

FENNEL This herb attracts ladybugs and lacewings that take care of aphids and other soft-bodied insects. It's also a popular nectar source for butterflies.

LAVENDER Bees really enjoy lavender and it can be planted anywhere. To create a relaxing part of your deck or garden, plant lavender for its aromatic scent.

LEMONGRASS The plant is used to attract bees for honey production.

MINT Bees are attracted to the sweet nectar in the blue flowers of the mint plant. Mint is a very hardy perennial.

CATNIP People like catnip because of the tea (stress reducing), but bees consider the white blossoms as another nectar source.

ROSEMARY This plant is native to the Mediterranean area. Grown indoors and outdoors for flavouring of dishes and fragrance, rosemary is a tasty treat for bees.

SAGE Used mostly for sausage and stuffing for fowl or meats, it's also one of the oldest medicinal herbs. Worker bees go after the purplish blossoms.

THYME Bees will come to the thyme plant when it's in full bloom and shows the small pink blossoms with tiny grey-green leaves.

NINE
INDOOR PLANTS

The Indoor Plant Shopper

Just as you would do for outdoor plants, always purchase quality indoor plants at fair prices from people who know their plant material. General retailers (grocery stores, supermarkets, variety stores) receive their shipments of plants with the goal of quickly selling the plants before they wilt (expire). These retailers don't have the full knowledge of the plants they are selling other than the time of the year (Mother's Day, Valentine's Day) and the price.

In general, the deciding factor where you shop is usually price and convenience. General retailers use the same grower or wholesaler who ships large orders of plant species direct from tropical regions. If the plants had poor care for even one week, you're usually looking at plants that had seven full days of inadequate lighting, too much or too little watering, and possible contact with diseases and insects.

The garden centre/nurseries employ staff who are knowledgeable about growing indoor plants. They can recommend plants based on your individual needs and advise on the plant's care. You rarely see an insect infestation from a reputable garden centre/nursery. Their reputations are on the line, and they will destroy unsatisfactory plants rather than lose a customer.

Plants for Cleaning the Air

Air pollution in the house, condo, confined office area or school is well known. Which indoor plants are the most effective for your environment? Each indoor plant has its light requirement, and this must be a consideration when purchasing the appropriate plant.

Plants have the necessary job to remove air pollutants (gases), such as benzene, trichloroethylene and formaldehyde. When you introduce greenery to your indoor space, you are benefiting your health and mind. The award-winning scientist Bill C. Wolverton said, "Nature has built into plants the ability to use our waste for their nourishments."

Plants absorb carbon dioxide and release oxygen. By adding plants, you are increasing the oxygen levels in your interior space — breathing becomes easier.

Plants release roughly 97% of the water they take in and will increase the humidity around you. The chance of colds, dry coughs, sore throats and other respiratory ailments are decreased. Before you purchase a humidifier machine to soften the air, consider buying a plant or two.

Air is purified as plants remove the toxins. We breathe the same air again and again, and there's the potential of inhaling harmful substances that are trapped indoors. Indoor plants help to remove pollutants, including volatile organic compounds (VOCs) that can cause headaches, nausea and many more aliments. In addition to filtering unwelcome chemicals, plants also emit clean air, improving the air quality surrounding them.

In the 1980s, NASA conducted a study to determine which plants were best able to filter the air of the space station. NASA's research confirmed that living, green and flowering plants could remove several toxic chemicals from the air in building interiors. Of all the plants, NASA deemed the spider plant as the best indoor plant for "scrubbing" indoor air pollution. The following selection of air-purifying plants is based on the NASA study.

Common Name (Cultivar)	Botanical/ Scientific Name	Exposure	Benefit	OPALS Ranking
Chinese evergreen	*Aglaonema aracea*	Medium light	Purifies air; removes formaldehyde from the air	5
Dragon tree	*Dracaena draco*	Low light	Purifies air; removes formaldehyde, benzene, toluene and xylene from the air	4 – 6, varies
Gerbera daisy (Transvaal)	*Gerbera jamesonii*	Medium/high light	Releases oxygen at night; purifies air by removing benzene and trichloroethylene	5
Parlor palm	*Chamaedorea elegans*	Bright light	Purifies air; removes formaldehyde from the air	f = 1, m = 7
Peace lily	*Spathiphyllum spp.*	Low light	Removes mould from the air	2
Snake plant (Variegated)	*Sansevieria trifasciata*	Low light	Purifies air; removes formaldehyde and nitrogen oxide	1

Common Name (Cultivar)	Botanical/ Scientific Name	Exposure	Benefit	OPALS Ranking
Spider plant	*Chlorophytum comosum*	Low light	Purifies air rapidly; removes formaldehyde; doesn't like tap water because of chlorine or fluoride (common cause of brown leaf tips); use distilled water or water that has sat out for at least 24 hours	f = 1, m = 6

Legend:

m = male; f = female plants

According to OPALS ranking: 1 = low and 10 = high, very allergenic

Let's Talk About Light

To achieve ultimate success in growing indoor plants, careful planning is required to expose them to the optimum light level for their species.

Bright light-loving plants need to receive at least five hours of direct sunlight per day, usually a south- or west-facing window.

Indirect light-loving plants need to be at least 60 centimetres (2 feet) from a south-facing window or for the window to have a sheer curtain to filter the light.

Low light-loving plants flourish with little attention from you. They also require very little light to flower. Plants can be placed in east or north-facing foyers, stair landings, windows or anywhere that doesn't get direct sunlight.

Medium light-loving plants are low fuss. They can tolerate some direct light, but not a lot. They like light, so bright light is good, but not direct light. They're good to go near a west or south-east window.

High light-loving plants need a lot of light (high light) to do their best. Place them in south or west windows — locations that get direct light most of the day. Windows that face south receive the most direct sunlight and are often too bright and hot for most indoor plants. Look at achieving indirect light when needed.

Which Plant... Which Window

When you want to garden, whether it's indoors or outdoors, always check the sun's position at noon. Does the front or rear of your house get morning or afternoon sun? Knowing this information, you can determine if the sun's location is suitable for your plant selection.

Indoor plants need varying amounts of light. Look at the window you want to place your plant in. Is it north-, east-, south- or west-facing? Few buildings face the exact direction of the four compass points, so you may have a combination, for example, southeast, northwest, etc.

The following list will help you strategically place your favourite plants in the classroom, home, hospital, and medical and home care facility.

Location	Common Name (Cultivar)	Botanical/Scientific Name	OPALS Ranking
East window (East-facing windows receive very good light levels and natural sources of heat without either being extreme.)	African violet	*Saintpaulia ionantha*	1
	Boston fern (Sword fern)	*Nepholepsis exaltata*	3
	Caladium	*Caladium bicolor*	4
	Dracaena (Fragrant)	*Dracaena deremensis*	4 – 6, varies
	Geranium	*Pelargonium*	3
	Gloxinia	*Sinningia speciosa*	2
	Ivy (Oakleaf)	*Cissus rhombifolia*	4
	Moth orchid	*Phalaenopsis*	1
	Peperomia	*Peperomia spp.*	3
	Philodendron	*Philodendron spp.*	3
	Pothos (Golden)	*Epipremnum aureum*	2
	Rubber plant	*Ficus robusta*	2 – 3, varies
	Wandering Jew	*Tradescantia fluminensis*	4
	Wax plant	*Hoya spp.*	3

Location	Common Name (Cultivar)	Botanical/Scientific Name	OPALS Ranking
North window (Windows facing north don't get any sunlight coming through. If the window is facing northeast, or northwest, you will get some sunlight in the mornings/ evenings, especially during the summer.)	Arrowhead	*Syngonium podophyllum*	2
	Asparagus fern	*Asparagus densiflorus*	3
	Baby's tears	*Soleirolia soleirolii*	3
	Cast-iron plant	*Aspidistra lurida*	1
	Chinese evergreen	*Aglaonema araceae*	5
	Dracaena	*Dracaena spp.*	4 – 6, varies
	Norfolk pine	*Araucaria excelsa*	f = 1, m = 7
	Philodendron	*Philodendron spp.*	3
	Pothos (Golden)	*Epipremnum aureum*	2
	Rubber plant	*Ficus maclellandii*	2 – 3, varies
	Snake plant (Variegated)	*Sansevieria trifasciata*	1

Location	Common Name (Cultivar)	Botanical/Scientific Name	OPALS Ranking
South or west window (The strongest rays from the sun flow through south-facing windows from late morning to mid-afternoon. As the afternoon progresses, the sun will eventually start shining through the west-facing windows right up until the sun sets. Overheating can be a problem.)	Amaryllis	*Amaryllidinae*	3
	Azalea	*Rhododendron spp.*	4
	Cacti and other succulents	*Schlumbergera spp.*	2
	Calla lily	*Zantedeschia*	4
	Coleus	*Coleus blumei*	1
	Cyclamen	*Cyclamen persicum*	1
	Daffodil	*Daffodil*	4
	Easter lily	*Echinopsis oxygona*	2
	Gardenia	*Gardenia jasminoides*	4
	Geranium (Martha Washington)	*Pelargonium x domesticum*	3
	Peace lily	*Spathiphyllum spp.*	2
	Tuberous begonia	*Begonia tuberousa*	2
	Tulip	*Tulipa*	1 – doubles, 3 – singles
	Wax begonia	*Begonia semperflorens*	4

Legend:

m = male; f = female plants

Doubles = double-flowering varieties; Singles = single-flowering varieties

According to OPALS ranking: 1 = low and 10 = high, very allergenic

If you have artificial light, put the plant anywhere you choose as you control the light conditions. I prefer using natural light as much as possible; it's the cheapest and easiest light source.

You're the Plant Doctor

Growing plants indoors is easy and just as much fun as having an outdoor garden. Nothing beats a flowering plant, such as an African violet, when the snow starts swirling and the icy temperatures keep you indoors. That doesn't mean that you won't be faced with a few plant challenges.

Before throwing out a plant that is experiencing some distress, let's train you to be a plant doctor and rally the plant back to health.

Q. What causes soil in the container to go white?

A. This is caused by hard water – lime deposit. Use distilled water.

Q. Why are the leaves yellowing and then dropping off?

A. This is a case of overwatering. Only water when the soil feels dry to the touch.

Q. What causes rotten lower leaves on my plants?

A. This is a case of overwatering. Try cutting back on the amount of water and frequency.

Q. Why are the flower buds falling off before the flower blooms?

A. The cause could be dry air or overwatering. Place your plant on a tray with pebbles and water to improve water retention or drainage.

Q. Why is green slime forming on the container?

A. This is caused by high humidity or overwatering.

Q. How can I stop browning on the leaf edges?

A. This is caused by too much direct sunlight, cold draughts or potassium deficiency. First, try to relocate the plant.

Q. Why is grey mould forming on the leaves and stems?

A. There's too much humidity in the area.

Q. What is causing wilted leaves and stems?

A. The cause could be either underwatering or disease. Water when the soil feels dry to the touch.

Q. What is the cause of patches of brown and yellow leaves?

A. This indicates underfeeding and the plant's need for some TLC.

Q. Why isn't my plant growing?

A. Stunted growth of plants is caused by underfeeding and underwatering. Use 15-15-15 or 10-5 fertilizer made specifically for houseplants. Mix or dilute according to the manufacturer's recommendations. Establish a regular regimen to address the problem.

Q. How do I know if there's too much light for the plant?

A. Look for leaves curling, wilting (especially when the light is shinning on them), fading (becoming less green), scorching or turning brown, or when new leaf growth is much smaller than the existing one.

Q. How do I know if there's too little light for the plant?

A. Look for leaves turning yellow or pale; variegated leaves losing the variegation; plant becoming spindly; bending toward the window; no flowers; no new growth in the growing season; plant is dropping older leaves, and new ones are sporadic and smaller.

WARNING SIGNS

As we just discussed, there are a lot of warning signs to some very common plant ailments. Often, it's just as simple as reconsidering the plant's location, increasing the frequency of watering or decreasing the watering frequency. Light problems, such as fading of leaf colour or variegation, may take a while to develop. Now that you know the symptoms of a plant in distress, you will be able to "doctor" your indoor garden in a timely manner.

Care of Your Cacti and Ferns

Cacti are fleshy plants that require less care because they are slow growers. All cacti are succulents, but not all succulents are cacti. Succulents are specialized plants that store water in their leaves/stems. They adapt well to harsh climates where water is scarce or occurs sporadically. Although succulents are often thought to be native to arid regions, such as deserts, you will also find them in forest settings, high alpine regions, and coastal and dry tropical areas.

Cacti belong to one of several succulent groups. Of the two kinds of cacti, the desert cacti are more known than the forest cacti. Desert cacti come from areas where there's plenty of sun and little moisture for long periods of time.

Forest cacti, such as the Easter and Christmas cacti, come from the rain forest region of tropical South America. They need shade from the very warm sun and water most of the year. Forest cacti are also called leaf cacti because the leaves (actual stems) are flat.

There's minimal care involved once the basic needs of the succulents are met. Let's take a look at the requirements of each type of plant.

DESERT CACTI

1. Fertilize in summer to encourage flowering.

2. Keep roots pot-bound to improve flowering. Re-pot when the roots begin to show through the drainage holes at the bottom of the pot.

3. Full sun is needed; provide some shade on hot days.

4. Keep soil moist in summer with little water and almost no water in winter.

5. Don't mist these cacti.

FOREST CACTI

1. Plant requires only slightly diffused light.

2. Mist in summer and when there are no flowers.

3. Keep soil moist. When in the dormant period, keep soil barely moist. Dormant periods are February and March for Christmas cacti, and from October to early February for Easter cacti.

> **Just a Thought***...*
>
> *Cacti or cactus? Cacti is the Latin plural of cactus. Like many names of plants, cactus is sometimes treated as plural.*

FERNS

Ferns are among the oldest plants on earth. Most come from tropical or subtropical regions. If you grow ferns indoors, provide a temperature of 15° – 22°C (59° – 71°F), dappled (indirect) light and fresh air. A north-facing window is ideal, although during the winter months, when the sun is low on the horizon, an east window is also acceptable for the plant. Avoid south- and west-facing windows, as the intense sunlight may scald the leaves or fronds of the fern, depending on the intensity of the light.

Although plant diseases are rare in ferns grown indoors, you may find they suffer from infestations of mealybugs, mites and scale insects. Pesticide sprays may injure ferns. If you must use, choose the least toxic product for the pest and read the label carefully before applying. As a preventative measure, check your plant at least weekly to catch pests early. If ferns are infested with scales, the easiest solution is to cut off affected fronds. If infestation is out of control, you may need to discard the plant before the rest of your houseplants are infected.

In addition:

1. Don't let the soil dry out; even in winter, keep the roots moist.

2. Drainage is very important.

3. Moist air in summer is essential. Mist the plant often.

4. Ferns like indirect light and are not shade lovers. Keep out of direct sun during the summer.

5. Fertilize in summer at half the recommended rate. Strong solutions damage the roots, and the fern doesn't absorb the water.

The following ferns can be grown as houseplants, which don't produce flowers and seeds but are reproduced by spores: bird's nest fern (*Asplenium*), Boston fern (*Nephrolepis*), brake fern (*Pteris*), button fern (*Pellaea*), holly fern (*Cyrtomium*), maidenhair fern (*Adiantum*), rabbit's foot fern (*Davallia fejeensis*), deer's foot fern (*Davallia*) and staghorn fern (*Platycerium*). Your local garden centre/nursery can also provide you with recommendations based on your needs.

Common Indoor Plants to Consider

There are many varieties of indoor plants to put on your windowsill. We'll look at a couple that you can add for perfect living decorations. Overwatering seems to be a common problem with many houseplants, so be sure to first check the soil before watering.

AFRICAN VIOLET (*SAINTPAULIA IONANTHA*)

This plant is one of the most popular of the indoor plants. Most African violet varieties have a unique and fun name, such as Rainbow's Quiet Riot (blue flowers flecked with white specks and streaks). *Saintpaulia* species are African violets to which all modern hybrids trace their ancestry. They can still be found growing on the hillsides in East Africa.

The interesting feature of the African violet plant is the ability to grow flowers several times a year. The flowers are 2 – 3 centimetres (3/4 – 1 3/16 inch) in diameter, with a five-lobed, velvety corolla (petals), and they grow in clusters of 3 – 10 or more on slender stalks.

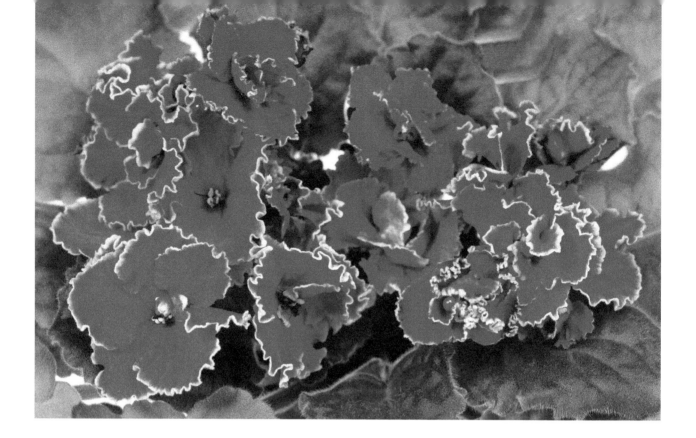

There are African violets for every taste, from Fancy Pants with single, frilled, red-and-white flowers, to Pip Squeak (Squeek) that has single pink rosette-shaped flowers. From spring until fall, African violets require bright, filtered light. In the winter, direct sunlight is best.

There are two ways of watering an African violet: using room temperature water at soil level, or placing the pot in a shallow dish with water. Chamomile tea is very pleasant tasting, but it can also be used to rejuvenate an African violet. Let the tea cool and add it to a spray bottle to give the foliage of your African violet plants a good misting. The tannins in the tea help to trigger the plant to set flower buds.

Re-pot all plants every 6 – 12 months using a peat-based, soilless mix that consists of at least 30 – 50% coarse vermiculite/perlite. Most standard African violets grown as a houseplant will require a 10 – 12 centimetres (4 – 5 inches) pot at maturity.

CHRISTMAS CACTUS (*SCHLUMBERGERA SPP.*)

Another very popular indoor plant is the Christmas cactus (*Schlumbergera spp.*, listed as *Zygocactus truncatus*). Flowers appear at the tips of the stems and are available in shades of coral, pink, red, purple, yellow or white.

The trick to get it to bloom in time for the holidays can be a challenge. For some lucky people, their Christmas cactus blooms without any special attention. But for others, some additional help is needed. Around October 20, place the cactus in total darkness from 5:00 p.m. to 8:00 a.m. Move the plant into a dark closet each evening or loosely cover completely with a black cloth. Keep the soil barely moist but not too dry as it will become shrivelled, with limp stems. Once it starts budding, don't move the plant as this could cause it to drop its buds and flowers. Also keep the plant away from drafty areas.

After your Christmas cactus finishes blooming, it will require a one-month rest. Water sparingly and stop using fertilizer until new growth forms in spring. If you want a fuller plant, spring is the best time to prune it back. Use sharp, clean scissors to prevent tearing of the stems. Cut a stem off between segments (the place where they're joined together by a mid-rib).

Re-potting your Christmas cactus is only necessary every 2 – 3 years. It likes to be slightly pot-bound. Wait until spring or early summer to re-pot.

DIEFFENBACHIA (*ARACEAE*)

This plant is known by several names, such as mother-in-law's tongue or dumb cane. Dumb cane gets its name because of the sap that is poisonous if ingested. Best to keep the plant away from pets and small children who may like to play with or chew on plant leaves.

The plant offers a single, thick trunk that unwinds into several trunks as it matures. The attractive broad leaves are about 25 centimetres (10 inches) long and are splashed, streaked or speckled in green and white.

This plant likes bright, filtered light during spring, summer and fall. During winter, place the plant in the brightest place possible. Water moderately and fertilize with liquid fertilizer diluted by half every two weeks.

Re-pot in spring or early summer using soilless potting mix, when the plant seems to have outgrown its pot. You will want to use a container with drainage holes to prevent from soggy soil.

You can diagnose any problems by looking at its leaves. It's normal for the older leaves to turn yellow and drop off. If you see new leaves fall off, this signals that the plant is in a cold area. Brown leaf tips are caused

by sporadic watering, so set a regular water schedule, but don't let the soil get too soggy. Curled, crisp leaf tips could mean you are using too much fertilizer. Scorched leaves with dry brown spots are caused by strong, direct sunlight.

Gardening Tip...

To determine if a plant needs water, test the soil by poking your finger about half an inch down into it; you will be able to feel how wet or dry it is. Always water your indoor plants with room temperature water. It allows water additives to evaporate or settle out in the water.

Growing Cat Grass

Each time a cat cleans itself, it swallows fur (hair), resulting in "fur" or "hair" balls. Cat grass can act as a laxative and help with the passage of hairballs through your cat's system. While it helps cats digest, it can also help them to regurgitate hairballs. Keep in mind that not all cats will eat the grass and may just demonstrate some curiosity toward it. Cat grass can provide nutrients that cats are not always getting from other food sources.

There are two main species of grass referred to as cat grass: *Dactylis glomerata* (also known as orchard grass or cock's foot) and *Avena sativa* (oat grass). Other common types of "cereal" grass that can be grown as cat grass include barley, oat, rye and wheat. Although you can buy cat grass at most garden centres/nurseries and pet stores, you can easily grow it from seed. You may purchase the seeds at any grocery store that has a bulk section or from a bulk store.

Don't be confused by catnip, as it's not the same as cat grass. Catnip is considered an aromatic herb, not grass.

Use a heavy flower pot (any size) or perforated plastic tray. Place an old face cloth or layer of gravel on the pot's bottom and fill with indoor potting soil. Next, sprinkle oats, wheat or other cereal grass over the soil. Tamp the seeds down and cover lightly with the indoor potting soil. Water lightly so the soil is moist but not wet. Every couple of days, water lightly as the sprouts grow.

Germination of the seed, an important step, will happen after 5 – 7 days. Good germination is keyed by light, moisture and reasonable warmth. Depending on the light conditions and how you water the grass, the germination process could take a few days or weeks. It's subject to where you have placed the growing pot. Use chicken wire or fine mesh over the pot or container. Why? The cat won't scratch the soil and make a mess all over the floor.

Once the grass is an inch or two long, move the pot to a spot easily accessible by your cat. For homeowners looking to discourage cats from chewing on indoor plants, it's a good idea to keep the cat grass away from the other plants.

TEN
KITCHEN HELPERS

Cooking Enhancements

When you watch your favourite television cooking show, you will see the chef add a dash of this and that during food preparation. I recommend cooking with fresh herbs, but when it's not practical or you lack time to wait for the plant to mature, using dried herbs is perfectly suitable. When using dried herbs, give them a pinch with your fingers to release the flavour and aroma before adding to the dish.

To cut fresh herbs for cooking, use clean, sharp scissors to remove the leaves at the top of the plant. The big leaves at the bottom of the plant act as a sturdy base. Only cut what you need for the recipe to retain freshness.

Before reaching for the salt shaker, try the following herbs, spices or flavourings to elevate your dish. Many of these herb and vegetable pairings can be easily grown by you. You and your dining companions will taste the "fresh" difference. Just remember not to over-season, as you can always add more as you cook to intensify the flavour.

Vegetables	Try Cooking with this Herb/Spice/Flavouring
Asparagus	Curry, dill, marjoram, mustard, nutmeg, oregano or rosemary
Beets	Basil, chives, dill, ginger, lemon or thyme
Broccoli	Basil, dill, fennel, garlic, ginger, lemon, marjoram or oregano

Vegetables	Try Cooking with this Herb/Spice/Flavouring
Brussels sprouts	Caraway, garlic, marjoram, mustard, nutmeg, oregano, parsley, rosemary or thyme
Cabbage	Caraway, chives, coriander, dill, fennel, garlic, ginger, marjoram, mint, nutmeg, parsley or thyme
Carrots	Basil, cinnamon, cloves, dill, marjoram, nutmeg, paprika, parsley, rosemary or sage
Cauliflower	Basil, coriander, dill, fennel, garlic, ginger, mint, oregano, paprika, parsley or thyme
Corn	Dill, basil, cumin, curry powder, onion, paprika or parsley
Cucumber	Basil, chives, dill, coriander, garlic, mint, parsley or rosemary
Eggplant	Basil, garlic, ginger, mint, oregano, parsley, rosemary or sage
Green bean	Chives, dill, lemon juice, garlic, oregano, rosemary or thyme
Leafy greens	Basil, coriander, garlic, ginger, marjoram, onion, oregano, nutmeg or rosemary
Peas	Basil, garlic, marjoram, mint, onion, parsley or sage
Potatoes	Chives, garlic, mustard, onion, oregano, paprika, parsley, rosemary, thyme or sage
Summer or winter squash	Allspice, basil, cinnamon, cloves, curry, nutmeg, onion, paprika, parsley, sage or thyme
Spinach	Allspice, basil, chives, dill, garlic, ginger, nutmeg or thyme
Tomatoes	Basil, cilantro, chives, dill, fennel, garlic, mint, oregano, parsley, pepper or thyme
Zucchini	Basil, chives, dill, garlic, marjoram, onion, oregano, pepper or thyme

Fish/Poultry/Meat	Try Cooking with this Herb/Spice/Flavouring
Fish	Basil, chive, dill, fennel, lemon balm (or lemon juice), marjoram, mint or pepper (or lemon pepper)
Meat (beef)	Basil, chive, garlic, marjoram, onion, oregano, pepper, rosemary, sage, savory or thyme
Pork	Basil, bay leaves, dill, garlic, lemon verbena, marjoram, onion, oregano, rosemary, sage, savory or thyme
Poultry	Chili powder, coriander, marjoram, oregano, paprika, parsley, rosemary, sage or thyme

Just a Thought...

Always read food labels because processed and prepared foods, and condiments that contain sodium, account for most of the salt consumed in our diets.

Edible Flowers

When you think about it, you may often eat flowers without realizing, such as artichokes, broccoli, Brussels sprouts and cauliflower. But eating "flowery" flowers like impatiens, pansies or nasturtiums is different. Many herbal flowers have the same flavour as their leaves.

By adding edible flowers to your food, you can introduce colour and flavour that is master chef worthy. As I mentioned in Chapter 2 – Gardening 101, not all flowers are edible, and some may be poisonous when ingested. Only eat flowers you know to be safe for consumption. Plus, by growing edible flowers in your garden, you will know that they aren't treated with pesticides or other harmful chemicals.

Did you know that for many generations, jelly makers dropped a flower and leaf of the sweet geranium into a jar of jelly with great results?

The nasturtium flower, leaves and seed pods are all edible. As pretty as they are, nasturtium flowers work as a scrumptious garnish for your plate. Its leaves make an ideal substitute for watercress in a salad or sandwich. The fresh seed pods can be pickled like capers.

The herb fennel tastes like licorice and is a lovely additive to a salad of clear gelatin (jello). Fennel is easy to grow and its bright yellow flowers look stylish when cooked with meat, vegetables or fruit.

Parsley is a biennial, meaning you can let it grow to flower and seed. The seedy heads of parsley flower for goodness and nutrition.

What about adding flowers in your soup? Yes, you can use a chive blossom or a piece of lemon or borage in your cream of mushroom or tomato soup. The following are suggestions of using flowers or herbs with your cooking.

Edible Flowers	Use for Cooking	Taste
Angelica	Flower	Pale lavender-blue to deep rose have a licorice-like flavour.
Bee balm	Flower	Red flowers have a minty flavour.
Calendula	Petal	Blossoms have a peppery, spicy and tangy taste.
Carnation	Petal	Petals are sweet and may have a clove-like or nutmeg scent.
Impatiens	Flower	Not much flavour, but make a pretty garnish.
Marigold	Petal	Blossoms have a peppery, spicy and tangy taste.
Nasturtium	Flower	Very popular for its sweet, floral flavour that bursts with a spicy pepper finish.
Pansy	Flower	Not much flavour (sweet green or grassy)w but makes a pretty garnish.
Rose	Petal	With petals intensely perfumed, their flavour is subtle and a bit fruity with complex undertones depending on variety and soil conditions.
Scented geranium	Flower	Range from citrus and spice to fruit flavour.
Violet	Flower	Sweet and tantalizing as a garnish in salads, desserts and drinks.

NOTE

Only consume pesticide- and chemical-free flowers grown for culinary use.

Edible Herb Flowers	Use for Cooking	Taste
Anise	Floret and flower	Has a licorice flavour, and its taste is very close to fennel or tarragon
Borage	Flower	Blossoms with lovely blue hue taste like cucumber
Chamomile	Flower	Flowers have a sweet flavour used often in tea. Ragweed sufferers may be allergic to chamomile.
Lavender	Floret	Sweet and spicy addition to savory and sweet dishes
Mint	Petal	Minty and cool to the tongue with an intensity that varies. May be sweet or lemon-scented or even with chocolate overtones depending on the type.
Oregano	Flowers	Subtle flavouring
Rosemary	Flower	Milder version of the leaf that can be used with meat, seafood or dressing
Sage	Flower	Subtle flavour that can be used in corn dishes, sautéed or stuffed mushrooms, or pesto sauce
Savory	Flower	Somewhat hot and peppery
Thyme	Flower	Milder version of the leaf

Gardening Tip...

Before eating, break up the individual florets. Don't use the whole blossom head consisting of the pistil or stamen.

Sprouting Seed Guide

Stretching the food budget to supply nutritious food to the table can be trying for parents and caregivers. One way to overcome nutrient deficiencies in our diets is to sprout seeds. These seed sprouts are a good source of vitamins A, B and C. They can be added to smoothies, salads, soups, stews, etc.

Put the seeds (see chart) into a litre (quart) Mason jar or similar size jar and add tap or bottled water. Cover the jar with cheesecloth or a nylon stocking cut to size, and affix with a rubber band to tightly close the jar. This is the "soaking time" process. Leave to soak as directed in the chart below, based on the seeds.

Next (twice a day during germination), refresh the water through the screen, shake the water and immediately drain excess water by tilting the jar over the sink. Set the jar in a dark place, for example, a kitchen cupboard. After 2 – 6 days' germination period, you will see texture forming. The flavour and nutritional value of these sprouts depend upon the size of the sprout. Use immediately when the sprouting seeds are ready to harvest.

Seed Type	Measurement Quantity for Jar	Soaking Time	Sprouting Time (Germination)	Yield
Alfalfa	45 ml (3 T)	4 – 6 hours	3 – 5 days	750 ml (3 c)
Beans	250 ml (1 c)	8 – 9 hours	3 – 5 days	750 ml – 1000 ml (3 – 4 c)
Chickpeas	250 ml (1 c)	10 – 11 hours	2 – 3 days	750 ml (3 c)
Green peas	250 ml (1 c)	10 – 11 hours	3 – 4 days	500 ml (2 c)
Lentils	250 ml (1 c)	6 – 8 hours	3 – 4 days	750 ml – 1000 ml (3 – 4 c)
Mung beans	250 ml (1 c)	8 – 9 hours	3 – 5 days	750 ml – 1000 ml (3 – 4 c)
Onion	15 ml (1 T)	4 – 6 hours	2 – 3 days	250 ml (1 c)
Sesame seeds	250 ml (1 c)	5 – 6 hours	2 – 3 days	250 ml – 500 ml (1 – 2 c)
Soybeans (yellow)	250 ml (1 c)	9 – 12 hours	4 – 6 days	500 ml – 1000 ml (2 – 4 c)
Wild rice	250 ml (1 c)	8 – 9 hours	3 – 4 days	250 ml – 500 ml (1 – 2 c)

Mixture suggestion: Combine 125 ml (1/2 c) mung bean seeds and 125 ml (1/2 c) rice seeds

---

NOTE

Sprouts can be subject to contamination that may result in bacterial growth such as E. coli, leading to food-borne illnesses. Always wash your hands thoroughly before handling foods, and keep sprouting equipment and all kitchen surfaces clean to avoid cross contamination. Consume sprouts immediately or within a few days, fresh and straight out of the fridge.

Here are some sprouts to try that are nutritious.

Type	Taste	Vitamins/Minerals
Alfalfa	Mild flavour with a delicate, crunchy texture that work well in sandwiches and salads.	Vitamins A, B complex, C, E and K, plus calcium, folic acid, magnesium, phosphorus, potassium, sodium and zinc
Beans	Many different types of beans, such as green, snap, kidney, lima or navy beans, have different tastes.	Good source of iron, phosphorus, potassium and protein
Chickpeas	Also called garbanzo beans, they have a mild, nutty taste.	Great source of fibre, niacin, protein and thiamine
Green peas	Freshly sprouted green peas are big and crunchy, and have a flavour sweeter than fresh green peas. Use as a salad topping, or drop some into a vegetable soup.	Have eight times more folic acid than bean sprouts. Four times the vitamin A found in tomatoes.
Lentils	Also called dahl, they're a meat alternative and a favourite for the vegetarian diet. Mixed in soups and stews. Mealy taste.	Good source of protein, fibre, iron, phosphorus and protein. Low in fat and sodium.
Mung beans	Nutty taste — mild and fresh. Can be enjoyed raw or steamed, and make an unusual and tasty garnish for salads and soups.	Rich source of amino acids and protein, as well as dietary fibre, minerals and vitamins.
Onion	Depending on the variety, most have a strong taste.	High concentration of thiamine, and vitamins A and C
Wild rice	Mealy taste	High iron content and calcium

Type	Taste	Vitamins/Minerals
Sesame seeds	Very mild flavour	Very high content of calcium, vitamin B and iron
Soybeans (yellow)	Very large, succulent sprouts with a mild flavour. Cooking improves the aroma and flavour.	Amino acids, minerals, protein and vitamins

ELEVEN
INSECTS – FRIENDS OR FOES?

Insects in the Garden

As we have discussed in earlier chapters, insects often get a bad rap. We need to think of our gardens as amazing tiny ecosystems with everything interconnected. Each insect has a role in the health of your garden — good or bad. Yes, there are some bad insects, but for each there's a helpful predator that can get rid of the nasty ones. Think of them as the "mighty terminators."

There are three kinds of beneficial "bugs" that are important to every gardener:

1. **Pollinators** are needed, otherwise our plants wouldn't be able to produce flowers or bear fruit. Ants, bees, sphinx moths and wasps are all important pollinators.

2. **Predators** help to control the insect population. Birds, ground beetles, lacewings, spiders, tachinid flies and wasps have a starring role as mighty terminators.

3. **Scavengers** work very efficiently to remove carcasses of dead animals. Ants, earwigs and carrion beetles are very important scavengers.

The "good guys" in the garden that eat insects are birds, butterflies, dragonflies, frogs, snakes and spiders. They offer "pesticide-free" pest control for gardeners. It's important to know how to attract them to your garden — not that you will go out of your way to attract a snake to your garden.

Let's look at a couple of the good insects to understand their role. Ladybugs eat aphids, spider mites and other soft-bodied insects. Some plants that attract ladybugs are coriander, scented geranium and Queen Anne's lace. Ground beetles like to hide under rocks and scramble fast when you uncover their hiding place. They eat a variety of caterpillars and other pest insects. Attract them to your garden by planting a coneflower or dill plant. Lacewings are flying insects that seem to like window screens. They eat aphids, spider mites, whiteflies and other small insects. Cosmos will attract lacewings to your garden.

The "bad guys" cause damage not only in our gardens but will attack our clothes, leaving holes, and destroy wood in and around our homes. Beetles (Colorado potato beetles, crucifer flea beetle, Japanese beetle, Mexican bean beetle), caterpillars, aphids, mealybugs, and others will eat flowers and vegetables. Don't be fooled by how tiny the aphid is, as it's the most destructive insect in the garden. Termites will eat wood and leave it like sawdust. A moth loves to take bites out of our clothes. Black flies, mosquitoes and wasps like to feast on our unprotected skin or sting us.

Pest of the Month Club

We just touched on some of the bad insects that like to invade your garden. Let's take a look when some of them will make an appearance so you are forewarned and can have controls in place.

JANUARY/FEBRUARY

Red spider mite

If you didn't do a thorough inspection of your newly purchased indoor plants, you may now find a common pest living on the underside (may be webbed) of the leaves. Red spider mites are very small. Using a magnifying glass, you can check for mites that have four pairs of legs. They are considered neither true insect nor spider. They like thin-leaved plants, such as ivies and spider plants.

Spider mites thrive in warm and dry conditions, and multiply rapidly. The number of generations per season varies with the temperature. Adults and young suck plant juices from the leaves, destroying the green chlorophyll and producing bronze-yellow or gray spots on the leaves. Ultimately the leaves discolour and drop, or with a heavy infestation, the plant will die.

Organic control calls for insecticidal soap as per instructions on the container or make your own. Mix a litre (quart) of water, 5 millilitres (1 teaspoon) each of liquid dish soap and cayenne or red pepper. Check the plant regularly and repeat spraying if needed.

MARCH/APRIL

Rodents

Although not an insect, I would be remiss if I didn't include rodents in the pest of the month club. The melting of snow during these months reveals some unwanted surprises, such as chewed bark on fruit trees, ornamental trees or flowering shrubs. Field mice and rabbits are the prime suspects.

If the chewing has gone through the outer layers of the bark and completely girdled the trunk, the plant will die. The lesson is to protect bark during the fall with plastic or burlap trunk wrap. If the injury is not severe, the plant might survive on its own. Wrap the chewed area of the tree to retard the drying of the live tissues. Remove the wrap in late summer. Use trunk guards in the fall and rodent repellent in areas our pets can't find it!

MAY/JUNE

Tent caterpillar

Caterpillars build tents in their favourite trees. They spend the winter as eggs on trees. In spring, the eggs hatch and larvae begin to eat. After about six weeks, they leave the tree and spin a cocoon. About three weeks later, the adult moth emerges, mates and lays eggs in circles around the twigs. They produce only one generation per year. The tent caterpillar can completely strip the leaves of a tree. The tree can produce a second set of leaves, but it weakens them.

In early spring, after the leaves are out, check the trees every week for "tents." The caterpillars eat the leaves during the day and return to the tents at night. For smaller trees with small webs or nests, if reachable from the ground or safely from a ladder, you can extract them from the tree. Flatten the web and dispose as organic matter. If larger, you can break apart the web with a wooden pole, so the larvae are exposed to natural predators. If using a pole or pole pruner in trees, you must be aware of any overhead wires as there's a potential danger to be electrocuted. Seek professional help if there are wires in the tree or within easy reach.

If you are contemplating any spray-based control method, seek environmentally-friendly compounds. Follow the directions carefully on the label.

LATE JUNE/JULY/EARLY AUGUST

Japanese beetle

The Japanese beetle is a very destructive garden pest. It feeds on well over 300 varieties of plants, shrubs, trees and vines. It's not found on evergreens. You may see them making lace work of your rose bush's leaves. They are about 1.25 centimetres (1/2 inch) in length with copper backs, metallic blue-green heads, small white hairs lining each side of their abdomen and tan wings.

The Japanese beetle spends the winter deep in the soil. In spring, it moves up to eat the roots of grass. In mid-summer, it emerges as an adult beetle. Adults feed until fall, when they lay the eggs in the soil. After about 10 – 12 days, the eggs hatch and the grubs start eating the grass roots. It then burrows deep into the soil for the winter. The life cycle takes one to two years.

For organic control, I recommend using Pyrethrum. Beetle traps can be used too, as the paper sliders in the trap are treated with a chemical that kills the beetle. You may also plant garlic near some of your plants to ward off the Japanese beetle. In mid-summer look for the adults (they are black) as they will damage flowers, fruit and leaves. Check at least every week throughout the growing season.

Grubs

White grubs are the larvae of Japanese beetles, June beetles or masked chafer beetles. The grubs can destroy a lawn and the adults chew on flowers, fruit and leaves. They are frequently found feeding on the roots of turf and pasture grasses. Damage is most severe in the spring and fall when the grubs are increasing in size and feeding near the surface.

Grubs have soft, white, C-shaped bodies with tan or brown heads and six prominent, spiny legs. During the colder days of fall, they go deep in the soil and remain there during the winter. With only a three-year life cycle, the grubs seem to cause the greatest damage during the second-year.

In Chapter 12 – Lawn Care Plus, I have included how to get rid of grubs that invade your lawn.

Fall Webworm

The summer is almost over, and the cool days of fall appear. Forest and hardwood shade trees change colour or drop their leaves. Dropping of the leaves can also be the result of the fall webworm. During June, the white with brown-striped adult moth begins to lay eggs in masses on the underside of the leaves. About mid-July, the grayish-brown haired caterpillar spins a web over the leaves. The leaf will be eaten, except the mid-rib and the veins. It will feed on almost 90 species of deciduous trees. It commonly attacks birch, cherry, crabapple, hickory and walnut. In most cases, the damage is aesthetic, but because the defoliation happens during the fall, it can retard the growth of the tree.

Two generations of the fall webworm are produced each year. The first is in late spring and the second in late summer. It's advisable to spray organic insecticide in mid-July when the larvae become visible. The entire infested plant doesn't need to be treated. Only the webs and the associated foliage should be thoroughly covered with insecticide.

NOVEMBER/DECEMBER

Aphids

These are also called plant lice. The small, soft-bodied insects vary in colour (black, brown, grey, light green, white or yellow) and some have wings, while others don't. Most of the time they feed in clusters and are seen on stems and the underside of the leaves. Quite often you will see ants because aphids secrete a sticky substance that attracts them.

The adults and their young suck the juices from fruit, flowers, leaves, stems and roots. A sign that aphids might be the culprit is that leaves will curl up and die. Plants may turn yellow, become weak and can die. The aphid spends the winter as eggs, hatch in spring, and in summer the females deposit the young on any plant. Aphids multiply very fast and can produce 20 or more generations a year.

Since aphids multiply quickly, you will need to control infestations before reproduction starts. Generally, heavy thunderstorms can sometimes reduce populations to more tolerable levels. Watering the shrub or tree to help offset the moisture loss in the plant is very helpful. This can be by the trickle method, where an open-ended hose is placed about 30 centimetres (12 inches) from the base of the shrub or tree and left on as a trickle for an hour or so. Monitor to see if there is run-off to the curb or outside of the plant canopy and reduce pressure as needed to prevent overland flow outside of the roots.

You can use commercially available biological controls, or spray with insecticidal soap or horticultural oil. You can also get rid of aphids by wiping or spraying the leaves of the affected plant with a mild solution of water and a few drops of dishwashing detergent. Mix a litre (quart) of water, 5 millilitres (1 teaspoon) each of liquid dish soap and cayenne or red pepper. Plants can also be dusted with flour or baby powder (constipates the pest) to quell an aphid infestation. Planting chives and garlic will repel aphids when placed near lettuce, peas or rose bushes.

Herbs as Insect Repellent

Herbs have double value in your garden. Take, for instance, **BASIL,** a well-known herb for cooking but also a pest repellent. When you plant basil beside your tomato plants, you will reduce insect and fungus damage. Grow some basil in a container on your balcony, deck or porch, and it will repel flies and mosquitoes. When you are planning to grow basil from seeds, plant outside at the same time as the tomatoes. Both like rich and warm soil.

The most potent flavouring herb and repellent is **GARLIC.** In the late fall, you can plant a few cloves near a peach tree as protection against the well-known peach borer. Roses are also well protected when you plant garlic cloves between the roses to deter aphids. Garlic keeps rabbits out of your garden, too.

The strong smell of **MINT** repels ants, cabbage butterfly and other small insects but still attracts bees, which are good for pollination. The growth habit of mint is very invasive. To overcome this problem, plant or seed the mint into a sonotube. These are available at your lumber dealer. Place the tubes 5 – 8 centimetres (2 – 3 inches) into the ground and leave about 4 centimetres (1 9/16 inches) above ground level. Fill the hole with lots of organic matter and good quality soil. If you like to grow mint close to your house in decorative containers or pots, it will repel mice and rats.

SAVORY is to the beans what basil is to the tomato. Summer savory can be started in the house or seeded outdoors beside the bean plants. The beans grow well with the savory as a companion planter and will repel Mexican beetles. Savory is also planted to protect onions. Summer savory is, in general, sweeter and less sharp in taste than the winter savory.

TANSY is a well-known perennial plant that can be used as a natural insecticide in the house. Hang branches in the basement or attic. Grow around the house, and it will keep ants away. Tansy can also be used between grape vines and raspberries to protect against Japanese beetles.

RUE planted between your roses keeps Japanese beetles away. This herb gives off a bitter and strong aroma. The rue's flowers are greenish-yellow and bloom from June until frost.

Insect Calendar Guide

The following guide shows when our gardens are most susceptible to insects. Insect development varies because of the environmental conditions in your area and can change from year to year.

Month	Plant/Shrub/Tree	Insect
April	Douglas fir	Spruce gall
	Pine	White pine weevil; European pine shoot moth
	Spruce	Spruce spider mite; spruce gall
May (early)	Flowering fruit trees	Eastern tent caterpillar
	Honey locust	Honey locust plant bug
	Pine	Sawflies; pine needle scale
May (mid)	Birch	Birch leafminer
	Holly	Holly leafminer
	Oak	Oak scale

Month	Plant/Shrub/Tree	Insect
May (late)	Ash	Oyster shell scale; lilac borer
	Birch	Bronze birch borer (first spraying)
	Common lilac	Lilac borer; scale
	Euonymus	Euonymus scale (first spraying)
	Hemlock	Hemlock scale
	Juniper	Juniper scale
	Sycamore	Sycamore lace bug
June (early)	Ash	Ash borer
	Azalea (Mountain laurel, deciduous azaleas)	Rhododendron borer
	Birch	Bronze birch borer (second spraying)
	Dogwood	Dogwood borer
	Euonymus	Euonymus borer (second spraying)
June (mid)	Azalea	Azalea scale
	Pine	European pine moth
June (late)	Arborvitae	Black weevil
	Linden	Japanese beetle
	Pine	Pine scale
	Yew	Fletcher scale; black weevil
July (early)	Fruit trees	Peach tree borer
	Black locust	Locust leafminer
	Maple	Maple scale

Month	Plant/Shrub/Tree	Insect
July (mid)	Euonymus	Euonymus scale (second generation)
	Hemlock	Pine needle scale

Insect- Versus Wind-Pollinated Flowers

There are two different ways that plants are pollinated: by insects and by wind. In this section, we'll look at the differences between both. Pollination by insect occurs with the transfer of pollen grains from the anther (inside the flower) to the stigma of a flower. For example, apple, horse chestnut, wild cherry and willow trees are pollinated by insects.

Wind pollination is typical for grasses, gymnosperms that produce cones, and many shrubs and trees that flower in winter and early spring. For example, common alder, hazel and sweet chestnut are pollinated by wind.

The pollinating agents include wind, insects and birds. Although we are only going to discuss two common methods of pollination, it should be noted that some plants have the ability to self-pollinate. A dandelion can be pollinated by insects or can do the job itself. Tomatoes can also self-pollinate, although a greater quality of fruit can result from insect pollination. Insect-pollinated flowers are different in structure than wind-pollinated flowers.

Insect-Pollinated Flowers	Wind-Pollinated Flowers
Large, brightly coloured petals to attract insects	Small petals, often brown or green; no need to attract insects
Large, brightly coloured petals often sweetly scented to attract insects	No scent to attract insects
Usually contain nectar	No nectar to attract insects
Small quantity of pollen, which means less waste compared to pollinated pollen	Most pollen doesn't reach another flower
Pollen is often sticky, rubs off on the insect	Pollen is very light and can easily be blown by the wind

Insect-Pollinated Flowers	Wind-Pollinated Flowers
Anthers are solid and inside the flower to brush against insects	Anthers are loosely attached and dangle out of the plant to release the pollen into the wind
Stigma is inside the flower, so the insects brush against it	Stigma hangs outside the flower to catch the drifting pollen
Stigma has a sticky coating that the pollen will stick to	Stigma is like a feather or net-like to catch the drifting pollen

INSECT-POLLINATED PLANTS FOR BEES

Bees are excellent pollinators for a variety of reasons and are well adapted to pollinate a range of flowers due to the size and shape of their furry bodies, differing tongue lengths, etc. The hairy bodies of bumblebees make them ideal pollinators, as the pollen sticks to its hairs and is transferred from one flower to another. Some bee species pollinate by releasing pollen from the anthers.

Honeybees pollinate apple trees (*Malus domestica*), apricot trees (*Prunus armeniaca*), black locust (*Robinia pseudoacacia*), elderberry (*Sambucus nigra*), plum and peach trees (*Prunus domestica* and *Prunus persica*), sweet and sour cherry trees (*Prunus avium* and *Prunus cerasus*), and tulip trees (*Liriodendron*).

> **Just a Thought...**
>
> *A honeybee visits 50 to 100 flowers during a collection trip.*

Benefit of Wasps in the Garden

If you have ever been stung by a yellow jacket wasp, as I have, you will understand their bad rap. Wasps often build nests close to our homes and will aggressively defend the nest. We tend to use the general term of "wasp" to describe the nearly 500 species at large. The paper wasp, hornet and yellow jacket all belong to the same family, Vespidae. Each social wasp colony includes a queen and some female workers. New queens and male drones are produced toward the end of the summer.

Did you know that in the garden wasps are quite beneficial? They feed on harmful insects such as caterpillars, flies and spiders that attack plants. Wasps need the protein to survive. In late summer, yellow jackets are attracted to the sweet flower nectar and other sources of sugar, which are necessary for the next season's queen wasps. Many wasp species contribute to the pollination of plants. And that's a good thing.

If their papery nest doesn't pose an immediate threat to your family or pets, it can be left until a safe winter removal.

Keep Flies Away

There are thousands of known species of flies. Flies belong to the order diptera, meaning two-winged. The most common are blow flies, deer flies, fruit flies, gnats, horse flies, house flies and sand flies. Flies can be a nuisance outdoors as well as indoors. Odours seem to attract these restless insects as they flit around. Since flies are prime carriers of diseases, you will want to keep them away from meat and other food items.

To keep the flies away, there are different ways of going about it:

1. Try cleaning your mirrors and windows with an onion solution. Add a few slices of a very fine sliced onion to a sauce pan of boiling water. After cooling, remove the onion slices from the water. Add the liquid to a spray bottle to spritz on your mirrors and windows. Flies won't attach to windows or mirrors again.

2. To keep flies off meat before cooking, place freshly sliced onion rings on your meat.

3. Keep a sponge soaked in bay leaf oil beside you on the bedside table. Flies don't like the smell.

4. Lemongrass oil has strong insect repellent properties. It can also keep your home with the scent of fresh lemons. Mix 20 – 25 drops of lemongrass essential oil with 125 millilitres (1/2 cup) hot water. Add the cooled mixture to a spray bottle and apply it along your doorways, windows or other fly-infested areas. Citronella oil, eucalyptus oil, lavender or peppermint oil work just as well.

5. Flies don't like the odour of cloves. Cut a lemon into two-halves and poke 6 – 12 cloves into each half of the lemon. Take the plate of lemons outdoors when you are having a barbecue.

6. Those pesky fruit flies frequently found in the kitchen are attracted to any fruit you may leave out. Try placing a glass of apple cider vinegar and a few drops of liquid lemon dish soap on the countertop during fruit fly season.

7. To repel flies in the kitchen and bedroom, hang some lavender or grow some in a container.

8. Keep your garbage bins and cans clean and sanitized with weekly washing.

9. Repair any screening (doors and windows) so that there's no possible opening for flies to get through.

10. Light a piece of camphor or citronella candle on the deck or porch to repel flies, as they hate the odour of smoke.

11. In the garden, plant some herbs like basil (*Ocimum*), lavender (*Lavandula*) and mint (*Labitae*) to deter flies.

12. Walnut trees (*Juglans spp.*) keep flies away, but the tree is **highly allergenic** with an OPALS ranking of 8 – 9.

These are only a few suggestions for repelling flies around your house and garden. The Internet is a wealth of other helpful suggestions that may offer a perfect solution to your respective problem.

Helpful Gardening Tips to Limit Pests

Whether you are new to gardening or a seasoned professional, this section will present a few handy tips to get the best results from your garden. I am always searching for inexpensive and eco-friendly methods to get rid of garden pests with products or ingredients found around the house.

PEST REPELLENTS

- For any "natural" pest repellents, space the plants about 1 metre (3 feet) among your other plants.
- To keep mice away from the house or compost bin/pile, plant mint (herb) in containers around the affected area. Mint is a very invasive plant, but you can control the growth by planting in clay pots or plastic pots dug in the ground.
- An easy insecticide mix is 30 millilitres (2 tablespoons) of dishwashing soap and a litre (quart) of water. Mix and spray on plant foliage to ward against aphids, mealy bugs and scale insects. Never use washing machine detergents; they are harmful to our environment.
- Spread black pepper around your summer or winter squash to deter the squash vine borer.
- Wood ashes sprinkled around cabbage and onions will repel maggots.
- Cayenne or red pepper can be used to repel ants.
- Plant onions around your carrots to prevent the carrot fly.
- Aphids don't like chives, coriander, fennel or mint. Plant near your roses to keep them insect-free.
- Plant mint or thyme next to leafy cole crops (broccoli, Brussels sprouts, cabbage and kale) to prevent root maggot infestation.
- Plant rosemary or sage (herbs) to prevent insects eating the carrots.
- Slugs don't like ginger. Purchase powdered ginger in bulk and spread this on the infested area.

- Cats don't like the odour of coffee grinds. After you have made a pot of coffee, dry the coffee grounds in the microwave, on the counter or in the sun. Sprinkle the dried grounds in the place where cats visit your garden to do their "business."

TWELVE
LAWN CARE PLUS

Lawn Grasses

We all know it by its familiar name, but grass is actually from the family of plants called *graminae.* There are over 6,000 species of the *graminae* family. Grass grows at the crown, a part of the stem that is at or near the surface of the ground. Not only does grass reproduce by the seeding process, the stems that emanate from the crown play a role. Stems that **grow above** the surface are stolons, and **stems below** the surface are rhizomes.

There are many varieties of grass for your landscaping needs, and it can be a bit overwhelming to know which one is perfect. Selecting the correct grass variety for your area of the country depends largely on sun exposure and temperature conditions. There are two categories of grass: cool-season and warm-season. For example, cool-season grasses can handle cooler spring and fall weather. They need regular watering and care to withstand hot summer weather. Warm-season grasses like hot summer months, and when temperatures dip they can experience some problems, such as turning brown.

All grass types require some sunlight to flourish. It's important to observe the extent of sun exposure to help with your selection.

If your lawn is blocked (shaded) by trees, bushes or another obstruction, you will need to consider a s**hade grass.** Just remember that even shade grass can't grow in complete darkness. There are some shade varieties that require about four hours of sunlight per day, even if it's dappled sunlight (similar to partial shade).

For colder northern climates, fescue grass thrives with little sunlight and is drought tolerant. There are over 100 different sub-species of fescue grasses. Intense heat does make planting shade grass more difficult, so look at carpetgrass, St. Augustine or *zoysia*.

I am including a few grass selections that will depend on your region's climate and the type of shade or sun conditions you may have.

	Kentucky Bluegrass	Creeping Red Fescue	Chewing Fescue	Annual Ryegrass	Perennial Ryegrass
Climate Conditions	Cool-season grass found in the northeastern, northwestern, midwestern, and mountain regions of Canada and the US	Cool-season grass commonly found in Canada and the Northern US	Cool-season grass found in Canada and the Northern US	Cool-season grass and can withstand cooler spring and fall weather	Cool-season, and can withstand cooler spring and fall weather, but doesn't like hot, dry weather
Colour and Leaf Texture	Greenish-blue colour and fine texture	Deep dark green colour and is a thin-bladed grass	Usually dark green and medium fine texture	Glossy leaves and a yellow-green base	Dark green with fine to medium texture
Dormant Period	During drought and high temperatures	Somewhat dormant in hot or cold temperatures	During winter's cold temperatures	Grows only once and then dies when temperatures heat up	Somewhat dormant in hot or cold temperatures
Growth Pattern	Rhizomes	Rhizomes	Bunch	Bunch	Bunch

	Kentucky Bluegrass	Creeping Red Fescue	Chewing Fescue	Annual Ryegrass	Perennial Ryegrass
Rate of Growth	Slow	Medium	Medium	Fast	Fast
Wear Tolerance	Very good	Good	Good	Very good	Very good
Drought Tolerance	Good	Very good	Very good	Fair	Fair
Shade Tolerance	Poor	Excellent	Excellent	Good	Good
Seeding Rate	3 lbs. p/1,000 sq. ft.	5 lbs. p/1,000 sq. ft.	5 lbs. p/1,000 sq. ft.	7 lbs. p/1,000 sq. ft.	7 lbs. p/1,000 sq. ft.
Seeds per Pound	1,500,000 – 2,000,000	500,000	500,000	250,000 – 300,000	250,000 – 300,000
Watering	Regular watering with emphasis on periods of drought and high heat	Moderate watering needed during periods of drought and high heat	Moderate watering needed during periods of drought and high heat	Requires regular watering	Heavy user of water

Legend:

Rhizomes – Creeping stems that grow below the surface, producing new shoots and roots at the nodes.

Bunch – Plant develops tillers at or near the soil surface, without producing rhizomes or stolons.

Tillers – A grass stem developing from a side shoot at the base of a stem, above the ground.

Stolons – A stem on or just below the soil surface producing new leaves, roots, nodes and stems.

Roots – Grass roots are always fibrous, (many lateral) branched and without tap roots.

Here are some answers to questions you may have about your lawn.

Q. What do I need to look for when purchasing grass seed?

A. When purchasing grass seed, it's important to read the label to determine the kind (mixture), amount and quality of seed in the container or bag. Some of the information to look for is the kind and variety of grass seed listed in order of predominance, percentage by weight of pure seed of each species and variety, germination percentage, percentage by weight of other crop seed, percentage by weight of weed seed, etc. Often, more than one seed species/variety will be included in the container or bag.

Q. What is germination?

A. The germination percentage that is included on the label will indicate the viability of the seed. Seed germination is simply the growth process that occurs when the seed absorbs sufficient moisture to start sprouting. When germination begins, if there's a significant change in the temperature, the seed or sprout will likely die. You would need to wait until conditions improve before repeating the seed sowing process.

Manufacturers calculate the germination rate based on the number of seeds that germinate during testing. Look for a rate of 90 – 95%, but you will find some grass varieties will typically be in the 80% range.

Q. What are the requirements for grass seed germination?

A. There are four requirements for successful germination: light, moisture, oxygen and warmth. There must be adequate moisture throughout the process so that the seeds won't dry out. Use caution, though, as too much moisture (watering) will result in the seeds rotting. Cool-season grass requires a minimum of 7° – 12°C (45° – 55°F), whereas warm-season grass needs a minimum of 12° – 18°C (55° – 65°F). This is based on soil temperatures that are usually cooler than air temperatures. As the grass sprout breaks through the seed, there's a need for oxygen to help in the growth process.

If the soil is too wet, oxygen will be depleted, and the sprout won't be able to grow. If your soil is too compact, this too can present an oxygen problem. If the seeds are buried too deep, the photosynthesis (light) process is hindered and won't be able to create the food needed for the plant's growth.

Q. How do I choose the right sod?

A. You may opt to purchase sod rather than reseeding your yard. Sod is grown professionally under conditions that, when done correctly, are weed-free. Grass plants are sown closely together, so that bare patches don't form to allow weeds to germinate. You will still need to know what type of sod is best for your yard, based on cool-season or warm-season climates. Sod will be in peak condition when it's first laid, so it will require periodic watering. Once it takes root in your yard environment, there will be more care needed, such as fertilizing, mowing and watering. Inspect the sod thoroughly to check for uniform blades with no bare patches or thatch.

What's Wrong with My Lawn?

Green is the colour of life, creating the calm of nature all around us. Lawns that are green and lush signal to us growth, renewal and health. But what happens when lawn problems arise? The problems with your lawn can be due to poor soil and growing conditions, inadequate lawn care maintenance or extreme weather conditions. Others can be through fungal diseases or insects.

The following is a guide to help you decide what conditions might be causing the problems in your lawn. Once you are aware of what you are up against, you can nurse your lawn back to optimum health.

Winter kill – large areas of straw-coloured grass, especially where exposed to the wind with little snow cover.

Water and ice damage – straw-coloured or rotted grass where water collects in the frozen soil.

Salt damage – dead or yellowed grass along the sidewalk or driveway where salt has been applied during the winter months.

Snow mould – pink, grey and white mould forms in circular patches on wet grass.

Low-nutrient levels – yellowed, slow-growing lawn.

Treatment of common lawn conditions include:

1. Once the snow has melted and the ground is completely thawed, de-thatch your lawn. You will want to rejuvenate your lawn by removing thatch buildup from old grass clippings, dead grass stems, dead roots and other debris that has built on top of the lawn's soil. Carefully rake your lawn to remove the buildup. You can use a standard garden rake or a de-thatching rake.

2. Aerate your lawn to break up the soil and allow oxygen and other nutrients to reach the grass roots. You can aerate your lawn with many different tools. The most inexpensive way is with a pitchfork or spading fork. This tool is useful for aerating small areas. You need to punch holes as deep as possible in the turf layer and then rock the fork to enlarge the holes. You can also rent an aerator (coring machine) or hire a lawn care service to do this task. Powered aerators rapidly punch holes in the sod and remove plugs that are then deposited on the lawn's surface.

3. Apply lawn fertilizer that is rich in nitrogen. The nitrogen (first number on the bag) will help jump start the lawn to form new lush, green growth. Read the fertilizer bag and follow the recommended rate. Apply the fertilizer with a broadcast spreader (either handheld or push).

4. Water your grass deeply once or twice a week. The goal is to provide your lawn with 2.5 centimetres (1 inch) of water per week over one or two waterings. Too much water deprives the roots of oxygen, will stunt the growth, and promote root and crown rots. Too little water will cause wilt (blue-green colour where your footprints are visible), and then you will start seeing browning and death of the grass

planting. Water early in the morning to allow the grass blades to dry before they have a chance to be scorched by the sun's rays. Night watering isn't recommended during hot, humid weather because of susceptibility to diseases.

5. Mow the lawn at 5 centimetres (2 inches) height to avoid scalping in irregular or bumpy areas. During hot and dry weather set the lawn mower to cut 8 centimetres (3 inches) high. Never remove more than 1/3 of the total length of the grass blade. If the grass blades appear brown and shredded, it's time to sharpen the lawn mower blade. Most types of grass release pollen only when they grow tall. The pollen comes from a feathery flower that grows at the top and is known to trigger seasonal allergies.

6. Check your lawn as it progresses with new growth throughout the season. That way you will be able to be proactive in setting a treatment regime.

7. Apply a fall winterize fertilizer to promote robust root development to help your grass through a harsh winter. Read the fertilizer bag and follow the recommended rate. Apply fertilizer with a broadcast spreader (either handheld or push).

Insects Are Attacking My Lawn

Insects are present in most lawns, but you can keep them under control with basic maintenance and some organic methods. Thatching the lawn every spring will go a long way to remove dead organic matter from the soil. By doing this maintenance step, you are reducing the food supply for some lawn insects. Applying a homemade detergent solution will also help drive insects to the surface.

Let's take a look at some of the insects you may be up against.

White grubs are dirty, white and soft-bodied insects that cause gradually increasing patches of thin turf grass; this looks like drought stress. (Drought stress is a lawn condition that causes areas of your lawn to turn brown due to lack of water.) When the turf is lifted to expose the grubs, they are usually lying on their sides in a C-shaped position. Sometimes we can't blame white grubs because the real culprits behind the large chunks of missing grass are skunks or raccoons. These animals are scavenging for a source of food — grubs.

Chinch bugs are quite small in length, change colour as they mature and have piercing mouth parts. They will suck the sap from the crown and stems of turf grass. The damage usually begins as localized dead patches and can look like drought stress. Chinch bugs thrive in hot, dry weather. They are also attracted to sunny areas.

Sod webworms are small moths that fly just above the ground at sundown. Damaged areas begin as small patches that spread into larger areas. Look for silken-lined tunnels in the thatch that typically occur in the centre of browning spots. You won't see the worms themselves unless you drive them out, as they are nocturnal.

Armyworms feed at night, and you may not see the caterpillars right away. Look for an increase of birds in your yard as this may indicate armyworms. Birds will eat the caterpillars but don't eat enough of them to keep the infestation under control. Brown spots on your lawn are often the first warning sign that you have an armyworm problem.

ORGANIC TREATMENT

1. Mix a solution of 60 millilitres (1/4 cup) powder or liquid laundry detergent to 4 litres (1 gallon) of water in the bucket. Pour the solution over the brown and yellow area. The solution will treat about .91 square metre (1 sq. yard) of surface area. The detergent solution will drive any insects or grubs to the surface in approximately 15 minutes.

2. Collect the insects and dispose of them. You can do this by raking the area. If no insects surface over the treated area, the problem may be a soil or grass disease. Consult your local garden/nursery or lawn care service provider for disease remedies.

INSECTICIDE TREATMENT

1. Spray the grass heavily with a liquid insecticide always following the manufacturer's directions. Granular insecticides are less effective against insect infestations than the liquid type. In Chapter 2 – Gardening 101, I recommended using *Bacillus thurengiensis kurstaki* (Btk) as an organic garden solution.

2. Leave the sprayed lawn for at least three days before mowing or watering. Keep pets and small children off the lawn during this period.

The World of Dandelions

From ancient times to the present, the common dandelion (*Taraxacum officinale*) has been considered one of the most enjoyable garden vegetables. Dandelions were brought to Canada by European settlers as both a food and herb.

The name is derived from the French "dent de lion" or "lion's tooth" because of its coarse toothed and long leaves. The dandelion is a stemless perennial herb with a long taproot and milky sap (latex). Dandelions have very small flowers collected together into a composite head. Each single flower in a head is called a floret. The yellow flower heads are 2.5 – 5 centimetres (1 – 2 inches) across, with top hollow stalks. Mature fruit forms the well known "puffballs," and lots of seeds. The botanical explanation — *Taraxacum officinale* — means "the official remedy for disorder." Due to a deep tap root, dandelions withstand droughts better than most lawn grasses and also bring up minerals from the subsoil.

The dandelion is a rarity in that we can eat all the parts of this plant. The young leaves can be used for dandelion tea, boiled like spinach or raw in salads. The taste is like endive (similar to a sweet, nutty flavour with a pleasantly mild bitterness). The roots are peeled and sliced for salads, eaten roasted on the barbecue or pan fried. Dandelion root coffee can be made with water, ground-roasted dandelion root, ground-roasted chicory root and cinnamon. The yellow blossoms can be eaten, deep fried or mixed into pancakes. The blossoms are used to make excellent wine too. Dandelions are a very good source of iron, copper, potassium and other minerals.

The least attractive feature of dandelions is that a perfectly green lawn can quickly turn into a sea of yellow. Dandelions are prodigious plants that produce large amounts of seeds, which can blow into your yard from your neighbours' yards. They tend to flower abundantly in spring but can also re-flower in the fall. Dandelions are aggressive feeders and eliminate neighbouring plants through competition and release of an ethylene gas that inhibits the growth of other plants.

Where there's a ban on pesticides, a more organic solution is required to combat this infestation problem. Here are some helpful tips:

1. When you have dandelions in your lawn, this could indicate a calcium deficiency. Dandelions love acidic, low-nutrient soil. Use gypsum or dolomite lime at 1.8 kilograms (4 pounds) per 90 square metres (968 sq. yards) of lawn. Apply the lime with a broadcast spreader (either handheld or push).

2. Dandelions can reproduce if the taproot is broken into pieces. The **whole** taproot must be removed from the ground if the plant is to be eradicated physically. This can be difficult because the taproot is contractile. Contractile means "locks in" to the soil and contracts as the rosette grows, keeping the growing point near the soil surface. There are digging tools sold in the marketplace that can help with this arduous task.

3. Spray white vinegar (or natural horticulture vinegar that has a 20% acid content) on the offending weed from head to base. The grass around the dandelion will be killed if you use too much. This method will still require frequent re-treatment to deplete the reserve of "food" stored in the roots of the dandelion.

4. Spread corn gluten meal (a by-product of corn starch production) on your lawn. It will prevent any broad leaf seed that comes into contact with it from germinating. Apply 9 – 18 kilograms (20 – 40 pounds) per 1,000 square metres (12,000 sq. yards) in early spring or about the time that tulips, crocus and daffodils are in bloom. If you need to re-apply, do this in late summer when temperatures turn cooler.

5. Mow your lawn high and mow often. Scalping your lawn is an open invitation for weeds to take root. A weed can't form seed heads when its topmost growth keeps getting cut off.

6. The timing of fertilizing is very important. The goal is to feed your lawn, not your weeds. Fertilizing in the heat of the summer will only promote more weeds to overtake your lawn. Also, you don't want to burn your lawn.

> **Gardening Tip...**
>
> *Control dandelions before they go to seed... this will go a long way to reduce the numbers in the future. The thicker and lusher your grass grows, the less chance for dandelions to take root.*

Crabgrass and Thatch Control

The three most common "grass" frustrations that gardeners deal with are crabgrass, dandelions and thatch. A healthy lawn that is thick, lush and thriving is the best defence against all three. We just discussed dandelion invasion, so let's take a look at how we can get rid of that pesky crabgrass and thatch.

Crabgrass typically germinates between mid-March and mid-May, but this will depend on the plant, the weather and your location. Although crabgrass is mostly killed by cold winters, the seeds remain for next year. Crabgrass looks for areas in your yard that have bare soil and receive sunlight. This often appears around the edge of the driveway, sidewalk or soil surrounding shrubs or trees.

Here are some suggestions to avoid crabgrass:

1. Seed any damaged areas in the fall and again in early spring to try and prevent bare areas. Crabgrass will look to settle in bare spots.

2. Use a liquid or granular fertilizer in the spring and fall to help reduce the amount of salt in the soil. Salt is prevalent in wintery locations where treatment is applied to icy driveways, sidewalks and roadways.

3. Mow the lawn at the recommended height of 8 centimetres (3 inches). If it's too short, crabgrass will feel welcome with good light to grow.

4. Water no more than twice a week, as daily watering will help crabgrass seeds to sprout. Follow the watering instructions I have suggested in this guide.

5. Rake the grass in the fall to help get rid of some of the crabgrass seed that will otherwise be dormant as it awaits spring temperatures.

Here are some treatment options to get rid of crabgrass:

1. Use a weed pulling tool to manually get rid of crabgrass. This may be labour intensive, so you may need to consider another solution.

2. Spray white vinegar (or natural horticulture vinegar that has a 20% acid content) on the offending crabgrass. The surrounding grass around the crabgrass will be killed if you use too much.

3. Spread corn gluten meal (a by-product of corn starch production) on your lawn following the package instructions for application rate.

4. Look for a fertilizer with crabgrass preventer. Apply it when you normally would and just before it rains to work both the fertilizer and the herbicide into the soil.

5. Fight crabgrass with a healthy lawn.

Thatch is a layer of grass stems, roots, clippings and debris that settles on the surface of the soil just below the grass line and usually out of sight. It will slowly decompose or accumulate over time. Thatch buildup is commonly found in lawns where grass has been allowed to grow tall, mulch is frequently left and the lawn has never been aerated. Warm weather seems to be the most common time to form thatch.

Dethatching is the process of removing thatch and debris from your lawn. Aerating can be a better option to dethatching if your lawn doesn't have excessive amounts of thatch.

There are typically two ways to dethatch your lawn:

1. Use a leaf rake, garden rake or dethatching rake for small- to medium-size lawns. This is time-consuming but tends to be less stressful on the lawn.

2. Use a power dethatcher (vertical cutter) to manually dethatch the lawn. You can rent a dethatcher or hire a lawn care service to do this task. A power dethatcher resembles a power lawn mower, but the

machine is very heavy due to the numerous blades. The cutting blades need to be calibrated to the correct height for each type of grass.

Whichever option you use, be sure to check that all the thatch and debris have been cleaned. Next, fertilize your lawn/re-seed it depending on the extent of thatch. Extra watering after the dethatching process will help to support new grass growth, especially during times of high temperature and drought conditions.

Moles in the Lawn

Looking out at your carefully tended lawn, you see unsightly raised patches of grass and broken earth. Tunnelling and mounds of dirt thrown onto the lawn are typical signs a mole has taken residence. Depending on the species, moles are approximately 10 – 20 centimetres (4 – 8 inches) in length from nose to tail. They have powerful outward digging claws, small ears and eyes. The snout of the common star-nosed mole has 22 short "tentacles." These assist them in sensing the surrounding environment. The pointed nose distinguishes them from meadow voles and shrews. Moles make two types of tunnels in your lawn or garden: one is near the soil surface and the other is 15 – 45 centimetres (5 – 18 inches) deep.

The holes close to the soil surface are the **feeding tunnels** and are only used once. The deeper tunnels are the **main routes** between the feeding area and living areas that provide cover against predators.

Moles have a perfect sense of smell, which makes up for their limited eyesight, but they can detect the difference in light and dark. Moles belong to the insectivore species that also includes bats. The diet of a mole consists of slugs, snails, earthworms and other insects. Your lawn is a prime feeding spot.

Moles seldom eat plants but may "unearth" them while tunnelling, whereas voles are plant eaters. The tunnelling requires a tremendous amount of energy as moles remain active day and night in search of food. They often eat 60 – 100% of their body weight daily. During spring and fall, moles are most active early in the morning and late afternoon on a cloudy day in search for high moisture-content soil.

The only time you see moles together is during the breeding season in early spring. After a 4 – 6 weeks' pregnancy period, the females produce one litter of 3 – 5 young each year. Sometimes, there can be seven moles in a litter. The "birthing" place is constructed 30 – 45 centimetres (12 – 18 inches) underground, under a large stone sidewalk or tree. The young moles leave the nest when they are 6 – 7 weeks old and become sexually active at the end of the first year. Generally, moles live up to four years. The enemies of moles are cats and dogs, foxes, hawks, owls, skunks and snakes.

They do serve a useful purpose, in that:

- ✓ Their tunnels loosen the soil and improve aeration
- ✓ They help to mix deeper soils with organic surface matter
- ✓ They eat Japanese beetles and many larvae/adult pest insects.

There are several home remedies to eliminate moles from your lawn and garden:

1. Mix a spray of 170 millilitres (6 ounces) of castor (bean) oil (also called ricinus oil) and 30 millilitres (2 tablespoons) of liquid dish detergent with 4 litres (1 gallon) of water. Soak the tunnels and the entrances. Moles are carnivores, and with their food source seasoned with castor oil, they will go elsewhere. You may need to repeat this treatment as when the scent goes away because the mole may well move back to familiar territory.

2. The best solution is to try trapping (known as the "pit trap") if you have a persistent mole problem. Use a humane trap and release the mole at least five miles from your home in a rural setting.

3. Sprinkle cayenne or red pepper in its tunnel entrances.

4. Sprinkle coffee grounds on the soil to keep moles from tunnelling.

5. Keep your lawn in good condition by not overwatering (moles are drawn to wet earth), and mow your grass so that you can easily see any signs of mole tunnels.

When all else fails, consider calling a professional pest control service.

THIRTEEN
NATIVE PLANTS

Native Pollinator Plants

Native plants are those that are indigenous to a certain geographical area. They include plants that have developed, occurred naturally or existed for many years in a given area. Native plants include flowers, grasses, trees and other plants. Some native plants have flourished in very limited, unusual environments, harsh climates or exceptional soil conditions.

Native plants are best obtained from garden centres/nurseries that specialize in purchasing from reputable growers and promote sustainable growing practices. I encourage you n**ot** to disturb native plants' ecosystems by collecting from the wild, such as greenways, forests, parks and other natural settings. Native plants in the wild form a "plant community," where several species or environments work in harmony.

Why choose native plants?

- ✓ They are low-maintenance because they are hardier and more adaptable to the growing conditions/environment area than most non-native plants.

- ✓ They provide a "natural" source of food for many different types of animals, birds and insects.

- ✓ They help to create a variety of pollinator species for your garden.

- ✓ They protect plant extinction that affects other species.

- ✓ They have developed defences against many pests and diseases.

✓ They promote biodiversity and ecological health to protect watersheds, mitigate erosion, moderate climate and provide shelter for animals.

The following list is comprised of native pollinator plants that will attract bees, beetles, butterflies, flies, moths, wasps, and — if native to your area — hummingbirds.

Bloom Period	Common Name (Cultivar)	Botanical/Scientific Name	OPALS Ranking
June – August	Beardtongue	*Penstemon digitalis*	2
July – September	Bee balm	*Monarda didyma* 'Scorpion'	3
July – September	Blazing star	*Liatris spicata*	4
June – October	Blue vervain	*Verbena hastata*	3
July – August	Butterfly weed	*Asclepias tuberosa*	3
July – September	Cardinal flower	*Lobelia cardinalis*	4
August – September	Culver's root	*Veronicastrum virginicum*	5
August – October	Ironweed (New York)	*Vernonia noveboracensis*	4
July – October	Purple coneflower	*Echinacea purpurea*	5
June – August	Sea holly	*Eryngium planum*	4
September – October	Smooth aster	*Symphyotrichum laeve* 'Bluebird'	4
June – September	Spiderwort	*Tradescantia spp.*	4
July – August	St. John's wort	*Hypericum perforatum*	5
July – September	Stoke's aster	*Stokesia laevis*	5
July – September	Swamp milkweed	*Asclepias incarnata*	3

Legend:

According to OPALS ranking: 1 = low and 10 = high, very allergenic

Use Native Plants to Attract Butterflies

Create a butterfly garden to add some brightly coloured wonders to your backyard. Butterflies can be a welcome addition to your garden, not only for their beauty but also for their usefulness in pollinating flowers. You will need to incorporate plants that serve the needs of all life stages of butterflies. The insects need places to lay eggs, food plants for larvae (caterpillars), places to form chrysalides, and nectar sources for adults.

Adult butterflies feed only on liquids: the nectar of flowers, tree sap from wounded trees and water. Some flowers attract butterflies more than others. I have included a variety of native plants that will make your garden attractive to butterflies. The bloom period will depend on the growing zone and the environmental conditions in your area.

Bloom Period	Common Name (Cultivar)	Botanical/Scientific Name	OPALS Ranking
April – June	Alyssum	*Alyssum maritimum*	5
July – September	Bee balm	*Monarda didyma*	3
August – September	Black-eyed Susan	*Rudbeckia hirta*	5
June – September	Blue vervain	*Verbena hastata*	3
May – July	Butterfly bush	*Buddleia davidii*	3
August – September	Butterfly weed	*Asclepias tuberosa*	3
August – October	China aster	*Callistephus chinensis*	2 – doubles, 4 – singles
June – August	China pink (Dianthus)	*Dianthus chinensis*	1 – 3, varies
June – August	Common milkweed	*Asclepias syriaca*	3
May – July	Cornflower (Bachelor's button)	*Centaurea cyanus*	3
June – September	Cosmos	*Cosmos bipinnatus*	5
June – September	Crown vetch	*Coronilla varia*	3
Summer	Dill	*Anethum graveolens*	3
June – August	English lavender	*Lavandula angustifolia*	5

Bloom Period	Common Name (Cultivar)	Botanical/Scientific Name	OPALS Ranking
May – June	Field pussytoes	*Antennaria neglecta*	f = 1, m = 5
June – August	Fleabane	*Erigeron spp.*	4
June – September	Forget-me-not	*Myosotis scorpioides*	2
June – September	French marigold	*Tagetes patula*	3 – 6, varies
July – September	Gayfeather	*Liatris spicata*	4
May – September	Geranium	*Geranium*	3
May – September	Giant hyssop	*Agastache spp.*	3
August – September	Hollyhock	*Althaea rosea*	2 – 3, varies
June – September	Honeysuckle	*Lonicera spp.*	5 – 6, varies
May – September	Jewelweed (Touch-me-not)	*Impatiens capensis*	1
May – June	Knapweed (American basketflower)	*Centaurea americana*	3
June – September	Lanceleaf coreopsis	*Coreopsis lanceolata*	3 – 5, varies
June – August	Lupine	*Lupinus perennis*	3
July – September	Meadow blazing star	*Liatris ligulistylis*	4
June – July	Meadow phlox (Summer)	*Phlox maculata*	3
June – August	Meadowsweet	*Spiraea latifolia*	5
June – August	Nannyberry	*Viburnum lentago*	3 – 5, varies
June – September	Nasturtium	*Tropaeolum*	3

Bloom Period	Common Name (Cultivar)	Botanical/Scientific Name	OPALS Ranking
September – October	New England aster	*Symphyotrichum novae-angliae*	2 – doubles, 4 – singles
May – September	New Jersey tea	*Ceanothus americanus*	4
May – June	Ninebark	*Physocarpus opulifolius*	4
July – August	Pearly everlasting	*Anaphalis margaritacea*	f = 1, m = 6
July – September	Purple coneflower	*Echinacea purpurea*	5
June – August	Silky beach pea	*Lathyrus littoralis*	3
March – April	Snowberry	*Symphoricarpos albus*	3
August – September	Sunflower	*Helianthus spp.*	1 – 6, varies
July – August	Swamp milkweed	*Asclepias incarnata*	3
June – August	Sweet William (Dianthus)	*Dianthus barbatus*	1 – 3, varies
June – September	Trailing nasturtium (Climbing)	*Tropaeolum lobbianum*	3
May – September	Violets	*Viola spp.*	1
July – September	Wild bergamot	*Monarda fistulosa*	3
June – August	Yarrow (Common)	*Achillea millefolium*	4
June – September	Zinnia	*Zinnia spp.*	3

Legend:

m = male; f = female plants

Doubles = double-flowering varieties; Singles = single-flowering varieties

According to OPALS ranking: 1 = low and 10 = high, very allergenic

Native Wildflowers Growing Conditions

Native wildflowers are naturally adapted to their geographic location, and they resist disease and insects. Cultivating native wildflowers in your garden provides pops of colour and contrast by using nature's "natural" wildflower beauties in the appropriate native environment.

When deciding on placement of your wildflowers, consider the view from a location they will best be seen. Will the wildflowers only be seen from the street by passersby, or from both the street and your front windows? Will they be randomly planted with other non-native plants for visual interest? Will there be sunlight available for the full day, part of the day or not at all? The idea is to provide natural beauty to your garden (flower beds, hillsides, meadows, etc.) by considering all aspects of wildflower placement.

Each wildflower is unique with its own needs to thrive in the sun, soil and water with what nature has provided them. Here are a few lists of wildflowers and their optimum growing conditions.

SUNNY AND DRY CONDITIONS

Common Name (Cultivar)	Botanical/Scientific Name	OPALS Ranking
Anise hyssop	*Agastache foeniculum*	3
Bee balm	*Monarda didyma* 'Scorpion'	3
Black-eyed Susan	*Rudbeckia hirta*	5
Blazing star	*Liatris spicata*	4
Blue false indigo	*Baptisia australis*	2
Butterfly weed	*Asclepias tuberosa*	3
Carolina pink catchfly	*Silene carolinia spp.*	1 – 5, varies
Prairie aster	*Symphyotrichum turbinellus*	2 – 4, varies
Purple coneflower	*Echinacea purpurea*	5

Legend:

Light requirement: Sun – 6 or more hours of sun per day; soil moisture: dry – soil doesn't exhibit visible signs of moisture

According to OPALS ranking: 1 = low and 10 = high, very allergenic

SHADY AND MODERATE CONDITIONS

Common Name (Cultivar)	Botanical/Scientific Name	OPALS Ranking
Black cohosh	*Actaea racemosa*	3
Bleeding heart	*Dicentra spectabilis*	4
Bloodroot	*Sanguinaria canadensis*	3
Bugbane	*Actaea matsumurae*	3
Crested iris	*Iris cristata*	1 – 4, varies
Dutchman's breeches	*Dicentra cucullaria*	4
Eastern red columbine (Wild red)	*Aquilegia canadensis*	1
Solomon's seal	*Polygonatum biflorum*	2
Wild geranium	*Geranium maculatum*	3
Woodland phlox	*Phlox divaricata*	3

Legend:

Light requirement: shade – less than 2 hours of sun per day; soil moisture: moderate – soil looks and feels damp

According to OPALS ranking: 1 = low and 10 = high, very allergenic

SHADY AND DRY CONDITIONS

Common Name (Cultivar)	Botanical/Scientific Name	OPALS Ranking
Blue wood aster	*Symphyotrichum cordifolium*	2 – 4, varies
Bowman's root	*Gillenia trifoliata*	2
Nodding onion	*Allium cernuum*	2
Small's beardtongue	*Penstemon smallii*	2
Woodland stonecrop	*Sedum ternatum*	2

Legend:

Light requirement: shade – less than 2 hours of sun per day; soil moisture: dry – soil doesn't exhibit visible signs of moisture

According to OPALS ranking: 1 = low and 10 = high, very allergenic

Native Plants for Clay Soils

If your garden has a clay soil, you know that it can be a challenge to find plants that will thrive. Clay soils, because of the density, hold moisture during wet spells and can become waterlogged. The same soil patch may quickly go from wet to dry as the weather conditions fluctuate.

Careful planning of this particular site is required before adding any plants. Patience and perseverance are also needed by the gardener, while the plant's root system develops over the first year. The deep roots are what keeps the plant surviving during periods of drought. If the plant's roots have a difficult time expanding into the hard clay, the roots will start to circle the plant, resulting in a root-bound plant. The plant won't grow as large or as healthy as it should.

Before you plant, top dress the entire planting area with 15 – 20 centimetres (6 – 8 inches) of very coarse sand. To improve drainage, you will need to vigorously turn the soil over to break up the clay particles. If digging into a clay base is too hard on your back, you may want to consider using a tiller. Cover the turned soil with several layers of newspaper, or work in at least 20 centimetres (8 inches) of organic compost matter. The newspaper also works as a composite aid to enrich the soil. The garden bed can be planted immediately. Robust foliage and bloom will be the reward once the plant system establishes itself. I recommend adding more organic matter on top of the bed once a year. By doing so, you are continuing to offset any settling.

Here's a list of native plants that will do well in clay soil once you prepare the garden bed.

Common Name (Cultivar)	Botanical/Scientific Name	OPALS Ranking
Anise hyssop	*Agastache foeniculum*	3
Beadtongue	*Penstemon digitalis*	2
Blue false indigo	*Baptisia australis*	2
Bottle gentian	*Gentiana andrewsii*	1
Common ninebark	*Physocarpus opulifolius*	4
Compass plant	*Silphium spp.*	5
Eastern red columbine (Wild red)	*Aquilegia canadensis*	1
Meadow rose (Smooth wild rose)	*Rosa blanda*	4
New England aster	*Symphyotrichum novae-angliae*	2 – 4, varies
Prairie blazing star	*Liatris pycnostachya*	4
Purple poppy mallow	*Callirhoe involucrata*	2
Red chokeberry	*Aronia arbutifolia*	2
Showy milkweed	*Asclepias speciosa*	3
Spiderwort (Ohio)	*Tradescantia ohiensis*	4
Tickseed	*Coreopsis grandiflora*	3 – 5, varies
Virginia bluebells	*Mertensia virginica*	1
White false indigo	*Baptisia lactea*	2
Wild bergamot	*Monarda fistulosa*	3
Yellow coneflower	*Echinacea paradoxa*	5

Legend:

m = male; f = female plants

According to OPALS ranking: 1 = low and 10 = high, very allergenic

Species of Native Shrubs and Trees

When the first book on native trees in Canada was written in 1917, authors B.R. Morton and R.G. Lewis defined a native tree as "a single-stemmed perennial woody plant growing to a height of more than ten feet, and which is indigenous to Canada." At that time, there were no concerns about allergy-producing plants. How things have changed!

Similar to flowering plants, native species of shrubs and trees provide rich ecosystem benefits in our landscapes. In respect of these benefits, shrubs and trees help to:

✓ Fertilize the soil with important nutrients

✓ Provide shelter for the animals that live among the branches

✓ Hold the soil intact with its roots by preventing runoff of nutrients in the topsoil and pollutants that fill up streams and waterways when it rains

✓ Put clean oxygen back into the air as they process carbon dioxide from the atmosphere, regulating greenhouse gases

✓ Support recreational and spiritual uses

✓ Provide a significant food source of nuts, berries and insects for pollinators, birds and animals

Native shrubs and trees generally grow well and require little care when grown in proper soils under the right environmental conditions for the location and geographical area. Where possible, select a variety of native species to prevent future local extinctions of animals, shrubs and trees. Here's a selection of native shrubs and trees with the OPALS ranking.

Common Name (Cultivar)	Botanical/Scientific Name	Type (Shrub or Tree)	OPALS Ranking
Amur chokecherry	*Prunus maackii*	Shrub/Tree	5
Arrowwood	*Viburnum dentatum*	Shrub/Tree	3 – 5, varies
Balsam fir	*Abies balsamea*	Shrub/Tree	2
Bindweed, hedge	*Convolvulus sepium*	Shrub	2
Black elderberry	*Sambucus nigra*	Shrub	5

Common Name (Cultivar)	Botanical/Scientific Name	Type (Shrub or Tree)	OPALS Ranking
Blueberry (Cranberry)	*Vaccinium myrtilloides*	Shrub	2
Bunchberry	*Cornus canadensis*	Shrub	5
Bushy cinquefoil	*Potentilla paradoxa*	Shrub	3
Cinquefoil	*Potentilla spp.*	Shrub/Plant	3
Common strawberry (Wild)	*Fragaria virginiana*	Shrub	1
Currant	*Ribes americanum*	Shrub	f = 1, m = 6
False indigo	*Amorpha fruticosa*	Shrub	4
Fragrant sumac	*Rhus aromatica*	Shrub	f = 1, m = 10
Gooseberry (Wild and Prickly)	*Ribes spp.*	Shrub	f = 1, m = 6
Mock orange	*Philadelphus spp.*	Shrub	3 – doubles, 4 – singles
Nannyberry	*Viburnum lentago*	Shrub	3 – 5, varies
Ragwort	*Senecio spp.*	Shrub	4 – 10, varies
Red chokeberry	*Aronia arbutifolia*	Shrub	2
Smooth sumac	*Rhus glabra*	Shrub	f = 1, m = 10
Spicebush	*Lindera benzoin*	Shrub	f = 1, m = 6
Spreading dogbane	*Apocynum androsaemifolium*	Shrub/Plant	4
American chestnut	*Castanea dentata*	Tree	f = 1, m = 1 6 = monoecious*
American holly	*Ilex opaca*	Tree	f = 1, m = 7
Chokecherry	*Prunus virginiana*	Tree	5
Eastern redbud	*Cercis canadensis*	Tree	4
Flowering dogwood	*Cornus florida*	Tree	5

Common Name (Cultivar)	Botanical/Scientific Name	Type (Shrub or Tree)	OPALS Ranking
Green hawthorn	*Crataegus viridis*	Tree	3
Honey locust	*Gleditsia triacanthos*	Tree	f = 1, m = 7
Jack pine	*Pinus banksiana*	Tree	4
Kentucky coffeetree	*Gymnocladus dioica*	Tree	f = 1, m = 8
Magnolia	*Magnolia spp.*	Tree	4 – 6, varies
Maple	*Acer spp.*	Tree	f = 1, m = 10
Persimmon	*Diospyros virginiana*	Tree	f = 1, m = 6
Pitch pine	*Pinus rigida*	Tree	4
Poplar	*Populus spp.*	Tree	f = 1, m = 8
Red dogwood	*Cornus sericea spp.*	Tree	5
Serviceberry	*Amelanchier spp.*	Tree	3
Tamarack (Larch)	*Larix laricina*	Tree	2
Tulip tree	*Liriodendron tulipifera*	Tree	3
White spruce	*Picea glauca*	Tree	3
Yellowwood	*Cladrastis lutea*	Tree	5

Legend:

m = male; f = female plants

Doubles = double-flowering varieties; Singles = single-flowering varieties

*Monoecious: having both the female and male reproductive system and can reproduce all on its own.

According to OPALS ranking: 1 = low and 10 = high, very allergenic

NOTE

Do you wonder why the ash tree has not been listed as a native tree? Well, yes, you are correct that it's a native tree. The reason I haven't included it in any plant list is the emerald ash borer (EAB) insect that feeds on ash species. This highly destructive wood-boring beetle feeds under the bark of ash trees. All ash trees except the blue ash (*Fraxinus quadrangulata*), will likely be extinct in less than 30 years. If you have had ash trees removed due to the EAB, please don't move the wood offsite yourself. The cut logs need to be properly disposed of by a professional tree trimming service to an approved site if available. This will help slow the movement of this destructive insect pest.

FOURTEEN
RAISED BED GARDENING

What Is Raised Bed Gardening?

During the time of the Maya Indians, about 350 – 700 A.D., the population of two million lived in what is now known as Guatemala. The Maya Indians were known for their knowledge of arithmetic and astronomy. But when they had to grow more food — such as corn, beans, peppers and squash — they developed the raised bed system.

Raised beds are gardens that have been raised above normal soil level. Unlike a planter or garden box, they don't have bottoms as they are built directly on top of the ground. The present-day gardener can use this method for growing flowers, herbs and vegetable gardens.

Here are some of the benefits of raised bed gardening:

✓ Longer growing season as the soil warms up earlier

✓ No compaction, since you don't walk on the soil

✓ Soil composition is improved because you make your own mixture with top soil/compost/peat moss and organic fertilizer

✓ Easier for planting, weed control and harvesting

✓ Ideal for growing small plots of flowers, herbs and vegetables where space is limited

✓ Improved use of space by inter-planting that increases the yield per square metre/yard

✓ No more problems with poor drainage of the soil

✓ Excellent horticultural therapy for people to learn new skills or regain those that are lost through disease, illness or injury.

It's quite possible that during their lifetime, seniors and individuals with a disability have had something to do with gardening. This might have been a garden on the farm, at home or in a city lot. Be sure to consult them when planning a raised bed garden. Their input is very important because a certain plant might bring back fond memories.

Raised Bed Garden Structures

Raised bed gardens can be made with or without structured sides. If you make a raised bed without structured sides, avoid building the beds higher than 45 centimetres (18 inches), because the top layer of the soil might drain too fast and dry out.

A raised bed can be a permanent addition if you use brick, blocks, untreated lumber or railroad ties. The last one is n**ot** recommended for vegetables because of the creosote used to treat railroad ties.

Framing may be built of redwood, rough cedar or fence posts. Don't use any lumber that has been treated (toxic preservative coating), as it could leach into the soil. The height of the raised bed will be determined by the individual and how accessible they need it to be. Keep the width of the raised bed within 1.2 metres (4 feet) for easy cultivation of the crops. It's recommended to use galvanized nails for the construction.

You may wish to consider an A-frame raised bed garden. Unlike a typical raised bed, the A-frame doesn't rest in the soil. It's a table top garden with legs that give the A-frame its strength. You can construct or purchase a hinged A-frame trellis to support peas, beans, tomatoes or other vining plants. This will maximize your harvest of a wide range of herbs and vegetables on the deck or patio.

There are many wonderful online sources for ideas on building or purchasing kits or preassembled raised bed structures.

I caution you to position the raised bed garden exactly where you want it, because it can be cumbersome to move later. It's not as easy as a clay pot to transport to another location once the soil and plants have been added. You will want to place the raised bed to maximize the amount of light it will receive. Vegetables require light, so look for a spot with a minimum of eight hours of sunlight. For vegetables and plants that prefer less sun, consider introducing taller vegetables as shade cover or use a trellis with a vine vegetable to cover more sun-sensitive plants. In Chapter 7 – Healthy Vegetable Garden, I wrote about companion plantings that you might want to consider for your raised bed garden.

Give plenty of space to move around the raised bed as you don't want to climb across it or make a long trek around to get to the opposite side. Think about a smaller, unattached bed for greater mobility. If there's a need for wheelchair access, you will require additional space between raised beds with wide aisles.

NOTE

The area around the raised bed garden should be flat with an anti-slip surface. Water outlets and a storage area for horticultural tools should be conveniently located for easy access. Tables to work on (seeding/transplanting) and benches for seating should be available at all times.

Plants for Raised Bed Gardens

Once the raised bed structure is installed, it's time to think about what type of plants. When selecting flowering plants, look for colour profiles to enhance the area. You may wish to consider growing for multi-purpose use, for not only the plants' beauty but also to use in fresh or dried floral designs. Taller plants can be selected for lower raised beds, whereas shorter varieties of plants should be cultivated in higher raised beds for ease of ongoing maintenance and harvest.

There's an extensive list of wonderful plants that would flourish in raised beds, and I am including just some ideas to plant for flower, herb and vegetable beds.

FLOWERS, ANNUALS AND PERENNIALS

Common Name (Cultivar)	Botanical/Scientific Name	Type (Annual or Perennial)	OPALS Ranking
Celosia (Cockscomb)	*Celosia argentea*	Annual	4 – 5, varies
China pink (Dianthus)	*Dianthus chinensis*	Annual	1 – 3, varies
Cosmos	*Cosmos bipinnatus*	Annual	5
Geranium	*Pelargonium*	Annual	3
Gerbera daisy (Transvaal)	*Gerbera jamesonii*	Annual	5
Impatiens	*Impatiens spp.*	Annual	1
Lavender lace cuphea	*Cuphea hyssopifolia*	Annual	2
Pansy	*Viola x wittrockiana*	Annual	1
Petunia	*Petunia*	Annual	2
Scarlet sage	*Salvia splendens*	Annual/Perennial	1 – 4, varies
Snapdragon	*Antirrhinum majus*	Annual	1
Tuberous begonia	*Begonia tuberousa*	Annual	2
Vinca (Periwinkle)	*Vinca minor*	Annual	2
Wax begonia	*Begonia semperflorens*	Annual	4
Zinnia	*Zinnia elegans*	Annual	3
American alumroot	*Heuchera americana*	Perennial	1
Astilbe	*Astilbe arendsii*	Perennial	4
Bleeding heart	*Dicentra* 'King of Hearts'	Perennial	4
Catmint	*Nepeta x faassenii*	Perennial	2
Coneflower	*Echinacea*	Perennial	5
Freesia	*Freesia*	Perennial	3

Common Name (Cultivar)	Botanical/Scientific Name	Type (Annual or Perennial)	OPALS Ranking
Gayfeather	*Liatris spicata*	Perennial	4
Lanceleaf coreopsis	*Coreopsis lanceolata*	Perennial	3 – 5, varies
Monkshood	*Aconitum carmichaellii*	Perennial	4
Moonshine yarrow	*Achillea millefolium 'Moonshine'*	Perennial	4
Orange coneflower	*Rudbeckia fulgida*	Perennial	5
Penstemon	*Penstemon gloxinioides*	Perennial	2
Peony	*Paeonia spp.*	Perennial	3 – full doubles, 1 – singles
Pineapple sage	*Salvia elegans*	Perennial	1 – 4, varies
Sea holly (Amethyst)	*Eryngium planum*	Perennial	4
Showy stonecrop	*Sedum spectabile*	Perennial	2
Snowcap shasta daisy	*Leucanthemum x superbum*	Perennials	4 – doubles, 6 – singles
Tickseed	*Coreopsis grandiflora*	Perennial	3 – 5, varies
Western bleeding heart	*Dicentra formosa*	Perennial	4

Legend:

Doubles = double-flowering varieties; Singles = single-flowering varieties

According to OPALS ranking: 1 = low and 10 = high, very allergenic

Some ideas for growing herbs are basil, dill, chamomile, lavender, lemon balm, lemongrass, marjoram, oregano, parsley, rosemary, sage and thyme.

Try some of the following vegetables in your raised bed: beans, beets, carrots, cauliflower, peppers, tomatoes and watermelon. Certain vegetables, such as squash, melons and sweet corn, might do better in larger garden plots because of the extensive amount of space they require.

Refer to Chapter 7 – Healthy Vegetable Garden, for information on companion vegetable planting to grow healthy vegetable pairings that won't interfere with each other's root patterns.

Care of Raised Bed Gardens

Just as you would with flower, herb and vegetable garden plots, you need to care for your raised bed gardens.

Raised bed gardens are a saving grace for frustrated gardeners battling poor soil conditions. You are presented with the opportunity to garden in perfect soil. Fill your raised bed with a good mixture of quality garden soil, compost and manure. Using soil high in organic matter (like compost) helps your raised bed deliver all the nutrients required by your plants. Organic content allows the roots to gather available resources like nitrogen, phosphorus and potassium much more easily. Adding mulch will help to keep the weeds down. Once you have filled the raised bed and raked it so that the surface is level, you are ready to plant or sow seeds.

Moisture in a raised bed tends to drain faster than conventional garden beds, so you will need to set a regular watering schedule. The best way to monitor soil moisture is getting your hands dirty. Get your fingers down to the root zone, about 7 centimetres (3 inches) deep. The soil should feel lightly damp. Planting intensively in a raised bed garden helps to minimize moisture loss.

When weeds do crop up, you will want to remove them quickly so that your plants aren't competing for moisture, nutrients and root space. You can remove weeds with a cultivator or Dutch hoe or by hand.

Depending on what type of plants (beans, tomatoes, etc.) you plant, those needing extra support will benefit from garden stakes, poles or vegetable cages. Carefully stake the plant to avoid damaging the plant's root system and those of surrounding plants.

Crop rotation is important as plants need different nutrients in varying amounts and a heavy feeder in one year needs to be replaced by one that nourishes the soil. Crop rotation will help improve the sustainability of your garden. Make sure you plan for a good crop rotation and never plant the same bed with the same vegetables the following year.

Put your compost bin close by to make things more convenient. Your vegetable garden will produce waste material that needs to be dealt with, and composting is the best way to do it.

Spring or fall is a good time to top dress with fresh compost and manure to bring the level of your raised bed back up to where it was. In the fall, you can lightly dig in or sprinkle some slow-release organic fertilizer (granular) on the soil's surface and cover with additional compost.

Before replanting in the spring, inspect each raised bed for needed repairs. In the winter, when soil tends to get wet and heavy, the added weight can exert pressure on the corners of the bed's structure. You may need to dig down into the soil to provide access to insert nails or screws, and this is best done before adding any plants that may get damaged during the repair.

Just a Thought...

"Every flower is a bit of summer." — Ella Griffin, author of The Flower Arrangement

Planning for a Raised Bed Garden

What do we have to look for in the planning stage? The following ideas are for seniors and individuals with a disability, but you may take some of the information and use in your own gardens:

1. Raised bed gardens can be built at different levels. For gardeners in a wheelchair, I suggest "wheelchair" height and smaller structures for convenient planting, harvesting and cleanup.

2. There should be some source of shade to protect the gardener against the sun because certain medications may cause allergic reactions or sensitivities. Look for a tree to shadow the area or build a pergola structure to protect against the sun's powerful rays.

3. Include a seating area or benches for relaxation and rest.

4. Always use planting material that is easy to grow and commonly known. The colour and texture should stimulate interest and offer sensory richness.

5. Fragrant plants are a favourite and should be planted to make use of the breezes and prevailing winds. Dead-heading (pinching off dead flowers) is a hand and fingers exercise for gardeners and good for the plants.

6. The activities and work areas should be well coordinated throughout the year, with indoor and outdoor pleasantries to extend the gardening season.

7. Growing certain plants, such as herbs for drying, dried flower arrangements or pressing flowers, are gratifying activities.

8. The social aspect is important, and the area should be a group or private oriented but also provide one-on-one interaction.

9. Quiet areas with time for reading or meditation should be considered. The use of a garden statue increases the time of reflection. Build a drinking fountain if possible.

10. Instant satisfaction of the bounty within raised beds gardens is a beautiful testament to the wonders of nature and eases the stress of the day.

FIFTEEN
SHRUBS AND TREES

In this chapter, we'll discuss shrubs and trees to enhance your landscapes. The selection process can be a bit daunting when seeking the perfect shrub or tree to fit your needs. I am hoping you find the detailed information in this chapter beneficial to your quest. Let's first start by looking at shrubs.

Ten Fragrant Shrubs

A welcome addition to your garden is a fragrant shrub that will fill the air with its sweet flower scent. You will find that you won't be able to walk past the shrub without pausing to lift a bloom to smell its fragrant aroma. As you breathe in its smell, it may trigger some favourite memories.

People with allergies and those who are "fragrance susceptible" are advised to read the plant labels first. Here are my favourite top ten fragrant shrubs.

Common Name (Cultivar)	Botanical/ Scientific Name	Fragrance/Bloom Colour/Time	OPALS Ranking
Beauty bush	*Kolkwitzia amabilis*	A deciduous shrub with an arching vase-shape and outstanding spring flowers that appear in clusters	3
Daphne	*Daphne x burkwoodii*	Sweet scent; white to light pink tubular flowers in clusters; blooming May to June	5

Common Name (Cultivar)	Botanical/ Scientific Name	Fragrance/Bloom Colour/Time	OPALS Ranking
English lavender	*Lavandula angustifolia*	Aromatic foliage that attracts butterflies; deep purple bloom; bloom time is June to August	5
Fragrant snowball	*Viburnum x carlcephalum*	Fragrance attracts bees, butterflies and birds; small white/near white; blooms early to late summer	3 – 5, varies
Lemon thyme	*Thymus citriodorus*	Lemon-scented leaves on this perennial evergreen shrub; tiny pale lilac flowers; blooms in July	3
Meadow rose*	*Rosa blanda*	Fragrance attracts butterflies and other pollinators; pink to deep rose flowers with yellow centres; blooms May to July	5
Mock orange	*Philadelphus* 'Snowbelle'	Citrus-scented, double white flowers; bloom time May to June	3 – doubles, 4 – singles
Rose of Sharon	*Hibiscus syriacus*	A vigourous, upright, vase-shaped deciduous shrub with showy, large highly coloured flower petals. Although most hibiscus flowers have exposed pollen that attracts pollinators (butterflies, bees), few if any member of this family cause allergy	3
Sweet pepperbush (Summersweet)	*Clethra alnifolia*	Sweet scent attracts hummingbirds; white, pink or rose-coloured flowers; blooms in late summer	4

Common Name (Cultivar)	Botanical/ Scientific Name	Fragrance/Bloom Colour/Time	OPALS Ranking
Winter honeysuckle	*Lonicera fragrantissima*	Citrus-like scent attracts hummingbirds; flower colours include orange, red, yellow, and white depending on the species; blooms in spring to mid-summer	5 – 6, varies

Legend:

*Multiflora roses with highly fragrant small flowers are OPALS ranked 5. Recommended low-pollen and self-fertile are the flower carpet roses and many of the David Austin series.

Doubles = double-flowering varieties; Singles = single-flowering varieties

According to OPALS ranking: 1 = low and 10 = high, very allergenic

Gardening Tip...

If you love the look of the tropical hibiscus plant when travelling to the Caribbean, look to plant a Rose of Sharon (Hibiscus syriacus) shrub. Its large, brightly coloured flowers will transport your thoughts back to your favourite vacation spot.

Flowering Shrubs to Brighten Your Garden

One of the easiest ways to introduce colour to your garden is to include a flowering shrub to your landscape plan. By planting a flowering shrub, you can add a burst of colour, shape and texture to your garden bed. There are many reasons why I love flowering shrubs. Not only do they reward me with flowers during the spring and summer, but when the colder temperatures set in, I can still expect to be awed with the vibrant colour changes in the foliage. When you don't have enough room for a large garden bed, a flowering shrub is a practical solution for smaller properties.

Flowering shrubs are quite hardy, which will guarantee a long life in the garden. Remember to give your flowering shrub space to grow. Be sure to read the plant identification tag or label for further information on plant height and spacing.

The following chart will provide a wealth of gorgeous flowering shrubs to create variety in your garden.

Common Name (Cultivar)	Botanical/Scientific Name	OPALS Ranking
Beauty bush	*Kolkwitzia amabilis*	3
Big-leaf hydrangea	*Hydrangea macrophylla*	3
Black cherry	*Prunus serotina*	5 – 7, varies
Bluebeard	*Caryopteris x clandonensis* 'Dark Knight'	5
Bluebeard	*Caryoptueris*	5
Bush honeysuckle (Northern)	*Diervilla lonicera*	4
Chinese fringe flower	*Loropetalum chinense*	4
Compact lemoine deutzia	*Deutzia lemoinei* 'Compacta'	3

Common Name (Cultivar)	Botanical/Scientific Name	OPALS Ranking
Cornelian cherry	*Cornus mas*	5
Daphne	*Daphne x Burkwoodii* 'Carol Mackie'	5
Endless summer hydrangea	*Hydrangea macrophylla* 'Endless Summer'	3
Japanese kerria	*Kerria japonica*	2
Mohican viburnum	*Viburnum lantana* 'Mohican'	3 – 5, varies
Nannyberry	*Viburnum lentago*	3
Peegee hydrangea	*Hydrangea paniculata* 'Grandiflora'	5
Purpleleaf sand cherry	*Prunus cistena*	5 – 7, varies
Red chokeberry	*Aronia arbutifolia*	2
Red osier dogwood	*Cornus sericea*	5
Snowflake mock orange	*Philadelphus x virginalis* 'Minnesota Snowflake'	3 – doubles, 4 – singles
Spirea	*Spiraea nipponica* 'Snowmound'	5
Summer stars honeysuckle	*Diervilla rivularis* 'Morton'	4
Sweet pepperbush (Summersweet)	*Clethra alnifolia*	4
Tango weigela	*Weigela florida* 'Tango'	3
Virginia sweetspire	*Itea virginica* 'Henry's Mackie'	5
Weigela	*Weigela florida* 'Bristol Ruby'	3
Winter honeysuckle	*Lonicera fragrantissima*	5 – 6, varies

Legend:

Doubles = double-flowering varieties; Singles = single-flowering varieties

According to OPALS ranking: 1 = low and 10 = high, very allergenic

Shrubs for the Shade Garden

When gardening in shady spots, there are a lot of interesting plants from which to choose. Keep in mind that some shrubs can take almost full shade, whereas others will need so-called bright or high shade (dappled light or morning sun). The degree of shade in a landscape may change with the season. Assess how much light the shrub will receive to determine what plant will work best. Once you have this information, speak to the staff at your local garden centre/nursery for further recommendations.

If you want your shade garden to appear more luminous, select shrubs with white, pale pink, light yellow or peach-orange blooms. Darker colour blooms of blues, purples and reds seem to recede into the shaded background and be less noticeable.

Here are some shrubs for shady spots in your garden that will bring some life and colour.

Common Name (Cultivar)	Botanical/ Scientific Name	Characteristics	OPALS Ranking
Azalea	*Azalea spp.*	Good for acid soils around evergreens and pines. Vibrant colours and bloom earlier than other perennials in early spring. This plant is often confused with the rhododendron. The difference between azalea and rhododendron is that azalea bloom on branches before you see the leaves appear, and azaleas lose their leaves in fall. Rhododendrons bloom when in full leaf; most of them are evergreen.	3
Daphne	*Daphne spp.*	Recommended are the rose daphne and burkwood daphne. Requires acid soil and sheltered location. Very fragrant flowers in spring. The small fruit are highly poisonous if eaten.	5

Common Name (Cultivar)	Botanical/ Scientific Name	Characteristics	OPALS Ranking
Enkianthus	*Enkianthus*	Well-drained, acidic soil (add peat moss). Fragrant, creamy white flowers in spring. Fall colour, yellow-orange/scarlet.	3
Fothergilla	*Fothergilla*	Flowers are creamy white in the spring, and shaped like bottlebrushes and good fall colour. Easy to grow in wet soil. There are two species: *Fothergilla major,* which can reach 1.8 – 3 m (6 – 10 ft.) tall, and the smaller *Fothergilla gardenia* at 1 – 1.5 m (3 – 5 ft.) tall.	5
Peegee hydrangea	*Hydrangea paniculata*	Requires acid soil. Partial shade to sun and might need support. The flowers are large cluster in white, blue or pink in summer.	5
Kerria	*Kerria japonica*	Very showy plant in early spring with single yellow flowers. Bright green leaves in early spring that turn yellow in fall. Prune heavily after flowering.	2
Rhododendron	*Rhododendron spp.*	Always plant in spring and provide well-drained, acidic and rich organic soil. Plant rhododendrons with top of root ball slightly above soil level. These plants are surface rooters and benefit from pine needles or fir bark covering.	4

Common Name (Cultivar)	Botanical/ Scientific Name	Characteristics	OPALS Ranking
Snowball (Viburnum)	*Viburnum opulus*	Long lasting, white, snowball-shaped, fragrant flowers. Leaves turn to burgundy, reddish-purple in the fall. Planting viburnum is best in the spring or fall. Most viburnums prefer full sun, but many will also tolerate partial shade.	3 – 5, varies
Sweetspire (Hollyleaf)	*Itea ilicifolia*	Clusters of white, green, fragrant flowers in spring and very good fall colour, lasting into the winter. Attracts pollinators, such as bees.	5

Legend:
According to OPALS ranking: 1 = low and 10 = high, very allergenic

Edible Fruit Shrubs

Nothing beats biting into some scrumptious fruit and its flavours coming alive in your mouth. Seasonal fruit at its very finest. Planting an edible landscape will provide both food and ornamental value to your garden. The fruit from the edible shrubs can be eaten fresh, dried or used in pies, jellies and preserves. You may have some competition with some local wildlife for the berries and fruit.

Take heart that there are several edible fruit shrubs that rank low on OPALS for persons with allergies/ asthma.

Common Name (Cultivar)	Botanical/Scientific Name	OPALS Ranking
Allegheny blackberry	*Rubus allegheniensis*	1 – 10, varies
Allegheny serviceberry	*Amelanchier laevis*	3
American elder	*Sambucus canadensis*	4
Black raspberry	*Rubus occidentalis*	1 – 10, varies

Common Name (Cultivar)	Botanical/Scientific Name	OPALS Ranking
Chokecherry	*Prunus virginiana*	5
Cloudberry (Bakeapple)	*Rubus chamaemorus*	1 – 10, varies
Common fig	*Ficus carica*	2 – 3, varies
Dwarf crabapple	*Malus spp.*	3 – 4, varies
Garden black currant	*Ribes nigrum*	f = 1, m = 6
Hairy-stemmed gooseberry	*Ribes hirtellum*	f = 1, m = 6
Japanese quince	*Chaenomeles japonica*	2
Nannyberry	*Viburnum lentago*	3
Pawpaw tree	*Asimina triloba*	3
Prickly gooseberry	*Ribes cynosbati*	f = 1, m = 6
Purple flowering raspberry	*Rubus odoratus*	3
Red raspberry	*Rubus idaeus*	3
Saskatoon serviceberry (Western)	*Amelanchier alnifolia*	3
Velvet-leaf blueberry	*Vaccinium myrtilloides*	2

Legend:

m = male; f = female plants

According to OPALS ranking: 1 = low and 10 = high, very allergenic

Identify Evergreens

Evergreens are mostly described as plants that keep their leaves — as opposed to deciduous shrubs or trees that shed leaves at the end of a growing season. Because of Canada's northern climate conditions, that's in the fall. This may differ for your geographical zone.

Evergreens do shed their leaves (needles) throughout the year. Each species differs as to when needles drop, adding to the confusion. Pine needles may last 3 – 4 years on the plant, whereas spruce holds them even longer.

When we talk about the broad-leaved evergreen, there are no needles but broad leaves instead, which also drop or die off at different times. Examples of broad-leaved evergreens are boxwoods, hollies and rhododendrons.

Needles on a plant don't indicate it's an evergreen. It's common knowledge to expect that: needles = conifers = evergreen. However, bald cypress, larch and Dawn redwoods all have needles that discolour and drop in the fall.

Popular landscape trees, such as the spruce, fir and pines, are difficult to tell apart until you observe and remember a few basics. The main difference used for identifying them is the way the needles are attached to the branches, the shape and the number of needles, separate or in bundles. The contour of the needle is important, too.

Spruce (*Picea*) needles are short, stiff and sharp. Each needle attaches singly to the branch with a peg-like woody base. When the spruce needle falls off, there's a little projection left behind, which makes the older branches very rough. The needles grow spiralling around the shoot but show partly on the underside.

Firs' (*Abies*) needle base looks like a suction cup or plunger that leaves a scar on the branch. The needles are flat with a dull or blunt tip. Needles grow all around the branch but appear to flop to one side or part.

Pines (*Pinus*) are more challenging to identify because they have a different number of needles per bundle (two, three or five). Scots pine has two needles per bundle, whereas white pines have five. The base of each bundle has a little sleeve into which the needles fit together in a cross-section forming a complete circle. Pines are the largest group of conifers.

Evergreens Lose Needles and Leaves, Too

Fall is in the air, and we have had the first night frost. If you noticed that the old leaves or needles in the interior of your evergreen have turned yellow and then brown, please don't become alarmed. Evergreens remain green throughout the year because they don't lose all their foliage at one time. The leaf life ranges from one – six years depending on the species of plant. New leaves or needles are produced annually on the outer canopy of the tree or ends of the branches, and those closer to the bark will die and fall to the ground due to the lack of light to support photosynthesis.

During a rainy summer, most plants put on a heavy growth of new foliage. If the following summer is dry, there will be light growth, which won't hide the old yellowing leaves.

Among the evergreens that drop their leaves/needles are the arborvitae, holly, laurel and white pine. Trees that retain green needles from three – five years or more are the spruce, fir, hemlock, yew and pine, and have two or three needles in a cluster.

A year or two after evergreens are transplanted, effects of needle drop may be more prominent. Those evergreens planted in wet or poor drained soil will often show an abnormal amount of yellowing on inside branches.

If you don't water transplanted trees during a dry summer, leaf or needle drop may be earlier and more severe than normal. It's important that you fertilize evergreens in early spring to give them a good start.

Here are some common pines that grow in Ontario, Canada, and the number of years they retain their leaves (needles).

Years Needles Retained	Common Name (Cultivar)	Botanical/Scientific Name	OPALS Ranking
2	Eastern white pine	*Pinus strobus*	4
	Jack pine	*Pinus banksiana*	4
	Scots pine	*Pinus sylvestris*	4
3	Eastern white pine	*Pinus strobus* 'Fastigiata'	4
	Korean pine	*Pinus koraiensis*	4
	Japanese black pine	*Pinus thunbergiana*	4
	Ponderosa pine	*Pinus ponderosa*	4
4	Austrian pine	*Pinus nigra*	4
	Red pine	*Pinus resinosa*	4
	Swiss stone pine	*Pinus cembra*	4
5	Bosnian pine	*Pinus heldreichii*	4
	Mugo pine	*Pinus mugo*	4

Legend:

Most pine trees (*Pinus spp.*) have an OPALS ranking of 4, which is low pollen/allergy-friendly, with the exception of the lodgepole pine (*Pinus contorta*), which is ranked 8 and very allergenic.

According to OPALS ranking: 1 = low and 10 = high, very allergenic

Tree Terms Explained

Walking through a garden centre/nursery can be a bit intimidating with all kinds of terms on the plant identification tag or label, and we may not have a clue what it all means. This often happens, especially if you are new to gardening. Let me take some of the confusion away by explaining some common tree terms you may encounter.

Broadleaf trees have wide flat leaves that are generally shed annually. These trees produce flowers to make seeds. Most broadleaf trees are deciduous.

Conifer shrubs or trees are cone-bearing and belong mostly to the evergreen family. This includes the cedar, fir, pine and spruce. The yews are also included because they bear seeds, too.

Deciduous shrubs or trees lose their leaves at the end of the growing season. This means they are leafless during the winter months.

Evergreen shrubs or trees are green all the time during the dry seasons or winter. The leaves or needles of the past season are not shed until new ones have developed.

Hardwood is classified as an **angiosperm**: plants that produce seeds with some type of covering. It could be a fruit, such as an apple, or a hard shell, such as an acorn. The wood is from broad-leaf trees and has a slower growth rate. Hardwood isn't necessarily a harder (denser) material. For example, balsa wood is one of the lightest, least dense woods but is considered a hardwood. Other examples of hardwood trees include alder, beech, hickory, mahogany, maple, oak, teak and walnut.

Softwood is classified as a **gymnosperm**: where plants let seeds fall to the ground with no covering. The seeds are released into the wind once they mature, which spreads the plant's seed over a wider area. For example, pine trees (conifers) that grow seeds in hard cones are considered a softwood. Most of the time the conifers grow too fast to form a large, hard trunk. Other examples of softwood trees are cedar, Douglas fir, juniper, redwood, spruce and yew.

TREE CHARACTERISTICS

No two trees look alike. Since there are thousands of species of trees, this is not surprising.

Depending on the tree species, the parts of a tree — its leaves, flowers, bark, tree shape and fruit — can all be different. Each of these characteristics is unique to certain species and in combination can be helpful to identify a tree's common name. Even characteristics like colour, texture, smell and taste will often assist in naming a particular tree.

The size of a tree can be very different in terms of height, trunk width and span of branches.

The chart will help when shopping for the perfect tree to add to your landscape.

Common Name (Cultivar)	Botanical/Scientific Name	Soil pH	Mature Height	Tree Type	OPALS Ranking
Big-tooth aspen	*Populus grandidentata*	4.8 – 6.3	20 m	Deciduous; Hardwood	f = 1, m = 8
Black locust	*Robinia pseudoacacia*	4.6 – 8.2	25 m	Deciduous; Hardwood	5
Box elder (Manitoba maple)	*Acer negundo*	6.5 – 7.5	8 m	Deciduous; Hardwood	f = 1, m = 10
Japanese maple	*Acer palmatum*	6.0 – 6.5	8 m	Deciduous; Hardwood	5
Red maple	*Acer rubrum*	4.5 – 7.5	16 m	Deciduous; Hardwood	f = 1, m = 9
Silver maple	*Acer saccharinum*	5.5 – 6.5	18 m	Deciduous; Hardwood	f = 1, m = 9
Austrian pine	*Pinus nigra*	4.5 – 6.0	18 m	Evergreen; Conifer; Softwood	4

Common Name (Cultivar)	Botanical/Scientific Name	Soil pH	Mature Height	Tree Type	OPALS Ranking
Balsam fir	*Abies balsamea*	4.0 – 6.0	20 m	Evergreen; Conifer; Softwood	2
Colorado spruce	*Picea pungens*	6.1 – 8.0	20 m	Evergreen; Conifer; Softwood	3
Eastern larch	*Larix laricina*	4.0 – 7.5	26 m	Evergreen; Conifer; Softwood	2
Eastern white pine	*Pinus strobus*	4.5 – 6.5	18 m	Evergreen; Conifer; Softwood	4
Scots pine	*Pinus sylvestris*	4.6 – 6.5	18 m	Evergreen; Conifer; Softwood	4
White fir	*Abies concolor*	4.0 – 6.5	20 m	Evergreen; Conifer; Softwood	2
White spruce	*Picea glauca*	5.5 – 7.3	25 m	Evergreen; Conifer; Softwood	3

Legend:

m = male; f = female plants

According to OPALS ranking: 1 = low and 10 = high, very allergenic

Plant a Female Tree, Please

Every year, we promise ourselves that we'll spend more time in the garden. One of the things we can do while we're in the garden is to consider planting a tree. Trees are often cited in the improvement of property value, friendly to the environment and, when suitably planted, protect our house from the excessive heat of the sun's rays and the chill of the northern winds.

We select our tree based on criteria important to us, such as fast or slow growing, deciduous or evergreen, drought tolerant, native or non-native, foliage colour, whether or not it will have showy flowers, fruit and its location. Other tree-selection considerations should be allergies and asthma since these two afflictions affect so many people.

That means we have to consider pollen production in our tree selection since pollen is known to cause allergic reactions. To combat this, make sure you purchase females trees or low-allergen trees. **Female trees, quite simply, don't produce pollen.**

You could go to your favourite garden centre/nursery staff member and ask, "Where are your female trees?" However, as Thomas Ogren says, "If you go to a garden centre or nursery and ask for female plants, they will probably laugh at you."

In general, garden centres/nurseries sell male, clonal, low-maintenance or seedless trees. Female trees tend to be messier by dropping flowers, seedpods and fruit (plant-produced fleshy fruit or berry), and they require more clean up. Female plants attract, trap and remove pollen from males of their own species, and as such they are a first line defence against incoming pollen.

Low-maintenance male trees are therefore easier to sell. But the flip side is that more male trees mean more pollen. Some high-allergy trees bloom in late spring/early summer and some in the fall. The tree pollen allergy season is the worst in spring but lasts much longer than that because of global warming and extended growing seasons. Male pollen causes more common allergy symptoms, such as sneezing, runny nose and itchy eyes, during early spring. **Male trees don't produce pollen year-round.**

Knowing how to "rank" plants on an allergy scale is half the battle. Thomas Ogren, the creator of OPALS, took the guesswork out of that for us. His forward thinking has helped so many people now and for future generations. For that, we are incredibly grateful. Because of Thomas's extensive work, arborists, the USDA urban forestry, landscape architects, allergists and garden centres/nurseries all over the world are using the OPALS ranking in their landscaping plans and plant offerings. The first garden centre to promote OPALS was Queux Plant Centre, Castel, Guernsey (UK), with allergy-friendly plant identification tags on its extensive selection of plants, shrubs, and trees.

Tree Planting for Future Generations

When considering adding a tree to your landscape, look for one that grows best in the environment and growing conditions to fit your situation. Trees have their own characteristics, but follow this checklist to determine which tree is best suitable for you:

1. How much space does the tree need to grow? Do you have enough room for it?

2. Is the proposed location in a wide-open area or dense growth area?

3. What are the soil conditions where the tree will be planted — clay, rocky or sandy?

4. Are you looking for a tree that is fast, medium or slow growing?

5. What is the purpose of planting — privacy, shade, ornamental or windbreak?

6. What structures are nearby to the planting site, and is the canopy/root spread potentially going to affect the structure?

7. How is the tree's root growth? Shallow-rooted or deep- (tap-) rooted?

8. What is overhead that might be in conflict with the tree as it grows? If there are wires above, have them relocated by a professional. Trees should be several metres from wires to allow for normal canopy growth and to prevent possible downed wires and electricity interruptions.

9. Is the planting site near a driveway, roadway or walkway that may have road salt or de-icing material placed during the winter months? The salt can infiltrate the soil, affecting the tree's root health. The salt

spray or fine powder can land on twigs and buds, which can lead to twig dieback or present a "witch's broom" effect if repeated over several years. Witch's broom means that the growing points of branches can trigger the formation of brooms. Think of them as many smaller branches or twigs shooting up from the main branches. The term comes from the German word *Hexenbesen*, which means to bewitch (hex) a bundle of twigs (besom). Check to see what salt tolerance the plant possesses.

10. What is the tree's maintenance rating — low or high maintenance (watering, pruning and spraying)?

11. What is the OPALS ranking of the tree? This question becomes more important because of the increase of allergies and asthma with children, often before the age of five. What we plant in our garden, landscapes or new parks, often has a direct effect on our health.

As with the questions above, the key to picking the ideal tree for your garden or landscape depends on the function you want them to play. Do you want the tree to provide shade, create a focal point, screen a view or give a splash of colour or golden autumn foliage? Will the spreading, aggressive root system threaten the home, patio or wall foundation? Don't make the common mistake of choosing and planting a tree without considering the mature size of the specimen. You need to know the ultimate size of the tree when determining how far to plant from the house or structures. This is to prevent or minimize future canopy or root conflict. You want to plan for its inevitable growth! These considerations also apply to placing shrubs.

As you have read throughout this guide, the importance of allergy-friendly plants is never more crucial as we plant for future generations. Allergies and asthma rates are on the rise and show no sign of abating. We know that a male tree that produces lots of pollen will easily expose us to ten times more pollen than would a female tree. Yes, female trees can be messier than male trees, but the result is no pollen to fuel respiratory issues.

Look to plant disease-resistant varieties of trees. Black spot, mildew, rust and other plant diseases all reproduce by spores, and these spores cause allergies, too.

Try to achieve a landscape that averages 4 on the OPALS ranking. There are many useful female tree cultivars like the embers red maple (*Acer rubrum* 'Embers'), October glory maple (*Acer rubrum* 'October Glory'), red sunset maple (*Acer rubrum* 'Franksred') or redspire ornamental pear (*Pyrus calleryana* 'Redspire'). All have exceptional colour and are allergenic pollen free. Each has an OPALS ranking of 1, the least allergenic. If you do have a tree or hedge that has a high allergic potential and don't want to remove it, keep it heavily sheared so that it flowers less.

Some trees, such as the London plane and sycamore belonging to the *Platanus* family, although fast growing, have a very high allergy rating (OPALS ranking of 8). They produce fuzz on the leaves and stems. This fuzz causes a skin rash, itching and irritation of the eyes.

People with asthma or COPD who are in a hospital or retirement home are also at a heightened risk from excessive pollen. Trees planted near windows should be allergy friendly. Pollen particles are very small and can easily pass through the window screen.

> **Gardening Tip...**
>
> *Always look up to check if there are any overhead wires or utilities before doing any planting. If wires are present, have them professionally relocated to prevent future canopy interference and damage to the shrub or tree.*

Let's Talk about the Guernsey Girl

I am a proud board member of the Society for Allergy Friendly Environmental (SAFE) Gardening. You can find the contact information in the resource section of this guide. The society's goal is to make the world a healthier place by using allergy-friendly plants. My good friend and colleague Thomas Ogren is also on the board.

Nigel Clarke, board member of SAFE Gardening, from the Isle of Guernsey in the Channel Islands, developed the Guernsey Girl tree (*Laurus nobilis*). Guernsey Girl is a native tree to the United Kingdom and can be found at the Queux Plant Centre.

Pollinator-friendly, the Guernsey Girl is a female tree, just as her name suggests, and her nectar-rich flowers attract many beneficial pollinators. The tree has been given the best OPALS ranking of 1, a low allergen. Guernsey Girl can be grown as an evergreen shrub or small to medium-size tree. It can be grown indoors with high light, in containers outside or in the ground. Guernsey Girl's bright green foliage and tight growing pattern make it ideal for solid hedges, and it can be pruned to create stunning formal shapes to frame any entrance. It's fondly known as an alternative Christmas tree, an allergy-friendly living bay tree.

Don't we all like an easy-to-grow plant? Well, Guernsey Girl is drought tolerant and can be planted outdoors in shade or full sun. Since it produces no pollen and only traps pollen from other plants, it's child and pet safe. The leaves can be used fresh or dried to flavour soups, stews and other savoury dishes.

Edible Flowering Trees

There are many types of flowering fruit trees. You will need to do a bit of research to find the best variety for your region. Growing fruit trees does take an investment in time. You will need to prune and carefully monitor the tree for pests. Plenty of growing space is required so that the tree has ample area to spread. Fruit can't ripen without adequate sun, so check the plant identification tag or label for the ideal light conditions.

There are several trees that are self-pollinating. This means they don't require another tree to complete the pollination process. Typical examples are apricots, nectarines, peaches and sour cherries. Other trees, for example, most apples, pears, plums, and sweet cherries, require a pollinator to help them bear fruit. Bees play a huge part in the pollination process. You may need to plant at least two compatible-pollen varieties within 15 metres (50 feet) of one another.

There are several edible fruit trees that rank low on OPALS for persons with allergies/asthma.

Common Name (Cultivar)	Botanical/Scientific Name	OPALS Ranking
Apple*	*Malus domestica/Malus communis*	3 – 4, varies
Black cherry	*Prunus serotine*	5
Canada plum	*Prunus nigra*	3
Cherry (sour)	*Prunus cerasus*	5 – 7, varies
Cherry (sweet)	*Prunus avium*	5 – 7, varies
Cornelian cherry	*Cornus mas*	5
Downey serviceberry	*Amelanchier arborea*	3
Dwarf crabapple	*Malus pumila*	3 – 4, varies
Hollyleaf cherry	*Prunus ilicifolia*	5
Kumquat	*Citrus japonica*	1 – 5, varies
Peach	*Prunus persica*	3
Pear	*Pyrus communis* 'Bartlett'	3 – 4, varies
Persimmon	*Diospyros virginiana*	f = 1, m = 6

Common Name (Cultivar)	Botanical/Scientific Name	OPALS Ranking
Plum	*Prunus domestica*	3

Insect Observation on Trees

Insects can be found just about anywhere, indoors or outdoors, but when they start to attack our garden trees, it's time for immediate corrective action. Yet despite providing your tree with all the necessities for healthy growth, diseases and insects can still invade. In most cases, healthy, mature trees can fend off minor diseases and insects without our help. However, a tree that is already under stress from drought, climate, flooding, poor pruning, etc. is more likely to experience problems. Young, newly-planted trees are more susceptible to diseases and insects because they are already under stress from being transported, so insecticide or fungicide treatments may be needed to reduce further stress.

If, after reading the next descriptions, you're still not sure what type of disease or insect is attacking your tree, it may be time to call in a certified arborist. Here's a list of common insects, diseases and damage to look for to help you in your assessment.

BORING INSECTS

Borers will get at or below the bark and tunnel into the wood. Their damage can appear suddenly, or the tree's health can slowly decline over several years. You may observe thinning foliage, early fall colour, wilted leaves and branch rotting. The borers can be the Asian longhorn beetle, bronze birch borer, dogwood borer, elm bark beetle or emerald ash borer.

SUCKING INSECTS

These insects get their name because they feed on plants by sucking the juices out of the leaves or stems. After a while, the leaves will take on a shiny look and feel sticky. Examples of common sucking insects include aphids, leafhoppers, scale insects, spider mites or thrips.

CHEWING INSECTS

The mouth parts consist of two opposing mandibles, or jaws, that damage the host plant. Insects with chewing mouth parts are responsible for ragged leaves, foliage consumption and mining in leaves, stems and trunks of plants. They may burrow in or around branches, plant stems or trunks. Common chewing insects are apple maggot, spring or fall cankerworm, gypsy moth, leaf miners, Japanese beetle or tent caterpillar.

Signs of the foliage or leaf feeder damage are as follows:

1. **Notching** occurs when the insect feeds on the edge of the leaf, e.g., from the black vine weevil or holly looper.

2. **Defoliation** happens when leaves are totally eaten away, e.g., from the bagworm, gypsy moth, sawfly, tent caterpillar, and web or cankerworm.

3. **Skeletonization** occurs when you notice the feeding on the leaves between the leaf veins, e.g., from the elm leaf beetle or Japanese beetle.

4. **Mining** happens when the insects feed on the inside of the leaves and create tunnels, e.g., from the birch leaf miner, boxwood leaf miner or holly leaf miner.

Just as insects can do severe damage to trees, so too can diseases. It isn't possible to see the organism attacking the tree, and sometimes all you have to guide you is the tree's response to the problem. You may notice wilting leaves, which can be the result of a root rot fungus that is preventing the roots from taking in moisture. The symptom is the wilting leaves and not the fungus itself. Or you may see mushrooms growing around the base of the tree. In this case, you are seeing the actual parts of the fungus (mushrooms) that are causing the root rot.

Diseases are classified into two board categories:

1. Infectious are transmittable diseases caused by microscopic living agents, such as bacteria, fungi and viruses.

2. Non-infectious are non-transmittable diseases that are inherited or the result of non-living agents, caused by disorders that are 70 – 90% of all the plant problems. This can be compacted soil, fluctuations in moisture levels, nutrient deficiencies, pollutants and temperature extremes.

The following three items are required for a disease to develop: disease-causing agent (the presence of the virus), plant susceptibility and environment.

TREATMENT

The best treatment method for the particular insect or disease infestation will depend on the species involved, the extent of the problem and a variety of other factors specific to the situation. If you have any questions on treatment options, seek the advice of a certified arborist.

Bark Splitting on Trees

Bark splitting can happen at different times of the year because of environmental factors. The splits can occur on the trunk and the branches. Trees that are most susceptible are the thin-barked trees, such as certain fruit trees. Newly planted and young trees are also prone to bark splitting.

Bark splits are not likely to be fatal to the tree, but in some cases they will allow the entry of diseases that will cause decay. With proper treatment to promote the natural callous growth or new bark covering, the tree should be able to naturally close most of the wounds. Depending on the damage, a sharp, sterilized knife (dipped in 10% bleach solution or 70% alcohol for several minutes) can be used to remove loose bark from the area of the split. This will help accelerate the callous growth and prevent insects from hiding under the loose bark. The resulting bare patch on the trunk should be left alone to allow for bark growth. I don't recommend tree wound paints or tars as they won't help in the wound healing process. Dark coloured paints prevent or delay callous growth as the sun can heat the surface temperature to a point the tree cannot grow over the wound/damaged area. If you are in doubt about how to proceed, a certified arborist can advise you on the applicable treatment plan for the tree's care.

There's no single reason for bark to split on trees. We know that during late winter and early spring, severe cold followed by rapid thawing can result in bark splitting, also called frost cracks.

The frost cracks can start from a wound that was inflicted during the tree's development. Sometimes the crack may remain in the internal wood, but further frosts can cause the crack to expand and split the bark. A lot of late growth during the fall with warm temperatures, high humidity and high nitrogen levels (lawn trees are susceptible) can increase the chance of frost cracking. It has been noted that the sugar content in the sap can act as "antifreeze." The better the vigour and health of the tree, generally the higher the sugar content to help reduce the prevalence of frost cracks occurring.

Dry weather (which slows growth) followed by wet or prime growing conditions may cause vigourous growth that can lead to splits in the bark.

Sunscald, especially during the winter months, can cause bark injury to thin-barked trees. Susceptible are the Kwanzan cherry, maples and fruit trees. An exact split might not be noticed; the outer layer of bark will peel away from the infected area during summertime following the winter damage.

Sunscald injuries to the limbs or trunks of trees can be prevented by avoiding heavy pruning of trees that have dense canopies. Gradual pruning over a few years is recommended. Newly planted trees can be protected from sunscald by wrapping the main trunk with tree wrap. The wrap can be purchased at various garden centres/nurseries and is not to be confused with burlap. Burlap is usually suggested for fall planting applications to reduce the injury from voles or ground-based bark eaters. This burlap should be removed in the spring as the covering can prevent the tree from thickening the bark in response to the sun.

> **Gardening Tip...**
>
> *Be careful **not** to fertilize the trees late in the season because this promotes new growth and the chance of winter injuries that includes bark splitting. If fertilizing is recommended, generally low nitrogen or N number should be used to prevent prolonged leaf retention.*

Drought Injury to Trees

Drought injury to trees can be an immediate reaction or may take up to 2 – 4 years. The stress may not kill a tree, but the consequences of insect and disease infestations will be noticeably high for the coming years.

Symptoms of drought injury can be:

✓ Tree leaves wilting, curling and yellowing at the end

✓ Deciduous leaves turning brown on the outside edges

✓ Evergreen needles may turn yellow, red or purple.

When the tree is subject to continuous drought, its leaves may be smaller than normal and drop prematurely. Here are some common watering questions answered.

Q. Where do I water the tree to prevent drought injury?

A. You will need to water to a depth of 30 – 45 centimetres (12 – 18 inches) **below** the soil level. To do this, drench the soil around the "drip line" (the outer edges of the tree branches). For evergreens, water 7 – 12 centimetres (3 – 5 inches) **beyond** the drip line around the plant.

The main objective is to water **slowly** and distribute the **water deep** down to the tree roots. Watering for short periods of time encourages shallow rooting, which can lead to more drought damage.

Q. How much water does my tree need?

A. During drought conditions, trees should be given **high priority** over watering your lawn. Caring for trees requires different watering methods than your lawn. How much water your tree should receive depends on the tree size.

A general rule is to **apply about 40 litres** (9 gallons) per 2.5 centimetres (1 inch) with the watering frequency based on the trunk's diameter. To calculate the diameter, measure the trunk at knee high.

Small trees: Diameter 2.5 – 15 centimetres (1 – 6 inches), water once a week.

Medium trees: Diameter 20 – 25 centimetres (8 – 10 inches), water three times per month.

Large trees: Diameter over 40 centimetres (15 inches), water twice per month.

If watering in heavy clay soils, you need to monitor the soil-absorbing ability to see if there is overland runoff. If runoff is noted beyond the tree roots, then shut the water source off and wait an hour or so before continuing to water again. Monitor as before. Dry, clay soils are like a dry towel that requires dampness to more quickly absorb water.

UNDERSTAND TREE ROOTS

Most people don't know what their tree looks like under the ground. Imagine the root as the non-leaf, non-nodes bearing part of the tree. As the roots spread they provide a strong foundation for the tree. This support is from large perennial roots and smaller, short-lived, feeder roots. As the tree grows and matures, its roots and branches increase in size and grow horizontally. Ninety per cent of all roots are located in the top 90 centimetres (3 feet) of the soil. Without a strong root foundation, the tree would topple.

TREE HEALTH

Tree roots require three conditions to grow to great depths: water, oxygen and soil compaction low enough to allow root penetration. You can do your part in preserving the health of the tree by an application of mulch 7 – 10 centimetres (3 – 4 inches) deep around (n**ot against)** the tree to prevent moisture loss. The mulch around trees also helps to prevent damage to the trunk from lawnmowers and grass trimmers. It's also an ongoing source of bio-nutrients. Think of organic mulch as giving back to the soil, which gives back to the tree.

I caution you n**ot** to fertilize a tree that is under drought stress. Instead, water the tree to bring it back to a healthy condition and then apply fertilizer according to the specifications on the package.

> *Gardening Tip...*
>
> *Stones and decorative rocks used as top dressing may look attractive around the base of a tree, but doing so robs the tree of needed oxygen and detours water from getting to the roots.*

Espalier System

Egyptian fig growers used espalier systems to train trees to grow against the wall of the pharaoh's garden. Garden plot size was limited, and this method was the perfect solution. The fig growers pruned the trees to be on one plane or flat surface. How can you incorporate the same technique into your garden when space is at a premimum? Look for a perfect blank wall, courtyard or fence area to create a privacy screen or horticultural focal point.

> **DID YOU KNOW?**
>
> Espalier (ess-pah-lee-AY) is French, originating from the Italian word *spalliera*, meaning "something to rest the shoulder against." It is a time-tested system (method) to protect fruit trees from frost. Vineyards have used the technique in the training of grapes for hundreds or perhaps even thousands of years.

If a fruit tree is trained against a south or southwest facing wall, the stones will store heat during sunny days and keep the buds warm during the cold nights. Using the espalier system allows you to grow fruit and ornamental trees and protect your house from the burning sun (UVR) rays. This, in turn, is environmentally-friendly to your house.

Patience, skill and creativity are necessary to have a successful project. Continued attention and pruning during the tree's lifespan are needed to keep the pattern of the tree. The trees are grown in five different shapes: candelabra, triple U (vertical), horizontal cordon, fan-shaped (low and high cradle) and Belgian fence.

Take the necessary time to prepare the planting site with good quality soil. The espalier tree or shrub should be planted 15 – 25 centimetres (6 – 10 inches) away from the wall. This is to allow room for air circulation and roots to develop.

I recommend the following shrubs and trees, but the list is dependent upon your plant hardiness zone.

Common Name (Cultivar)	Botanical/Scientific Name	Type (Shrub or Tree)	OPALS Ranking
Arrowwood	*Viburnum dentatum*	Shrub	3 – 5, varies
Flowering quince	*Chaenomeles spp.*	Shrub	2
Rose of Sharon	*Hibiscus syriacus*	Shrub	3

Common Name (Cultivar)	Botanical/Scientific Name	Type (Shrub or Tree)	OPALS Ranking
Weigela	*Weigela florida* 'Bristol Ruby'	Shrub	3
Apple	*Malus domestica*	Tree	3 – 4, varies
Crabapple	*Malus spp.*	Tree	3 – 4, varies
Eastern redbud	*Cercis spp.*	Tree	4
Japanese kerria	*Kerria japonica*	Tree	2
Pear	*Pyrus spp.*	Tree	3 – 4, varies
Peking cotoneaster	*Cotoneaster acutifolius*	Tree	5

Legend:

According to OPALS ranking: 1 = low and 10 = high, very allergenic

Did you notice that all the mentioned shrubs and trees are allergy-friendly (ranked low on OPALS)? When you are using an apple or pear tree, select a cultivar that produces a large number of spurs and is grafted on dwarf or semi-dwarf rootstock. Grafting is a horticultural technique whereby tissues of plants are joined so as to continue their growth together. Many vines, such as Japanese wisteria, climbing roses and scarlet runner beans (flowering climber), are also perfect choices.

HOW TO CREATE AN ESPALIER SYSTEM

You can purchase a ready-made wooden structure or build your own according to the area you want to cover. Chicken wire can be used, but remember heat is generated from the sun hitting the brick and metal. The structure must be strong enough to support a plant laden with fruit, if applicable.

If planting a fruit tree, look for one that is young with flexible shoots and about 0.9 metres (3 feet) high. The planting hole should be 0.9 metres (3 feet) square and 0.6 (2 feet) deep. Mix using a combination of the dug-up soil and triple mix. The branches should be 15 centimetres (6 inches) from the wall. You want to encourage growth and air flow.

When new growth begins from the main stem, carefully bend the new branches towards the espalier frame structure. You want to train the plant while branches are still young and flexible. Loosely tie the branches in place as soon as they are 30 centimetres (12 inches) long. Plastic ties, twine, strips of old pantyhose or other suitable material can be used. During the growing season, prune all other growth to maintain a main vertical stem and side branches to achieve the desired shape. You may need to prune 2 – 3 times a year to keep the tree's shape.

Dormant pruning should be done at the end of the first winter (January – March). Fruit trees can be pruned after bud break. Remove any vertical shoots and suckers, and shorten horizontal branches to create a fruiting spur (short branches with flower buds). The fruiting spurs will be the location of future fruit. Patience is required as it may take a few years to get the entire fruit tree structure in place.

At the end of the fourth growing season, all pruning should be done during the spring and summer months. During spring when the branches are 5 centimetres (2 inches) long, cut them off. You want to keep the shape and growth habit.

Tree Pollen Cross-Reactivity

People allergic to pollen from grass or trees may experience symptoms when they eat certain fruit, vegetables, spices and nuts. This is called cross-reactions or cross-reactivity. To put it simply, if I am allergic to pollen and eat an apple, then come in contact with active pollen from an alder tree, there's a strong possibility I will experience a cross-reaction or cross-reactivity. My normal allergy symptoms to pollen will be more severe due to eating a cross-reactive food (the apple).

The same principles apply when we look at tree-to-tree cross-reactivity and cross-reactive pollens. Birch allergens were found to cross-react with other trees, such as common alder (*Alnus glutinosa*), European hornbeam (*Carpinus betulus*), European filbert/hazel (*Corylus avellana*), European chestnut (*Castanea sativa*) and white oak (*Quercus alba*) pollens. It was then established that birch pollen alone was sufficient to desensitize patients to all of these tree pollens. In Southern Italy, scientists discovered that food sensitive, pollen-allergic patients are sensitized directly to oak and hornbeam without the influence of birch. This is an example of geography influencing an individual's reactivity pattern.

Swedish scientists, when studying birch tree pollen cross-reactivity, observed that it occurred not only between trees but also between trees and foods.

Specific food allergies were noted to occur during tree pollen allergy season, leading to a realization that tree pollen and food allergies are related.

Doctors noticed patients with springtime hay fever complained of itching and tingling of the lips, tongue and throat after eating hazelnuts during birch pollen season. The cluster of foods that birch-pollen-sensitive patients reacted to were termed "birch pollen related foods." Knowing this, if you have pollen allergies, you probably wouldn't want to landscape with birch trees.

It's possible that people with a pollen allergy can tolerate the cross-reacting foods when they have been cooked, baked or roasted.

In the chart, you will find some of the foods identified so far that may cross-react with tree pollen. If you have pollen allergies, you can see which foods may cause symptoms. It should be noted that not every pollen-allergic person will experience symptoms from all food mentioned. This is not to be considered an inclusive list, as there may be other food triggers for pollen allergic individuals.

Type of Food Allergy	Source	Pollen Allergy to Tree Type*
Fruit	Apple	Alder, Birch
	Apricot	Birch
	Cherry	Birch, Hazel
	Kiwi	Birch
	Mango	Birch
	Nectarine	Birch
	Orange	Birch, Oak
	Peach	Birch
	Pear	Birch
	Plum	Birch
	Prune	Birch
	Tomato	Birch
Herbs and spices	Coriander	Birch
	Fennel	Birch
	Parsley	Birch

Type of Food Allergy	Source	Pollen Allergy to Tree Type*
Legumes	Peanut	Birch
Tree nuts and seeds	Almond	Alder, Aspen, Birch
	Chestnut	Birch
	Hazelnut	Birch, Linden
	Walnut	Birch
Vegetables	Carrot	Birch, Beech
	Parsnip	Birch
	Pepper	Birch
	Potato	Birch
	Spinach	Birch

Legend:

*There's a possibility that more than one tree's pollen can cause cross-reaction with a listed food or spice, for example, alder, beech, birch, elm, hazel, linden, etc.

Another set of cross-reactive allergens finds its sensitizer in olive tree pollen (*Olea europaea*) that is cross-reactive with trees, such as privet (*Ligustrum vulgare*), ash (*Fraxinus spp.*), as well as lilac (*Syringa spp.*) and forsythia (*Forsythia spp.*), all of which belong to the olive family. However, olive cross-reacts with pine (*Pinus sylvestris*) and cypress (*Cupressus sempervirens*), members of the grass family, and non-related mugwort (*Artemisia vulgaris*). In addition to these pollens, a recently discovered olive pollen allergen cross-reacts with latex, tomato, kiwi, potato and peach. Therefore, a person sensitive to olive pollen might have allergy symptoms when exposed to any or all of these otherwise unrelated plant pollens and foods. They may also exhibit a latex sensitivity.

Invasive Shrubs and Trees

Before we move on to the next chapter, I would be amiss if I didn't address the topic of invasive shrubs and trees. Some shrubs, trees and other plants are not recommended for planting in our landscapes because they are considered invasive.

Invasive plants tend to spread, disrupt ecosystems and crowd out native plants. While they may not necessarily cause problems in your garden, they still may pose a serious threat when they spread to nearby natural areas. When they crowd out native plants, they ultimately deprive native animals of the food they need to survive. They also take all the available resources and displace the natural vegetation. This can cause native plants in the area to become endangered.

Birds and other animals that consume the fruit from shrubs and trees can deposit seeds in other areas, which spreads these species far from the original plant location. Some invasive shrubs and trees — such as Norway maple, tree of heaven and black alder — also have their seeds spread by the wind and water. The problem is that some of these shrubs and trees are still being sold as ornamental plants.

Once an invasive plant is introduced to the landscape, it's there to stay. It's very difficult and time-consuming, in some cases years, to remove an invasive plant after it becomes established.

Always look on the plant identification tag or label for the scientific name, which will assure you of the species. Some invasive species are simply referred to by a trademarked name, which causes confusion of what plant species you are purchasing.

In the chart, you will find some of the common invasive shrubs and trees in North America as researched by the Canadian Botanical Conservation Network. This is not to be considered an inclusive list, as there are too many species to note.

Common Name (Cultivar)	Botanical/Scientific Name	Type (Shrub or Tree)	OPALS Ranking
Bittersweet	*Celastrus scandens*	Shrub	f = 1, m = 6
European cranberry bush	*Viburnum opulus*	Shrub	3
Japanese barberry	*Berberis thunbergii*	Shrub	3
Japanese honeysuckle (Hall's)	*Viburnum japonica* 'Halliana'	Shrub	5 – 6, varies
Siberian peashrub	*Caragana arborescens*	Shrub	4

Common Name (Cultivar)	Botanical/Scientific Name	Type (Shrub or Tree)	OPALS Ranking
Variegated viburnum	*Viburnum lantana* 'Variegatum'	Shrub	3
Wayfaring tree (Wayfarer)	*Viburnum lantana*	Shrub	3
Black locust (False acacia)	*Robinia pseudoacacia*	Tree	5
European mountain ash	*Sorbus aucuparia*	Tree	4
Glossy buckthorn	*Rhamnus frangula*	Tree	f = 1, m = 9
Norway spruce	*Picea abies*	Tree	3
Scots pine	*Pinus sylvestris*	Tree	4

Legend:

m = male; f = female plants

According to OPALS ranking: 1 = low and 10 = high, very allergenic

---

NOTE

In Canada and the United States, there are various government departments or invasive plant work-groups that list invasive plants in your region that cause problems to ecosystems. We know an invasive plant can thrive and spread aggressively outside its native range. To combat this, I suggest you do your homework by contacting your local native plant society, department of national resources, botanical garden or conservation centre to help identify locally invasive plants. Your first line of defence is the gained knowledge to avoid introducing the identified plants, shrubs and trees to your garden. We can all do our part in preserving healthy native plant habitats.

SIXTEEN
US PLANTS

Understand USDA Plant Zones

If you are starting out as a novice gardener or have years of experience, you may have seen a map of different planting zones for Canada and the United States. A **zone** in the field of landscaping and horticulture refers to the overall temperature of an area, marking the annual lows. Other considering factors for the United States Department of Agriculture (USDA) Plant Hardiness Map include the length of growing season, timing and amount of rainfall, winter lows, summer highs, wind and humidity.

The zone map helps you to match a plant to a specific region. The zones for the United States range from 1 – 13, with three only appearing at the coldest parts of the north near Canada, and 10 – 11 showing in some parts of Florida, Texas and California. The southeastern region includes zones 5 – 11. The higher the zone number, the warmer the temperatures for gardening in the area. Zones are further broken down into an "A" section and a "B" section, representing 5°F difference (for greater precision), with an "A" being colder than "B."

Here's a handy chart of plant hardiness zones for you based on each state.

Hardiness Zone	USDA Plant Hardiness Zones*	States
Alaska	Zones 1a – 8b	Alaska
Hawaii	Zones 9a – 13a	Hawaii

Hardiness Zone	USDA Plant Hardiness Zones*	States
Northeast	Zones 3b – 8a	Connecticut, Delaware, District of Columbia, Illinois, Indiana, Kentucky, Maine, Maryland, Massachusetts, Michigan, New Hampshire, New Jersey, New York, Ohio, Pennsylvania, Rhode Island, Vermont, Virginia, West Virginia
Northwest	2b – 6a	Iowa, Minnesota, Montana, Nebraska, North Dakota, South Dakota, Wisconsin, Wyoming
North Midwest	2b – 6a	Iowa, Minnesota, Montana, Nebraska, North Dakota, South Dakota, Wisconsin, Wyoming
Southeast	5b – 11a	Alabama, Florida, Georgia, Mississippi, North Carolina, South Carolina, Tennessee
Southwest	4a – 10b	Arizona, California, Nevada, Utah
South Midwest	3a – 10a	Arkansas, Colorado, Illinois, Kansas, Louisiana, Mississippi, Missouri, New Mexico, Oklahoma, Texas

Legend:

*Zone numbers are subject to change due to average annual extreme minimum temperatures in a given year period. Check with the United States Department of Agriculture website for updates.

Gardening Tip...

Plant for the weather conditions in your geographical area.

Flowering Annuals of the States

Not sure what annuals will thrive best in your region of the United States? Well, I hope to take some of the mystery away with my suggestions. As we have discussed in earlier chapters, annuals are plants that have a flowering lifespan of one season.

Some of the plants mentioned in the lists are considered perennials in warmer states, but are used as annuals in colder (Northern) states. When shopping at your local garden centre/nursery, always check the plant identification tag or label for information on the best planting zones and hardiness temperatures. Not all annuals can be successfully grown in your garden.

BEST ANNUALS FOR SOUTHERN STATES

Here's a list of popular annuals for Southern climate gardens.

Common Name (Cultivar)	Botanical/Scientific Name	OPALS Ranking
Ageratum	*Ageratum spp.*	2
Annual daisy	*Bellis annua*	3
Black-eyed Susan	*Rudbeckia hirta*	5
Blood flower	*Asclepias curassavica*	3
Caladium (Angel wings)	*Caladium bicolor*	4
Celosia (Cockscomb)	*Celosia argentea*	4 – 5, varies
Coleus	*Solenostemon scutellarioides*	1
Flamingo flower	*Anthurium scherzeranum*	2
French marigold	*Tagetes patula*	3 – 6, varies
Golden shrimp	*Pachystachys lutea*	2
Impatiens	*Impatiens spp.*	1
Johnny-jump-up (Violets)	*Viola tricolor*	1
Lindheimer's beeblossom (Gaura)	*Gaura lindheimeri*	2

Common Name (Cultivar)	Botanical/Scientific Name	OPALS Ranking
Marigold	*Tagetes*	3 – 6, varies
Mexican sunflower	*Tithonia rotundifolia*	5
Pansy	*Viola x wittrockiana*	1
Periwinkle (Vinca)	*Vinca minor*	2
Petunia	*Petunia*	2
Shrimp plant	*Justicia brandegeana*	1
Spotted bee balm	*Monarda punctata*	3
Sweet alyssum	*Lobularia maritima*	5
Tickseed	*Coreopsis grandiflora*	3 – 5, varies
Treasure flower	*Gazania rigens*	4
Tuberous begonia	*Begonia tubersoua*	2
Wax begonia	*Begonia semperflorens*	4
Wishbone flower	*Torenia fournieri*	3
Zinnia	*Zinnia hybrids*	3

Legend:
According to OPALS ranking: 1 = low and 10 = high, very allergenic

BEST ANNUALS FOR NORTHERN AND MIDWEST STATES

Here's a selection of popular annuals for Northern and Midwest climate gardens.

Common Name (Cultivar)	Botanical/Scientific Name	OPALS Ranking
Alyssum	*Alyssum*	5
Blue daze	*Evolvulus glomeratus*	Not ranked
Caladium	*Caladium bicolor*	4

Common Name (Cultivar)	Botanical/Scientific Name	OPALS Ranking
Canna	*Canna*	3
Cineraria	*Cineraria*	5
Cosmos	*Cosmos bipinnatus*	5
Dahlia	*Dahlia*	2 – doubles, 5 – singles
Geranium	*Pelargonium*	3
Gerbera daisy	*Gerbera jamesonii*	5
Impatiens	*Impatiens*	1
Lavender lace cuphea	*Cuphea hyssopifolia*	2
Licorice plant	*Helichrysum petiolare*	4
Marguerite daisy	*Argyranthemum frutescens*	Not ranked
Marigold	*Tagetes*	3 – 6, varies
Million bells petunia	*Calibrachoa*	Not ranked
Morning glory	*Ipomoea purpurea*	4
New Guinea impatiens	*Impatiens hawkeri*	1
Petunias	*Petunias*	2
Pimpernel (Skylover)	*Anagallis monellii*	3
Pinks - annual dianthus	*Dianthus spp.*	1 – 3, varies
Snowstorm	*Bacopa*	2
Tickseed	*Coreopsis spp.*	3 – 5, varies
Zinnia	*Zinnia hybrids*	3

Legend:

Doubles = double-flowering varieties; Singles = single-flowering varieties

According to OPALS ranking: 1 = low and 10 = high, very allergenic

Here's a list of popular annuals for Hawaiian tropical gardens.

Common Name (Cultivar)	Botanical/Scientific Name	OPALS Ranking
Ageratum	*Ageratum spp.*	2
American black nightshade	*Solanum americanum*	Not ranked
Bitter melon	*Momordica charantia*	Not ranked
Celosia (Cockscomb)	*Celosia argentea*	4 – 5, varies
Climbing dayflower	*Commelina diffusa*	Not ranked
Field indian paintbrush	*Castilleja arvensis*	Not ranked
Florida tasselflower	*Emilia fosbergii*	Not ranked
Floss flower	*Ageratum houstonianum*	2
Greenleaf ticktrefoil	*Desmodium intortum*	Not ranked
Lilac tasselflower	*Emilia sonchifolia*	Not ranked
Littlebell	*Ipomoea triloba*	4
Moonflower	*Ipomoea alba*	4
Morning glory	*Ipomoea indica* 'Oceanblue'	4
Nasturtium	*Tropaeolum*	3
Sensitive plant	*Mimosa pudica*	2
Wedelia	*Wedelia trilobata*	3

Legend:

According to OPALS ranking: 1 = low and 10 = high, very allergenic

Here's a selection of popular annuals for Alaskan climate gardens.

Common Name (Cultivar)	Botanical/Scientific Name	OPALS Ranking
Columbine	*Aquilegia* 'Songbird Nightingale'	1
Cornflower (Bachelor's button)	*Centaurea cyanus*	3
Floss flower	*Ageratum houstonianum*	2
Marigold	*Tagetes*	3 – 6, varies
Nasturtium	*Tropaeolum*	3
Petunia	*Petunias*	2
Snapdragon	*Antirrhinum majus*	1
Sunflower	*Helianthus*	1 – 6, varies
Sweet alyssum	*Lobularia maritima*	5
Zinnia	*Zinnia spp.*	3

Legend:

According to OPALS ranking: 1 = low and 10 = high, very allergenic

Flowering Perennials of the States

Perennials are plants with a three or more years' lifespan. Some thrive for just a few years, while others are long-living in your garden. Keeping in mind the USDA zones, I have created some plant lists for zones similar to the ones we just discussed in the selections of annuals. As with any plant I mention in this guide, it's always best to check the plant identification tag or label for information on the best planting zones and hardiness temperatures. Not all perennials can be successfully grown in your garden.

BEST PERENNIALS FOR SOUTHERN STATES

Here's a list of popular perennials for Southern climate gardens.

Common Name (Cultivar)	Botanical/Scientific Name	OPALS Ranking
African lily (Lily of the Nile)	*Agapanthus africanus*	2
Agave	*Agave spp.*	4 – 6, varies
Amaryllis	*Amaryllidinae*	3
Blazing star	*Liatris spicata*	4
Bromeliads	*Bromeliad spp.*	2
Bulbine	*Bulbine frutescens*	3
Butterfly iris (African)	*Dietes iridioides*	2
Chenille plant	*Acalypha hispida*	f = 1, m = 7
Crinum	*Crinum americanum*	3
Firecracker flower	*Crossandra infundibuliformis*	2
Flamingo flower	*Anthurium scherzeranum*	2
Garden phlox	*Phlox paniculata*	3
Gaura	*Gaura lindheimeri* 'Whirling Butterflies'	2
Gayfeather	*Liatris spicata*	4
Golden candle	*Pachystachys lutea*	2

Common Name (Cultivar)	Botanical/Scientific Name	OPALS Ranking
Obedient plant	*Physostegia virginiana*	3
Orange plume flower (Mexican honeysuckle)	*Justicia spicigera*	1
Royal catchfly	*Silene regia*	1 – 5, varies
Scorpion tail	*Heliotropium angiospermum*	5
Soapwort (Max frei)	*Saponaria x lempergii*	3
Spider lily	*Crinum spp.*	3
Stokes aster	*Stokesia laevis*	5
Swamp sunflower	*Helianthus angustifolius*	1 – 6, varies
Tickseed	*Coreopsis grandiflora*	3 – 5, varies

Legend:

m = male; f = female plants

According to OPALS ranking: 1 = low and 10 = high, very allergenic

BEST PERENNIALS FOR NORTHERN AND MIDWEST STATES

Here's a selection of popular perennials for Northern and Midwest climate gardens.

Common Name (Cultivar)	Botanical/Scientific Name	OPALS Ranking
Anise hyssop	*Agastache foeniculum*	3
Aster	*Symphyotrichum spp.*	2 – doubles, 4 – singles
Astilbe	*Astilbe arendsii*	4
Balloon flower	*Platycodon grandiflorus*	2
Bee balm	*Monarda didyma*	3

Common Name (Cultivar)	Botanical/Scientific Name	OPALS Ranking
Black-eyed Susan	*Rudbeckia hirta*	5
Chrysanthemum	*Chrysanthemum*	4 – doubles, 6 – singles
Columbine	*Aquilegia spp.*	1
Coneflower	*Echinacea spp.*	5
Coral bells	*Heuchera sanguinea*	1
Cornflower	*Centaurea cyanus*	3
Garden phlox	*Phlox paniculata*	3
Hollyhocks	*Alcea rosea*	2 – 3, varies
Ladybells (Grannybells)	*Adenophora liliifolia*	Not ranked
Maiden pink	*Dianthus deltoides*	1 – 3, varies
Oriental lilies	*Lilium*	4
Painted daisy	*Tanacetum coccineum*	5
Peonies	*Paeonia spp.*	1 – doubles, 3 – singles
Speedwell	*Veronica spicata*	2
Tussock bellflower (Carpathian)	*Campanula carpatica*	1
Yarrow	*Achillea millefolium*	4

Legend:

Doubles = double-flowering varieties; Singles = single-flowering varieties

According to OPALS ranking: 1 = low and 10 = high, very allergenic

Here's a list of popular perennials for Hawaiian tropical gardens.

Common Name (Cultivar)	Botanical/Scientific Name	OPALS Ranking
Aster	*Symphyotrichum spp.*	2 – doubles, 4 – singles
Blue daze	*Evolvulus glomeratus*	Not ranked
Canna	*Canna*	3
Gazania	*Gazania rigens*	4
Geranium	*Geramium*	3
Gerbera daisy	*Gerbera ambigua*	5
Globe amaranth	*Gomphrena globosa*	4
Ilima papa	*Sida fallax*	Not ranked
Impatiens (New Guinea and Common)	*Impatiens hawkeri*	1
Kalanchoe	*Kalanchoe blossfeldiana*	2
Lanceleaf coreopsis	*Coreopsis lanceolata*	3 – 5, varies
Lantana	*Lantana camara*	2 – 6, varies
Lily of the nile	*Agapanthus* 'Peter Pan'	2
Periwinkle (Madagascar)	*Catharanthus roseus*	1
Tuberous begonia	*Begonia tuberousa*	2
Verbena (Peruvian)	*Verbena officinalis*	3
Wax begonia	*Begonia semperflorens*	4

Legend:

Doubles = double-flowering varieties; Singles = single-flowering varieties

According to OPALS ranking: 1 = low and 10 = high, very allergenic

Here's a selection of popular perennials for Alaskan gardens.

Common Name (Cultivar)	Botanical/Scientific Name	OPALS Ranking
Bellflower (Dickson's gold)	*Campanula garganica*	1
Bleeding heart	*Dicentra spectabilis*	4
Bugleweed	*Ajuga reptans*	1
Candy mountain foxglove	*Digitalis purpurea* 'Candy Mountain'	2
Candytuff	*Iberis sempervirens*	2
Dwarf columbine	*Aquilegia flabellata*	1
Foxglove	*Digitalis purpurea* 'Sugar Plum'	2
Geranium	*Geranium* 'Rozanne'	3
Greek yarrow	*Achillea ageratifolia*	4
Lady's mantle	*Alchemilla alpina*	4
Masterwort	*Astrantia major* 'Ruby Cloud'	3
Monkshood	*Aconitum napellus*	4
Rock cress (Snow cap)	*Arabis alpina subsp. caucasica*	1
Rocky Mountain columbine	*Aquilegia x caerulea*	1
Sea pink (Thrift)	*Armeria maritima*	1
Shasta daisy	*Chrysanthemum spp.*	4 – doubles, 6 – singles

Legend:

Doubles = double-flowering varieties; Singles = single-flowering varieties

According to OPALS ranking: 1 = low and 10 = high, very allergenic

Wildflowers of the States

What is a wildflower? It's a flowering plant that grows in the wild, as its name implies, or on its own without cultivation. Wildflowers that are indigenous, meaning they originate or occur naturally in a particular place, are called "natives." Naturalized wildflowers are considered common but not indigenous and have been introduced to the area from some other part of the world. Both types are adept at growing on their own.

Wildflowers may be grown in your landscape for a natural look. The best time to sow wildflower seeds is the spring after the possibility of frost. Most wildflowers are annuals and will bloom quickly and heavily before dropping their seeds when the weather either gets too cold or dry for the plant to live. Many plants will grow the following year because of the dropped seeds. Seeds must fall on the ground; then they rely on climate changes to germinate and grow. These annual wildflowers are called "self-sowing."

Since wildflowers grow naturally, they don't need much attention. If you do fertilize, use one with low nitrogen. You will want to first prepare the area to remove any weeds, whether you are planting wildflowers near trees, boulders, grassy areas or a nearby meadow. Mix your seeds with about 10-parts of light nursery sand or vermiculite to one-part seed. Many wildflower seeds are very fine and can fly away when sown. After you scatter the seeds, flatten the seeded area (either with your feet or board plank) so that the seeds will adhere to the soil. Water sparingly to keep the seeds from blowing away during germination, and until the plants become established.

Many wildflowers growing in natural settings (forests, green spaces, etc.) are considered rare, threatened or endangered. They are not to be picked or transported into your garden.

Here are some wildflowers that you can grow in your landscape. It's best to check the seed package, plant identification tag or label for the ideal planting zone.

Bloom Time	Common Name (Cultivar)	Botanical/Scientific Name	OPALS Ranking
Spring	Adam and Eve (Puttyroot orchid)	*Aplectrum hyemale*	Not ranked
Late summer	Aster (Hairy white oldfield, Frost, White heath)	*Symphyotrichum pilosum*	2 – doubles, 4 – singles
Summer	Bartram's rosegentians	*Sabatia decandra*	Not ranked
Mid-season	Beardtongue	*Penstemon digitalis*	2
Fall	Blue mistflower	*Conoclinium coelestinum*	Not ranked
Spring – summer	Daisy fleabane	*Erigeron vernus*	4
Mid-season	Desert marigold	*Baileya multiradiata*	Not ranked
Fall	Dotted horsemint (Spotted bee balm)	*Monarda punctata*	3

Bloom Time	Common Name (Cultivar)	Botanical/Scientific Name	OPALS Ranking
Early mid-season	Eastern red columbine (Wild red)	*Aquilegia canadensis*	1
Summer – fall	False foxglove	*Agalinis tenuifolia*	2
Early season	Five spot	*Nemophila maculata*	1
Mid-season	Globe gilia	*Gilia capitata*	3
Mid-season	Godetia	*Clarkia amoena*	2
Spring – summer – fall	Goldcrest	*Lophiola aurea*	Not ranked
Mid- and late season	Hibiscus (Rose mallow)	*Hibiscus moscheutos*	3
Fall	Ironweed	*Vernonia spp.*	4
Spring – Summer	Lanceleaf milkweed	*Asclepias lanceolata*	3
Mid and late season	Lemon beebalm	*Monarda citriodora*	3
Mid season	Mexican hat (red)	*Ratibida columnaris*	Not ranked
Summer – fall	Morning glory	*Ipomoea purpurea*	4
Spring – summer	Pitcherplant (yellow)	*Sarracenia flava*	3
Spring	Rain lilies	*Zephyranthes spp.*	3
Mid- and late season	Scarlet flax	*Linum grandiflorum var. rubrum*	4
Early season	Siberian wallflower	*Cheiranthus allionii*	3
Early spring	Texas bluebonnet	*Lupinus texensis*	3
Spring	Trillium	*Trillium spp.*	2
Spring – summer	Trumpet creeper	*Campsis radicans*	5
Mid-spring	White wild indigo	*Baptisia alba*	2

Bloom Time	Common Name (Cultivar)	Botanical/Scientific Name	OPALS Ranking
Spring	Yellow colic-root	*Aletris lutea*	Not ranked

> **NOTE**
>
> Check the wildflower seed package for any non-native invasive species that could kill native plants or overtake the areas where they grow. Be sure to search online for the various government departments or invasive plant workgroups lists of invasive wildflower plants in your region that cause problems to ecosystems.

Ground Covers, Shrubs and Vines of the States

There are many options for gardeners when planting attractive, blooming, colourful, fragrant ground covers, shrubs and vines. Gardeners in the Northern United States will need to contend with severe winters, whereas hot, high-humidity days are considerations for gardeners in the South. As with all the plants suggested in this chapter, it's best to check the plant identification tag or label for the ideal planting zone.

GROUND COVERS

Here's a list of ground covers to consider for your garden.

Common Name (Cultivar)	Botanical/Scientific Name	OPALS Ranking
Baby tears stonecrop (white)	*Sedum album chloroticum*	2
Balsam impatiens	*Impatiens balsamina*	1
Blue star creeper	*Isotoma fluviatilis*	5
Cardboard plant	*Zamia furfuracea*	f = 1, m = 6

Common Name (Cultivar)	Botanical/Scientific Name	OPALS Ranking
Carpet bugle	*Ajuga spp.*	1
Cast iron plant	*Aspidistra elatior*	1
Creeping mazus	*Mazus reptans*	1
False heather	*Cuphea hyssopifolia*	2
Florida arrowroot	*Zamia floridana*	f = 1, m = 6
Inkberry	*Scaevola plumieri*	3
Japanese ardisia	*Ardisia japonica*	3
New Zealand brass buttons	*Leptinella squalida*	5
Perennial peanut	*Arachis glabrata*	3
Periwinkle	*Vinca minor*	2
Pink quill	*Tillandsia cyanea*	Not ranked
Tampa mock-vervain	*Glandularia tampensis*	3
Trailing lantana	*Lantana montevidensis*	2 – 6, varies

Legend:

m = male; f = female plants

According to OPALS ranking: 1 = low and 10 = high, very allergenic

SHRUBS

Here's a list of interesting shrubs for your garden.

Common Name (Cultivar)	Botanical/Scientific Name	OPALS Ranking
Bayberry	*Myrica pensylvanica*	f = 1, m = 9
Butterfly bush (blue)	*Rotheca myricoides*	3
Bridal wreath spirea	*Spirea prunifolia*	5

Common Name (Cultivar)	Botanical/Scientific Name	OPALS Ranking
Bunchberry	*Cornus canadensis*	5
Carolina allspice	*Calycanthus floridus*	3
Chenille plant	*Acalypha hispida*	f = 1, m = 7
Emperor's candlesticks	*Senna alata*	5 – 7, varies
Firethorn	*Pyracantha spp.*	5
Florida hopbush	*Dodonaea viscosa*	f = 1, m = 9
Gold mound spirea	*Spiraea japonica*	5
Guava	*Psidium guajava*	3
Juniper berry	*Citharexylum caudatum*	Not ranked
Labrador tea	*Ledum groenlandicum*	4
Miniature holly	*Malpighia coccigera*	4
Mock orange	*Philadelphus microphyllus* 'June Bride'	3 – doubles, 4 – singles
Ninebark	*Physocarpus opulifolius*	4
Princess flower	*Tibouchina urvilleana*	2
Scrub palmetto	*Sabal etonia*	5
Snow bush	*Breynia disticha*	Not ranked
Spice bush	*Lindera benzoin*	f = 1, m = 6
Sticky currant	*Ribes viscosissimum*	f = 1, m = 6
Texas sage	*Leucophyllum frutescens*	2
Twinberry	*Lonicera involucrata*	5 – 6, varies
Weeping lantana	*Lantana montevidensis*	2 – 6, varies
Western serviceberry (Saskatoon)	*Amelanchier alnifolia*	3

Common Name (Cultivar)	Botanical/Scientific Name	OPALS Ranking
Wood rose	*Rosa gymnocarpa*	Not ranked
Yellow twig dogwood	*Cornus sericea* 'Flaviramea'	5

Legend:

m = male; f = female plants

Doubles = double-flowering varieties; Singles = single-flowering varieties

According to OPALS ranking: 1 = low and 10 = high, very allergenic

VINES

Here's a list of visually pleasing vines to add to your garden.

Common Name (Cultivar)	Botanical/Scientific Name	OPALS Ranking
American bittersweet	*Celastrus scandens*	f = 1, m = 6
American wisteria	*Wisteria frutescens*	4
Bower vine	*Pandorea jasminoides*	2
Bougainvillea	*Bougainvillea spp.*	1
Carolina jessamine	*Gelsemium sempervirens*	4
Clematis	*Clematis spp.*	5
Climbing aster	*Symphyotrichum carolinianum*	2 – 4, varies
Cross vine	*Bignonia capreolata*	5
Dutchman's pipe	*Aristolochia macrophylla*	3
Fox grape	*Vitis labrusca*	f = 1, m = 6
Ground nut	*Apios tuberosa (or Americana)*	Not ranked
Honeysuckle (Trumpet)	*Lonicera sempervirens*	5 – 6, varies
Star jasmine	*Trachelospermum jasminoides*	5

Common Name (Cultivar)	Botanical/Scientific Name	OPALS Ranking
Trumpet flower	*Bignonia capreolata*	5
Virginia creeper	*Parthenocissus quinquefolia*	4
Woodbine	*Clematis virginiana*	5

Legend:

m = male; f = female plants

According to OPALS ranking: 1 = low and 10 = high, very allergenic

ORNAMENTAL GRASSES

I am including an additional selection of ornamental grasses to this section if you are looking for foliage that will provide a big impact to your landscape. Some grasses are not only attractive but will also attract insects and birds. You can combine the ornamental grass with a variety of perennials to complement the area, for example, geraniums, chelone, daisies, hostas, etc.

I want to feature one type of grass — Buffalo grass. Native to Rocky Mountain areas, this is a drought-tolerant lawn grass. At this time, there's no type of Buffalo grass that can be grown from seed and be all-female. Look at some cultivars '609,' 'Prairie,' 'Legacy,' 'Buffalo Girl' and 'UC Verde' (selected for California and southern Arizona).

Here are some additional ornamental grasses to add captivating plumes that will also add soothing sounds to your garden as the grass waves in the breeze.

Common Name (Cultivar)	Botanical/Scientific Name	OPALS Ranking
Blue oat grass	*Helictotrichon sempervirens*	Not ranked
Blue sedge	*Carex flacca*	f = 1, m = 8
Pennisetum	*Pennisetum purpureum hybrid* 'Princess Molly'	1
Japanese blood grass	*Imperata cylindrica*	Not ranked
Lilyturf	*Liriope muscari*	3
Maidengrass	*Miscanthus sinensis*	Not ranked

Common Name (Cultivar)	Botanical/Scientific Name	OPALS Ranking
Mexican feather grass	*Stipa tenuissima*	Not ranked
Pink muhly grass	*Muhlenbergia capillaris*	Not ranked
Purple love grass	*Eragrostis spectabilis*	Not ranked
Salt grass	*Distichlis spicata*	f = 1, m = 9
Zebra grass	*Miscanthus sinensis*	Not ranked

Legend:

m = male; f = female plants

According to OPALS ranking: 1 = low and 10 = high, very allergenic

Gardening Tip...

Combine ornamental grasses with other flowers and shrubs to provide an interesting range of textures and colours — from the bluest of blues to green and reddest of red — to the garden.

Native Shrubs and Trees of the States

The word "native" describes species living in the area where the plant is found naturally. Every plant is native to some geographic area. Native plant gardens are wildlife habitats in that each plant contributes to the local biodiversity. The plants form an intricate part of the natural heritage of each state.

There are too many outstanding native trees to mention, but I would like to discuss one — the California black oak tree, native to Oregon and California. **Although a high allergen tree (OPALS ranking of 8), it does serve many purposes.** Over 50 species of birds are thought to use the tree, and the acorns provide a substantial winter diet for bears, deer, squirrels and woodpeckers. This species of oak tree has a longevity of 100 – 200 years, and occasionally up to 500 years. The tree has adapted to the wildfires common in this part of the country. According to the USDA, the tree's thick, insulating bark protects it from low- and most moderate-severity surface fires. The California black oak also re-establishes itself from acorns after a fire. At one time, the tree's black oak acorns were a food staple important to Native American tribes located within the oak groves.

Here's a list of native shrubs and trees that are used by the Minnesota Department of Natural Resources based on solid, scientific principles.

Common Name (Cultivar)	Botanical/Scientific Name	Type (Shrub or Tree)	OPALS Ranking
American elderberry	*Sambucus canadensis*	Shrub	4
Black chokeberry	*Aronia melanocarpa*	Shrub	2
Bush honeysuckle	*Diervilla lonicera*	Shrub	4
California lilac	*Ceanothus spp.*	Shrub	4
Creeping juniper	*Juniperus horizontalis*	Shrub	f = 1, m = 10
Highbush cranberry	*Viburnum trilobum*	Shrub	3
Inland serviceberry	*Amelanchier interior*	Shrub	3
Lowbush blueberry	*Vaccinium angustifolium*	Shrub	2
Nannyberry	*Viburnum lentago*	Shrub	3
Ninebark	*Physocarpus opulifolius*	Shrub	4
Snowberry	*Symphoricarpos albus*	Shrub	3
Beaked (Bebb's) willow	*Salix bebbiana*	Tree or Shrub	f = 1, m = 10
Common juniper	*Juniperus communis*	Tree or Shrub	f = 1, m = 10
Eastern red cedar	*Juniperus virginiana*	Tree or Shrub	f = 1, m = 10
Gray dogwood	*Cornus racemosa*	Tree or Shrub	5
Balsam poplar	*Populus balsamifera*	Tree	f = 1, m = 8
Big-tooth aspen	*Populus grandidentata*	Tree	f = 1, m = 8
Cottonwood	*Populus deltoides* 'Cordata'	Tree	f = 1, m = 8
Fireberry hawthorn	*Crataegus chrysocarpa*	Tree	3
Quaking aspen	*Populus tremuloides*	Tree	f =1, m = 8
Red pine	*Pinus resinosa*	Tree	4

Common Name (Cultivar)	Botanical/Scientific Name	Type (Shrub or Tree)	OPALS Ranking
Tamarack	*Larix laricina*	Tree	2
White pine	*Pinus strobus*	Tree	4
Wild plum	*Prunus Americana*	Tree	4

Legend:

m = male; f = female plants

According to OPALS ranking: 1 = low and 10 = high, very allergenic

Flowering Trees of the States

With their fragrant blooms adding a sweet perfume to the air, many species of flowering trees will produce edible fruit later in the season. The flowers attract pollinators to your landscape, and the tree's fruit feeds birds and small animals. If you are looking to add a showpiece to set the tone in your garden, there are many flowering trees available in your favourite colour palate. From vibrant reds, classic pinks, pure whites and soft purples, there's no limit in highlighting your creativity.

When you choose a flowering tree, think beyond spring flowering to introduce species that bloom in summer or early fall. When doing your research, look for interesting leaf shapes (rounded, tapered, heart-shaped), showy fall colour (brilliant scarlet, orange or yellow), and bright berries or fruit.

Many flowering trees will continue to dazzle with intense fall colour that will extend your garden's transformation. Flowering times may differ from plant hardiness zones, e.g., the chaste tree blooms in June in the South but not until August in the Pacific Northwest.

I have put together a list of flowering trees that are adaptable to various soil types and plant hardiness zones, and offer an attractive variety of colours.

Common Name (Cultivar)	Botanical/Scientific Name	Colour Notes	OPALS Ranking
Autumn cherry tree (Higan)	*Prunus subhirtella* 'Autumnalis'	Huge double blooms	5 – 7, varies
Callery pear	*Pyrus calleryana*	Masses of white flowers	4

Common Name (Cultivar)	Botanical/Scientific Name	Colour Notes	OPALS Ranking
Chaste tree	*Vitex agnus-castus*	Luminous lavender spikes of flowers	4
Crabapple	*Malus x moerlandsii* 'Profusion'	Deep pink flowers	3 – 4, varies
Crape myrtle tree (Muskogee)	*Lagerstroemia*	Lavender blooms	5
Eastern redbud	*Cercis canadensis*	Pink blooms	4
Empress tree	*Paulownia tomentosa*	Fragrant blue blooms	4
Flowering dogwood	*Cornus florida*	Pure white blooms	5
Golden rain tree	*Koelreuteria elegans*	Yellow flowers	4
Holywood (Lignum vitae)	*Guaiacum sanctum*	Purple/blue blooms	3
Jacaranda	*Jacaranda mimosifolia*	Blue flowers	4
Japanese snowbell tree	*Styrax japonicus*	Fragrant white blooms	4
Jerusalem thorn	*Parkinsonia aculeata*	Yellow flowers	5
Kwanzan cherry	*Prunus serrulata*	Vibrant pink blooms	5 – 7, varies
Okame cherry	*Prunus* 'Okame'	Gorgeous pink blooms	5 – 7, varies
Oklahoma redbud	*Cercis reniformis* 'Oklahoma'	Bright pink blooms	4
Pacific crabapple	*Malus fusca*	Spring bloom with late-summer red or orange fruit	3 – 4, varies

Common Name (Cultivar)	Botanical/Scientific Name	Colour Notes	OPALS Ranking
Portia tree (Milo)	*Hibiscus populneus*	Yellow flowers resemble those of the hibiscus plant	3
Queen's crape myrtle	*Lagerstroemia speciosa*	Intense lavender-pink flowers	5
Red osier dogwood	*Cornus sericea*	Flat clusters of small white flowers, with white berries in the fall	5
Santa rosa (Japanese plum tree)	*Prunus salicina*	White blossoms give way to ripe plums	3
Silky oak tree	*Grevillea robusta*	Gold (yellow-orange colour flowers)	5
Sweetbay magnolia	*Magnolia virginiana*	Showy white flowers	4 – 6, varies
Tree of gold	*Tabebuia caraiba*	Yellow flowers	5
Tulip tree (Yellow poplar)	*Liriodendron tulipifera*	Gold foliage with full yellow blooms	3

Legend:
According to OPALS ranking: 1 = low and 10 = high, very allergenic

Palms and Palm Equivalent Plants

What are you adding to your garden in the spring? We tend to think of palm trees only in tropical climates. Cold hardy palms will survive winter planting, as long as it's going to be warm for at least six months. They need soil temperatures preferably above 18°C (65°F) for new root growth. Otherwise, it will take the palm longer to establish itself, leaving it susceptible to secondary problems. In the Southern climates, soil warmth is less of a concern, allowing palms to be planted year-round. Regardless, you will want to ensure there's an available and adequate water supply.

Depending on the length of time and depth of a hard freeze (cold freeze), wind speed and ambient humidity, even a cold hardy palm tree can sustain destructive damage. Palm trees sheltered by other trees and shrubs may fare better than those palms fully exposed to the full brunt of winter cold. During a severe cold snap, you can protect your cold hardy palm by wrapping the trunk with a protective cover.

All palms require different levels of sun or shade. It's best to check before you expend time and energy planting in a less than an ideal location. As with any tree, they may be small now but, given time, when exposed to sun, rain, and the right conditions and depending on the species, they will grow tall and wide. This calls for a careful placement to avoid overcrowding and creating deeply shaded areas that make growing other plants difficult.

Common hardy species are ready to plant in the ground without acclimating (putting them in partial shade for an adjustment period). Less common species that may have been grown in greenhouses can experience some shock if immediately planted from the nursery to ground. If you live in a tropical climate, the acclimating process is less of a concern.

Did you know that palms have reasonably small roots compared to most trees? They don't grow a real tap root or have roots that branch out or get very thick like a tree. As the palm ages, it produces numerous roots that act as anchors and feeders to sustain the growing plant. Most palm species are perfectly content to live in smaller spaces (clay pots and containers). I would suggest leaving the root-bound root ball intact for this very reason. Palm roots don't like to be handled or disturbed.

You will want to dig a hole nearly the exact size and shape of the root ball. To make this task easier, a post hole digger would be preferable. Depending on the palm's size, when planting a large palm, you may want to add gravel, sand or other similar matter at the bottom of the hole to a 30 – 60 centimetres (1 – 2 feet) depth before adding back fill. This will prevent the palm's roots from drowning in poor drainage soils.

Palms require water right after planting to make the soil evenly moist. Care needs to be taken not to drown the roots. Water the newly planted palm frequently for a good six months as the plant establishes itself. If you have a clay soil, overwatering can cause the palm to drown. Large-trunked palms have a natural water reserve in them and can tolerate some drying before requiring water.

Palm roots are not ready to be fertilized for up to six months. Doing so could cause the inactive roots to burn. I suggest you speak with the expert staff at your local garden centre/nursery to discuss the fertilizer options best suited for your plant choice.

Here are some different palm species that are suitable for more Southern climates. Some are also cold hardy and will tolerate a wide variety of soil and weather conditions. Although the red abyssinian banana is not considered a palm, I have included the tropical plant in the chart for its spectacular showing in the garden.

The red leaf looks hand painted and spans up to 3 metres (10 feet) long. Depending on your plant zone, the height ranges from 2.4 – 5.4 metres (8 – 18 feet).

Common Name (Cultivar)	Botanical/Scientific Name	OPALS Ranking
Bamboo palm	Chamaedorea spp.	f = 1, m = 7
Bismarck palm	Bismarckia nobilis	f = 1, m = 7
Brittle thatch palm	Thrinax morrisii	2
Buccaneer palm	Pseudophoenix sargentii	5
Butterfly palm	Chrysalidocarpus lutescens	f = 1, m = 8
Cabbage palm	Sabal palmetto	5
Cardboard plant	Zamia furfuracea	f = 1, m = 6
Carpentaria palm	Carpentaria acuminate	6
Chinese fan palm	Livistona chinensis	1
Date palm	Phoenix dactylifera	f = 1, m = 9
Florida thatch palm	Thrinax radiata	2
Florida arrowroot	Zamia floridana	f = 1, m = 6
Formosa palm	Arenga engleri	3
Lady palm	Rhapis excelsa	f = 1, m = 6
Paurotis palm	Acoelorrhaphe wrightii	1
Red abyssinian banana	Ensete maurelii 'Red Abyssinian Banana'	2
Scrub palmetto	Sabal etonia	5
Silver palm	Coccothrinax argentata	1
California fan palm	Washingtonia filifera	3

Legend:

m = male; f = female plants

According to OPALS ranking: 1 = low and 10 = high, very allergenic

Here are some palms considered cold hardy to include for gardens in somewhat marginal climates. Windmill palms and Mediterranean fan palms are known to receive snowfall in their native habitats.

Common Name (Cultivar)	Botanical/Scientific Name	OPALS Ranking
Dwarf palmento	*Saval minor*	5
Mediterranean fan palm (European)	*Chamaerops humilis*	f = 1, m = 8
Mexican fan palm	*Washingtonia robusta*	3
Needle palm	*Rhapidophyllum hystrix*	5
Palmetto palm (Bermuda)	*Sabal spp.*	5
Parlour palm	*Chamaedorea spp.*	f = 1, m = 7
Pindo palm	*Butia capitata*	4
Sago palm	*Cycas revoluta*	f = 1, m = 6
Windmill palm	*Trachycarpus fortunei*	f = 1, m = 7

Legend:

m = male; f = female plants

According to OPALS ranking: 1 = low and 10 = high, very allergenic

Hummingbirds in Florida

There are about 16 different species of hummingbirds found in the United States. Over 11 species have been recorded in Florida. Native and most common in Florida is the ruby-throated hummingbird (*Archilochus colubris*). Migrating males are usually the first to arrive in early to mid-March and usually depart by the end of October. Females follow within two weeks. Some may stay in South Florida year-round, while most winter in Mexico and Central America.

Although we are focusing on attracting hummingbirds to Florida, seasonal movements of hummingbirds are also observed in Canada, Mexico, Central America and other US states.

To be successful in attracting hummingbirds to your garden, you must plant for them. Nesting hummingbirds need nectar from March to September. Your garden should have numerous nectar plants with tubular flowers, which hold large amounts of nectar at their base.

Here are some plantings to try in your gardens to attract hummingbirds.

Common Name (Cultivar)	Botanical/ Scientific Name	Plant Description	OPALS Ranking
Butterfly bush	*Buddleia davidii*	Summer blooming fragrant shrub or small tree in varieties of lilac, pink or white blossoms	3
Cigar plant	*Crossandra ignea*	Shrub blooms all winter if the temperature doesn't go below freezing	2
Coral honeysuckle	*Lonicera sempervirens*	Vine covering a trellis or fence will provide hummingbirds with a good source of nectar	5 – 6, varies
Cross vine	*Bignonia capreolata*	Showy flowers of the tall climbing vine are in shades of yellow and orange	5
Scarlet bush (Texas firebush)	*Hamelia patens*	Florida native shrub, grown from cuttings or from seeds	2
Flowering maple	*Abutilon spp.*	This isn't a "true" maple but related to the hibiscus family, cotton and okra. Non-native and frost sensitive.	3
Shrimp plant	*Justicia brandegeana*	Flowering shrub produces drooping yellow or reddish flowers that look like large shrimps	1
Trumpet vine	*Campsis radicans*	Blooms early in the spring with brilliant red and orange flowers	5

Legend:

m = male; f = female plants

According to OPALS ranking: 1 = low and 10 = high, very allergenic

SEVENTEEN
PRUNING 101

Pruning in the Garden

Pruning of shrubs, trees and evergreens is an essential part of gardening. When each plant type is correctly pruned, the gardener will be rewarded with superior appearance, vigour and healthy blooms. Don't be intimidated by the very thought of pruning. Proficiency of pruning plants just takes some time, experience and the right tools.

Common pruning tools include:

1. Handheld pruning shears (secateurs) for cutting stems up to 13 millimetres (.5 inch) in diameter.

2. Hedge shears or electric hedge trimmers used for trimming of formal hedges when a neat edge of foliage is the goal. Tool can be used to shape hedges and pyramidal evergreens.

3. Lopping shears for cutting through stems up to 39 millimetres (1.5 inches) in diameter.

4. Pruning saw used for larger branches.

Take the time to select the appropriate tool for the job. You don't want to damage the plant further by crushing the bark or making jagged cuts. Your goal is to remove dead, damaged and diseased branches to help your plant flourish. In addition, you will want to prune for aesthetic reasons to keep plant sizes manageable.

All gardening tools need care to keep their edges sharp and clean. To sharpen the edge, put a bit of oil (WD-40® or silicone lubricant) on the blade. Then with a handheld whetstone, file the blade at a 20-degree

angle. You can also use a file or a motorized sharpener. Care needs to be taken, and wearing work gloves and safety glasses are safe preventative aids. If you prefer, look for a professional sharpening service in your area. A professional can advise if the blade edge is beyond repair and the tool needs replacing.

PRUNING EVERGREENS

Evergreens, like fir and pine trees, need little trimming or pruning. When you do prune, your goal is to help evergreens keep their shape and to remove damaged branches. Most evergreens are best pruned in early spring while in the dormant stage, or when semi-dormant in mid-summer. New growth is referred to as "candles" due to the candle-like shape of the branch tips. When you cut back the candles halfway, done before the needles unfold, it will help keep the plant more compact. Depending on your zone and weather, candling occurs between late March and mid-May. I do caution not to prune once the needles have fully opened, as this may result in a misshapen plant. Most evergreens are unable to replace their growing tips.

The pruning of ornamental vines can be a problem for gardeners, often resulting in poor outcomes. The vines that are not "thinned-out" or not pruned become matted and heavy. Old and neglected vines damaged by the wind or a rainstorm, often pulled from their supports, should be cut back, and the weak and dead wood removed. The new shoots should be trained accordingly. You may need to tie vines to the structure with waxed garden string or twine.

Shrub pruning should be carefully considered. In general, most pruning is done once a year. But we have to separate this into two categories: spring flowering species and those that flower in summer and fall. The best rule of thumb is to prune immediately after flowering. When you prune spring flowering species too early, you prevent flowering. It's very important to think about how much pruning each shrub can take without damaging the specific species. If you have questions, contact the gardening experts at your local garden centre/nursery.

In the chart, you will find common shrubs with the ideal time to prune for optimum growth.

Shrub Name	Jan	Feb	Mar	Apr	May	Jun	Jul	Aug	Sep	Oct	Nov	Dec
Abelia	P	P	–	–	–	–	–	–	–	–	–	P
Allspice (Sweet shrub)	–	–	–	–	–	–	P	P	–	–	–	–
Azalea	–	–	–	–	P	P	P	–	–	–	–	–
Barberry	–	–	–	–	P	P	P	–	–	–	–	–
Bayberry	–	–	P	P	P	P	P	–	–	–	–	–
Beauty bush (Kolkwitzia)	–	–	–	–	–	P	P	P	–	–	–	–
Butterfly bush	P	P	P	–	–	–	–	–	–	–	P	P
Chaste tree	P	P	P	–	–	–	–	–	–	–	–	–
Deutzia	–	–	–	–	–	P	P	–	–	–	–	–
Flowering almond	–	–	–	–	–	P	P	P	–	–	–	–
Forsythia	–	–	–	–	P	P	P	–	–	–	–	–

Shrub Name	Jan	Feb	Mar	Apr	May	Jun	Jul	Aug	Sep	Oct	Nov	Dec
Hibiscus (Rose of Sharon)	P	P	P	–	–	–	–	–	–	–	–	–
Honeysuckle	–	–	–	–	P	P	P	–	–	–	–	–
Hydrangea	P	P	P	–	–	–	–	–	–	–	P	P
Kerria	–	–	–	–	–	P	P	–	–	–	–	–
Leucothoe	–	–	–	–	–	P	P	–	–	–	–	–
Lilac	–	–	–	–	–	P	P	–	–	–	–	–
Mock orange	–	–	–	–	–	P	P	–	–	–	–	–
Mohonia (Grapeholly)	–	–	–	–	P	P	P	–	–	–	–	–
Mountain laurel (Kalmia)	–	–	–	–	–	P	P	–	–	–	–	–
Pieris	–	–	–	–	P	P	P	–	–	–	–	–
Quince	–	–	–	P	P	P	P	–	–	–	–	–
Rhododendron	–	–	–	–	–	P	P	–	–	–	–	–
Smoke bush	P	P	–	–	–	–	–	–	–	–	–	–
Spirea (spring blooming)	–	–	–	–	P	P	–	–	–	–	–	–
Spirea (summer blooming)	P	P	–	–	–	–	–	–	–	–	–	–
Sweet pepperbush (Summersweet)	P	P	P	–	–	–	–	–	–	–	P	P
Viburnum	–	–	–	–	P	P	P	–	–	–	–	–

Shrub Name	Jan	Feb	Mar	Apr	May	Jun	Jul	Aug	Sep	Oct	Nov	Dec
Weigela	–	–	–	–	P	P	P	–	–	–	–	–

Shrubs grown for foliage should be pruned in the spring. The following chart details when to prune and the amount of pruning needed for common shrubs in the garden.

Common Name (Cultivar)	Botanical/ Scientific Name	Time of Pruning	Amount of Pruning
Allegheny serviceberry	*Amelanchier laevis*	Before flowering	Remove dead wood only
Butterfly bush	*Buddleja davidii*	Before growth start in early spring	Remove all two-year-old wood to ground level and prune back one-year growth each spring
Cotoneaster	*Cotoneaster spp.*	Prune lightly before and after blooming	Remove three-year-old wood to ground level
Currant	*Ribes spp.*	Prune after flowering	Remove dead wood only, cut out three-year-old wood to the ground
Deutzia	*Deutzia x lemoinei*	Prune after flowering	Remove dead wood only
Flowering almond	*Prunus glandulosa*	After flowering	Remove dead wood only
Forsythia	*Forsythia spp.*	Prune lightly before and after flowering	Prune dead wood only
Honeysuckle	*Lonicera tatarica*	Prune lightly before and after flowering	Remove dead wood only

Common Name (Cultivar)	Botanical/ Scientific Name	Time of Pruning	Amount of Pruning
Lilac	*Syringa species*	Prune after flowering	Remove seedpods after they have formed
Mock orange	*Philadelphus*	Prune after flowering	Prune three-year-old wood to the ground
Privet	*Ligustrum vulgare*	Prune before growth starts in early spring	Remove dead wood only
Spirea (early flowering)	*Spirea*	After flowering	Prune three-year-old wood to the ground
Spirea (late flowering)	*Spirea*	Before growth starts in spring	Remove all two-year-old wood, and prune back one-year-old wood
Weigela	*Weigela florida*	Prune lightly before and after blooming	Remove three-year-old branches to the ground

The following shrubs should be pruned before new growth begins: alpine currant, barberry, burning bush, dogwood, honeysuckle, ninebark, purple leaf sandcherry, smoke bush and sumac.

PRUNING ROSES

There are three reasons for pruning roses. When a rose's flower has faded, you will want to dead-head the spent blossom. General spring pruning keeps the plant healthy by removing damaged, dead or diseased wood. Prepare the plant for the winter months. In Chapter 18 – Winter Protection, I discuss how to prepare your rose bush for the winter months.

To dead-head, you need to cut the spent flower stem back to an outward-facing bud above a five-leaflet or seven-leaflet leaf. If the plant is weak or small, you may decide not to cut off as much of the plant. In this case, you may opt to prune only the old flower. To lessen the likelihood of rose disease, such as botrytis, dead-heading is suggested as a viable solution.

Most gardeners find pruning rose bushes very confusing, especially when considering how to best care for each species of English roses, hybrid teas, old garden (heirloom) roses, once-blooming roses and shrub roses. General pruning principles apply to all roses, but for certain classes of roses, there are differences you should know. For example, hybrid tea roses require the most severe pruning for optimum bloom and health. Climbing roses may need a few seasons to establish before pruning is necessary. To best understand the pruning needs for your particular rose bush, ask a gardening expert at your local garden centre/nursery.

The goal of spring pruning is to create an open-centred plant that allows for air and light to easily penetrate the plant.

Here are some basic pruning fundamentals for roses:

- Always use clean, sharp equipment — garden clippers, loppers or pruning shears.
- Cut at a 45-degree angle about .5 centimetres (1/4 inch) above the outward-facing bud. Slant the cut away from the bud.
- Look for dead or dying canes (stems) and remove them by pruning. Canes will appear shrivelled, dark brown or black.
- If you notice your rose bush has a tendency to be invaded by cane borers, seal the end of the cuts to prevent entry by the insect. White glue will work well.
- It's best to remove all thin, weak canes that are smaller than a pencil in diameter for the health of the plant.

PRUNING TREES

There's an important reason why I am not covering this topic — personal safety. We have all heard of too many people seriously injured or killed because they weren't trained or certified in tree pruning. Not only do you have to worry about personal accidents, but there is a possibility of property damage from falling tree limbs. Your life is too important to your loved ones. For this reason, I strongly recommend you hire a certified arborist for this job.

EIGHTEEN
WINTER PROTECTION

Winter Protection in Your Garden

In general, winter environments that are cold, icy and snowy create a problem for many plants, shrubs and trees. The change of temperature accelerates this dilemma. Winter damage is often caused by a combination of low temperatures, the wind, reduced soil moisture and sunlight.

There are steps we can take in the fall to protect our tender plants before snow blankets our gardens.

PERENNIALS

Most hardy perennials can sleep peacefully through the winter if covered under a thick blanket of snow. Others benefit from some special care to prepare for the winter season. Where soil drains poorly, winter wet can rot the crown of even the hardiest of perennials. After the first frost, cut the stems of the perennial plant about 5 centimetres (2 inches) above the base. Never cut a perennial to the ground while the foliage is still green, as the plant is still working on reserving energy for spring growth.

Apply a blanket of 5 – 10 centimetres (2 – 4 inches) of mulch (compost, peat moss or straw) in and around the base of your plants to stabilize the soil temperature from freezing and thawing. When the soil freezes, thaws and freezes again, it will eventually damage roots and may heave your plants out of the soil. Mulch doesn't keep your plant warm through the winter; rather, it helps the soil keep a constant temperature and retains moisture needed for the plant. I don't recommend using leaves for mulch, as they tend to mat and prevent air reaching the soil, resulting in damage to the plants.

SHRUBS AND TREES

Very low temperatures can damage shrubs and trees. To protect deciduous shrubs from winter damage, wrap them with garden ties or medium-weight string. If a heavy, wet snowfall or ice storm occurs, the plant is secure from having branches broken and maybe even the trunk snapping from the added icy weight. Narrow evergreens can be protected using plastic netting, like a stocking, over the shrub. Burlap makes for an inexpensive protective wrap for shrubs and evergreens.

Young and newly planted trees, especially thin-barked trees, such as crabapple, cherry, maple, honey locust and plum, are most susceptible to sunscald. Sunscald is the freezing of bark following high temperatures in the winter season, resulting in permanently visible bark damage. Older trees are less subject to sunscald because of the thicker bark. To prevent sunscald, wrap the trunk with commercial tree wrap or plastic tree guards. The wrap reflects the sun and keeps the bark at a more constant temperature. Newly planted trees should be wrapped for at least two winters and thin-barked species up to five winters or more.

If planting conifers in the fall, water well to help them prepare for the winter. It's advisable to protect or shield the shrub or tree from the winter sun by providing a burlap covering that is not in contact with the plant's branches. Using wooden support stakes, just outside of the canopy or branch ends, wrap the tree canopy with the burlap and staple the material to the stakes. This protection should be removed in early spring or when frost is no longer a factor in the soil. This can be done for the first two winters to help reduce the incidence of "winter browning" when the soil is frozen, and abnormally high temperatures open the needles, causing them to lose moisture and dry out. This can lead to the death of the tree.

The winter discoloration of evergreens occurs for four reasons:

1. Winter sun and wind result in foliage water loss (transpiration), while the roots are in the frozen soil but unable to replace the lost water. The result is the browning and desiccation of the plant tissue.

2. Sunny days during the winter warm the plant above the normal temperature, which in turn warms the cell structure of the plant. When the sun is rapidly in decline and temperatures drop fast, this injures the foliage and results in killing the plant.

3. During cold winter days, the chlorophyll in the foliage is destroyed and doesn't come back when the temperatures are below -2°C (28°F). You will notice the bleaching of the foliage.

4. Foliar damage caused by winter browning or burn often occurs on the south, southwest and windward sides of the plant. Your evergreen will show brown to red, dry foliage or needles.

> **Gardening Tip...**
>
> *Winter browning can affect all evergreens. Keep evergreens properly watered throughout the growing season into the fall.*

WINTER DAMAGE TO PLANTS

Plants suffering from frozen roots may wilt and slowly decline once spring resumes. As we just discussed, the addition of mulch helps to insulate most soils to prevent soil temperatures from falling below freezing.

In the winter, rodents, such as mice and rabbits, often damage young trees by feeding on the tree's bark. This usually happens when there's a prolonged, heavy snow cover, and available food sources are scarce. Mice tend to feed near the ground level, whereas rabbits are fond of the bark above the snow. Trees can be protected using hardware cloth or screen wire around the trunk of the tree. You can protect shrubs and trees with a repellent. The repellent is not a poison; rather, it simply has an undesirable taste or fragrance. Bait blocks (poison) are hazardous to humans, pets and wildlife.

What about deer damage? Plants can be painted or sprayed with a repellent, or heavy bags with repellent can be placed near the plant. But… if deer are hungry, there's little you can do. They will eat anything palatable.

Salt damage from the de-icing of walkways and driveways can cause winter injury and dieback. The salt runoff will not only injure the roots when it's absorbed by the plant but also result in damage to the foliage. Using burlap barriers around planting areas that tend to be salted will help to protect plants from the salt spray.

SPRING INSPECTION

Once the warming temperatures of spring start, it's time to inspect your plants for winter damage. It's possible that only a few branches on certain sections of the plant will show some damage.

Look for splitting or cracked branches or stems on plants, shrubs and trees. To determine if the plant has died over the winter months, you can use the fingernail test to scratch a tiny portion of the bark. If you reveal green tissue, the plant's stem is alive. Brown tissue under the scratch mark means that the portion of the stem is dead. Look at the leaf and flower buds. Do you see plump buds beginning to swell? If the buds look withered, limp, or with brown or black colour, pull one bud off. When you squeeze it between your thumb and finger, if it flakes, unfortunately, it's dead. Keep looking for signs of live buds on the stem.

Fertilize damaged plants in early spring, and water well. Prune the dead branches back to the "living" tissue after the last frost. In most cases, new growth will start to develop from that junction and will replace the newly pruned section. If possible, wait until late May to do any pruning to injured plants unless you are completely confident that the branches or stems are dead. Some plants may be slower than normal to bud out if there's an unusually harsh winter.

"Kindness is like snow. It beautifies everything it covers." — *Kahlil Gibran, poet*

Winter Protection of Roses

The "queen of the garden," our roses, are susceptible to winter damage and must be protected because of temperature fluctuations. While many of the roses that are classified as old garden (heirloom) roses are extremely tolerant to the cold, others such as hybrid teas, grandifloras and floribundas need special attention. Winter damage can be light with only the cane's tips dying back, or severe with the killing of the plant to the ground level.

While there are many methods to provide winter protection, the importance is to protect and keep the rose bush uniformly cold and frozen all winter long to prevent thawing and freezing effects. Before adding any protection, make sure that the rose bush is in the dormant stage. This is when the plant has stopped growing and is conserving its energy for the season and weather changes. Roses don't hibernate; rather, when temperatures lower, their metabolism slows. You don't want to cover the rose bush too early, as moisture trapped by mounding materials can cause fungal problems and rotting canes. Wait until a hard frost has caused most of the rose's leaves to fall.

The most common way to protect rose bushes is to pile or hill-up a combination of composted manure around the plant's base and slightly over the plant to a depth of about 25 – 30 centimetres (10 – 12 inches). After you have covered the soil, add some mulch, straw or even fir boughs for additional winter coverage.

Rose cones or collars are a good alternative and hold the soil in place. You may use Styrofoam rose cones also, but remember not to place them around the rose bush too early as this will cause heat to build up inside. If there are no ventilation holes in the rose cone, cut four, 5 centimetre (2 inch) holes in the top and bottom to prevent heat concentration on the inside during warm winter days. Mound soil around the crown. When using a rose collar, fill the collar with composted manure at the base of the rose bush.

Uncover roses after the threat of a hard freeze has passed in early spring. Look for nightly temperatures that are consistently over 0°C (32°F) before doing this task. Don't be concerned if a normal frost occurs after you have uncovered the rose bush.

When checking the health of the rose bush after the winter months, check if the branches are the colour of wood. If they are then the rose bush is most likely dead. If you scrape back a section of the branch, look for green inside. This indicates the rose bush is living and transporting nutrients. Rose bushes are deciduous, and in the winter will appear dead, so don't rush pulling from the garden bed. Another test is to bend a branch to test its flexibility. If the branch is stiff and perhaps cracks when gently bent, the rose bush is dead. Knowing what to look for will help you time a visit to the local garden centre/nursery to replace winter damaged plants.

Gardening Tip...

Roses that can withstand winter conditions are considered to be "hardy." Tender roses don't do well below 0°C (32°F), but proper winter protection can help them come through unscathed. It's better to overprotect rather than underprotect your delicate beauties.

NINETEEN
WILDLIFE INFORMATION

Keep Wildlife at Bay

As more homes are being built, displacing local wildlife from their natural surroundings, it can become a problem when they cohabitate in neighbourhoods around your town or city. Or perhaps your home is in a rural setting and wildlife is a common sight every day.

When the weather brings pleasant temperatures, we seem to gravitate to the cottage, camping site or favourite area in the great outdoors. While you're away, wildlife may take up residence in your vegetable patch or flower garden, decimating all your hard work. It's time for action.

We may take many things for granted, but for the new or experienced outdoor person, a few rules about deer and garden plantings should be kept in mind. If using "natural" pest control plants, space them about 1 metre (3 feet) among your other plants.

- Deer love nibbling on many ornamental shrubs. If deer are common to your area, this is important to know so that you aren't surprised when the shrub's leaves and berries disappear.

- The best way to keep deer away is to use ground covers, such as bugleweed, lily of the valley, pachysandra and vinca.

- Angel's trumpet, morning glories and poppies (annual and perennial plants) are mostly ignored by deer.

- Deer don't like alliums, chives and ornamental onions. These belong to the onion family, and deer don't like the taste.

- Deer don't like the following herbs: basil, catnip, lavender, lemon balm, mint (various), rosemary and thyme, to mention a few.

- Plants such as astilbe, daisies, ferns, foxglove, geranium, marigolds and verbena are fine in the garden, and deer won't eat them.

- Avoid planting cardinal flower, daylilies, hostas, phlox and roses as they will offer a tempting feast to deer.

- You may need to build a substantial fence to ensure deer stay out of the garden.

- Plastic netting, floating row covers or chicken wire can be added to protect small beds or specific plants or crops.

- Mothballs placed around the garden area work great for deterring deer and squirrels. Keep in mind that mothballs are poisonous to cats and dogs.

- Blood meal sprinkled around vegetable plants, such as corn, melons and tomatoes, will keep the deer at bay.

- Mice and squirrels hate the smell of peppermint. Put a few drops of peppermint oil on a bunch of cotton balls, and place in various areas of the garden. You may want to consider adding peppermint plants to your garden.

- Use chicken wire or garden stakes (upside down) in your containers to prevent squirrels from being able to dig.

Gardening Tip...

Is it a deer in my garden? Well, a deer has cloven hooves, and the clear print in the soft garden soil will resemble two half circles, often with just the tips pushed in on firmer ground.

Deer- and Rabbit-Discouraging Plants

Everyone who gardens at one time or another has problems with animals who like to devour plants, shrubs or trees, whenever possible. Most animals don't like fuzzy or thorny foliage. There are plants that rabbits or deer don't like, but... when deer are hungry, they will eat ANYTHING!

Here's a list of common plants that should help to keep deer and rabbits from feasting in your garden.

Animal	Common Name (Cultivar)	Botanical/Scientific Name	OPALS Ranking
Deer avoid	Ageratum	*Ageratum spp.*	2
	Black-eyed Susan	*Rudbeckia hirta*	5
	Columbine	*Aguilegia spp.*	1
	Foxglove	*Digitalis purpurea*	2
	Garden verbena	*Verbena x hybrida*	3
	Iris	*Iris*	1 – 4, varies
	Purple coneflower	*Echinacea purpurea*	5
	Tuberous begonia	*Begonia tuberousa*	2
	Wood sage (Salvia)	*Salvia x sylvestris*	1 – 4, varies
Rabbits avoid	Columbine	*Aguilegia*	1
	Foxglove	*Digitalis purpurea*	2
	Garden verbena	*Verbena x hybrida*	3
	Gladiolas	*Gladiolas*	3
	Hollyhocks	*Alcea rosea*	2 – 3, varies
	Impatiens	*Impatiens*	1
	Iris	*Iris*	1 – 4, varies
	Marigold	*Tagetes*	3 – 6, varies
	Morning glories	*Ipomoea*	4
	Snapdragon	*Antirrhinum majus*	1
	Sweet pea	*Lathyrus odoratus*	3

Legend:

According to OPALS ranking: 1 = low and 10 = high, very allergenic

TWENTY

HONEY "DO" CALENDAR

Garden Calendar

JANUARY

- Happy Gardening New Year!

- Try forcing the branches of the following species indoors: apple, cornelian cherry, flowering peach, flowering pear and forsythia (keep allergies in mind when doing so).

- Start a garden diary.

- Try sprouting grapefruit seeds.

- Save wood ashes to use in your garden in spring.

- Feed the birds now; they will eat insects later.

- Time to sow your geranium seeds indoors to be ready for spring planting.

- Check for insects under the leaves of your houseplants.

- Start sprouting alfalfa and other seeds for salads.

- Check websites for allergy-friendly plant information.

- Purchase an indoor plant for a friend — the gift that cleans the air.
- Check for browning edges of houseplant leaves as this indicates low humidity.

Gardening Notes (Honey "Do" List):	Supplies:	Dates to Remember:

FEBRUARY

- Try forcing the branches of the following species indoors: Japanese quince, magnolia and spicebush (keep allergies in mind when doing so).
- Prune the grapes and ornamental trees in the garden.
- Carefully remove snow from the evergreens.
- Time to take cuttings from your geraniums (that you brought in during the fall) and grow some plants for a nursing home or fundraiser.
- Plan your nutritious vegetable garden – vitamins A and C are cancer preventers.
- Tuberous begonias can be started indoors.
- Try to grow avocado or kiwi plants from seed.
- Re-pot any pot-bound foliage houseplants.
- Check ferns for scale insects.

- Start new houseplants from cuttings.

- Plan for late flowering perennials.

- Read about horticultural therapy; it might come in handy one day: www.chta.ca.

- Check for browning edges of houseplant leaves as this indicates low humidity.

- For children and grandchildren with allergies/asthma, check the website: http://healthyschoolyards.org, and inform your family, friends and school boards.

Gardening Notes (Honey "Do" List):	Supplies:	Dates to Remember:

MARCH

- Try forcing the branches of the following species indoors: flowering dogwood, flowering cherry, Japanese maple and lilac (keep allergies in mind when doing so).

- Finish pruning your fruit trees.

- Check the garden centre/nursery or seed catalogue for new ideas.

- It's time to separate African violets with multiple crowns.

- On warm days, check your perennials and press the soil back around plants that have heaved.

- Shady yard? Design a "shady" perennial garden.

- Maple or birch trees shouldn't be pruned now — wait until summer.

- Join a garden club or volunteer to share your knowledge at a school, as gardening with children is very rewarding.

- Keep compaction in mind by avoiding working in overly wet soil.

- Fertilize your indoor plants.

- Compost your garden waste.

- Volunteer to garden with people in nursing homes or senior residences.

- Read to people with low vision about gardening and plant a garden with textures and scents in mind.

Gardening Notes (Honey "Do" List):	Supplies:	Dates to Remember:

APRIL

- The following shrub species can be forced indoors: currant and mock orange.

- Prune winter damaged twigs on shrubs and trees.

- Start your dahlia tubers indoors.

- When the leaves are 1 centimetre (3/8 inch) high, spray to control iris borer.

- Vegetable gardens should get six hours of sun, so consider the location when planting a new plot.

- When soil is workable, prepare the vegetable garden.

- Remember Arbor Day; plant an allergy-friendly tree or donate one to an organization of your choice.

- Apply pre-emergence crabgrass killer after the forsythia blooms, but before the lilac blooms.

- Daylilies have very few pests and make a good addition to your garden.

- If the weather co-operates, you can take away the mulch from your perennials.

- Divide perennials as needed.

- Compost your garden waste.

- Before using clay pots, soak them in water for 24 hours so that they don't drain all the moisture from your potting soil.

- To keep cats out of your garden, plant rue, wormwood, alliums or marigolds.

- Hostas like shaded areas, and the end of April is the perfect time to transfer to another area in the garden.

Gardening Notes (Honey "Do" List):   Supplies: Dates to Remember:

_____   _____   _____

_____   _____   _____

_____   _____   _____

_____   _____   _____

_____   _____   _____

_____   _____   _____

- Plant your annuals and gladiolus bulbs.

- Fertilize your lawn, shrubs and trees.

- Prune and plant winter-hardy explorer or shrub roses.

- Prune spring-flowering shrubs immediately after blooming.

- Re-seed your "sparse" (winter kill) looking lawn.

- Plant dill for pickles and salads.

- Sow peas, radishes and sweet pea seeds in your garden.

- Use organic products against black rot on roses.

- Check your plants daily to prevent future problems.

- Weather permitting, take your houseplants outside to a shaded area.

- Plant allergy-friendly plants for persons with allergies/asthma.

- Plant garlic between roses to repel aphids.

- Keep ants away from the house by planting mint in containers.

- Consider adding parsley, tarragon, onion or garlic to your food for flavour.

- Attract hummingbirds to your garden by growing cleome, columbine, delphinium, foxglove, morning glory, nasturtium and salvia.

- To prevent cutworm damage, place a stiff cardboard collar (toilet paper holder) around the stem of your pepper and tomato plants.

- Lure butterflies to your garden by growing ageratum, cosmos, gaillardia, marigold, phlox, sweet William, verbena and zinnia.

- Add dried coffee grinds between carrots, onions and radishes when seeding outdoors to prevent worms from eating your plants.

- Keep moles away by placing fresh cat litter into their tunnels.

- Mites might be present on conifers, so do an inspection.

- Compost your garden waste.

- Seed or plant "cancer preventer" (high in vitamins A and C) vegetables.

Gardening Notes (Honey "Do" List):	Supplies:	Dates to Remember:
_____	_____	_____
_____	_____	_____
_____	_____	_____
_____	_____	_____
_____	_____	_____
_____	_____	_____

JUNE

- Remove old (spent) flowers to prolong the blooming phase.

- Trim the new growth of your evergreens to maintain shape.

- Pull weeds to reduce the stress on your grass and plants.

- Earthworms work well in your garden and composter, so don't remove them.

- Fertilize your hanging flower baskets every two weeks.

- Hunt for fireflies after sunset with the grandchildren.

- Plan for successive plantings of vegetables.

- Water your garden or lawn thoroughly and deeply once a week or let nature do the job.

- To kill weeds between interlocking stones, pour boiling water between them.

- Spot spray (organic means) the weeds in your lawn.

- Hang some lavender to keep flies out of the kitchen.
- Never place cut flowers near fresh fruit as the gases released from the fruit will damage the flowers.
- At the cottage, apply a few drops of vinegar on your hot stove to keep the flies away.
- Chapped hands? Rub your hands with sheep's wool.
- Watch for earwigs around the house foundation and in damp places, such as basements.
- Remove faded flowers on rhododendrons.
- Compost your garden waste.
- Prune cedar hedges carefully at the end of this month.

Gardening Notes (Honey "Do" List):	Supplies:	Dates to Remember:

JULY

- Save your back by bending your knees when lifting.
- Tall plants should be staked to support the stems.
- Pinch petunias to promote bushy growth.
- Prune your climbing roses after they bloom.
- Seed carrots, beans, beets and lettuce for a fall crop.

- To get rid of pesky fruit flies in the kitchen, take a small glass and fill with apple cider vinegar and a few drops of lemon dish soap.

- Check your lawn for lawn insects (chinch bugs).

- When the onion foliage folds, the bulb is full-grown.

- Side-dress flowers and vegetables with granular organic fertilizer.

- Remove the seedpods from perennials and shrubs.

- Be careful with grass trimmers around shrubs and trees.

- Compost your garden waste.

- Mid-to-late July, start grub control for your lawn.

Gardening Notes (Honey "Do" List):	Supplies:	Dates to Remember:

AUGUST

- Seed or sod your new lawn at the end of the month.

- Prune raspberry canes back to ground level after they fruit.

- Harvest your herbs around noontime for drying to avoid excess moisture.

- Ensure foliage is dry when you pick beans.

- Dry rose petals for sachets for sweet smelling cupboards or dresser drawers.

- Cut and dry everlasting flowers for winter enjoyment.

- Apply raw honey or a sliced clove of garlic to a cut or scratch.

- Take cuttings from impatiens for winter houseplants.

- Plan and plant a perennial section of your garden.

- Always remove old flowers from annuals and perennials.

- Harvest peppers at any time this month.

- Check your lawn for grubs and take action.

- Compost your garden waste.

- Transplant and divide peonies and phlox.

Gardening Notes (Honey "Do" List):	Supplies:	Dates to Remember:
_____	_____	_____
_____	_____	_____
_____	_____	_____
_____	_____	_____
_____	_____	_____
_____	_____	_____

SEPTEMBER

- Green tomatoes will ripen in a paper bag or wrapped in newspaper.

- Return your houseplants indoors (see the month of May).

- Divide and replant your daylilies.

- Plant some garlic cloves in your vegetable garden for next spring.

- Newly planted trees need staking to support them during the blustery winter months.

- Plant peonies in your garden for spring bloom.

- Plant spring flowering bulbs.

- Take geranium cuttings to over-winter inside.

- Fertilize your lawn one last time before winter sets in.

- Plan for an indoor herb garden.

- Compost your garden waste.

- Sow chives and parsley for indoor growing.

Gardening Notes (Honey "Do" List):   Supplies: Dates to Remember:

_____   _____   _____

_____   _____   _____

_____   _____   _____

_____   _____   _____

_____   _____   _____

_____   _____   _____

OCTOBER

- Clean and store your garden tools and equipment, and sharpen any clippers or shears for use next spring.

- Check your houseplants for insects.

- Water shrubs and trees before the ground freezes.

- Trim back any tall grass to discourage snow mould.

- Rake leaves and compost them, or put with yard waste for municipal removal.

- Have your soil tested to determine if you need to add organic matter.

- Place houseplants on pebble trays to increase the humidity in the house.

- Dig up and store summer flowering bulbs.

- Plant bulbs in pots for forcing indoors, such as crocus, daffodils, hyacinth and tulips.

- Cover perennials with mulch.

- Compost your garden waste.

- Place your fertilizers in a dry, safe place away from a child's reach in the garden shed or garage.

Gardening Notes (Honey "Do" List):	Supplies:	Dates to Remember:

NOVEMBER

- Use fresh or dried herbs that you grew yourself for cooking.

- Wrap tree trunks against mice damage and sunscald.

- Mound rose bushes with "good" garden soil after the first frost.

- You can burn 220 calories per hour by raking leaves.

- Prepare snow removal equipment and schedule maintenance if needed.

- Birdhouses might need cleaning to get rid of old nests and twigs.

- Reduce feeding your houseplants.

- Keep cut flowers in a cool place; they last longer.

- Pot paper white narcissus indoors for visual and sensory interest.

Gardening Notes (Honey "Do" List):   Supplies: Dates to Remember:

_____   _____   _____

_____   _____   _____

_____   _____   _____

_____   _____   _____

_____   _____   _____

_____   _____   _____

DECEMBER

- Check your stored bulbs for any decay or rot.

- Poinsettias don't like hot or cold drafts; plant is mildly toxic to pets if ingested (**High OPALS ranking**).

- Try growing a cactus garden indoors.

- Create some Christmas decorations from greenery and pine cones.

- Sprout seeds for salads.

- Yarrow increases the aroma and taste of all vegetables.

- Start amaryllis bulbs and paper whites indoors.

- Grow herbs in a sunny window for winter nutrient.

- Gardening books make for inspiring holiday gifts.

- Avoid walking on your lawn when grass blades are frozen.

- Support evergreen branches against snow damage.

- Keep bird feeders filled through the winter.

- Try cat litter, sand or sawdust instead of salt to melt snow and ice, and your plants and grass will thank you.

Gardening Notes (Honey "Do" List):	Supplies:	Dates to Remember:
_____	_____	_____
_____	_____	_____
_____	_____	_____
_____	_____	_____
_____	_____	_____
_____	_____	_____

Just a Thought...

Becoming a wise and skilled gardener may take time and experimentation, but for those of you who like a challenge, you will never be disappointed!

TWENTY-ONE
HONOURING VETERANS

Bravery Parks

Spurred on by the many international conflicts in which Canada and the United States are involved, I am inspired to create a park footprint to honour injured and fallen soldiers, as well as those who return safely to their homes. It's a tribute to their courage, bravery and dedication to freedom, also recognizing the sacrifices they have made to make this a better world for all of us. A Bravery Park™ can be created in any size village, town, city or municipality and takes only a fraction of the effort that these soldiers have undertaken.

There are four very important components to this project:

1. Honouring Canadian and United States soldiers — first and foremost. Nothing takes higher precedence than this. We honour those who put their country ahead of themselves. We show our recognition and appreciation of their service that sometimes results in the ultimate sacrifice. Some return home to face a life filled with even greater challenges, as they bear wounds that are not always visible to the human eye.

2. Assisting the millions of people with allergies/asthma in Canada and the United States to enjoy the parks by specifically planting allergy-friendly plants and trees (maple) is a secondary benefit.

3. The third benefit is that merely by planting trees, we are improving the environment as they sequester CO_2 from the atmosphere.

4. The *Veterans Gardening Guide* is specifically focused to encourage the healthy environment that our veterans and civilians deserve.

Visiting a Bravery Park will provide relaxation and a shaded recreational area for those who enjoy the outdoors and wish to remember the families of the brave men and women that have fought tirelessly for their country.

In Canada, maple trees have been specifically selected because they represent beauty and are our national emblem. The maple leaf is also shown on the Medal of Bravery that was established on May 1, 1972, and is awarded by the Governor-General of Canada.

The town of Orangeville, Ontario, is building a Bravery Park to honour hometown hero Cpl. Matthew McCully, who was killed in Afghanistan. The park will provide a place of thoughtful reflection for those who have served, their families, and those who are touched by the sacrifices of veterans. The project's goal is to rehabilitate and enlarge an existing park in need of repair.

Local sculptor Donna Pascoe, from Grand Valley, Ontario, has created a life-size statue (model) featuring a soldier in full gear, kneeling in front of two Afghan children, who are offering him a butterfly symbolizing peace, change and trust. Once bronzed, the statue will be featured in Orangeville's Bravery Park.

In Prince George, British Columbia, what was once known as Glenview Park was renamed the Cpl. Darren Fitzpatrick Bravery Park on July 13, 2011, after one of the city's most courageous citizens.

See my contact page to inquire how you can implement a Bravery Park in your area.

Gardening for Physically Challenged Veterans

Every year too many veterans are affected by physical and mental disabilities. These veterans like to garden, and we as a society have the opportunity to create something that the veterans can build upon. Planning a garden for veterans can be a very rewarding undertaking. But we have to keep costly mistakes to a minimum. Everybody should have some input into this project, such as family, medical care practitioners, recreational and administrative staff, and caregivers.

Let's not overlook the input from the veterans. The reason for planning a veteran's garden is to offer opportunities of physical exercise, along with mental and social stimulation. Take into consideration the age difference of the veterans when planning. Encouragement and commitment should be to:

- Improve the present environment
- Develop gardening as a hobby
- Retrain and strengthen motor and social skills

- Teach the basics of plant and animal life

- Encourage one-on-one conversations in a safe and pleasing indoor/outdoor environment

- Inspire visual gratitude of nature.

HOW TO ENSURE A GOOD GROWING SEASON

Here are a few steps to make gardening a positive experience for the veteran:

Watch for sun movement in conjunction of sun- or shade-loving plant material. A vegetable garden does well in a north-south direction.

1. Shelter veterans from too much sun and wind, as you want to create a comfortable outside environment.

2. Add security measures from the possibility of animal damage or human vandalism.

3. Purchase allergy-friendly plants that will attract birds, butterflies and hummingbirds.

4. Choose proper anti-slip paving stones.

5. Raised beds offer accessible gardening for those with physical conditions.

6. Situate bird-feeding stations to be observed from different sight lines.

7. Create a quiet, reflective area.

8. Provide water supply outlets, hose and tap lines within reach of the garden.

There's no greater joy than seeing new plants sprout from the soil and nature regenerating itself through the seasons. All veterans, regardless of their level of disability, can be filled with pride in participating in the garden.

Introduce veterans to the joys of the earth and watch their reactions as they get their hands dirty to help grow beautiful flowers and/or the bounty of homegrown vegetables.

Just a Thought...

Gardening knows no bounds!

Veterans Flower Garden Selection

This flowering pollinator garden selection was compiled to express our thanks to our highly respected veterans. Gardeners can start the plants from seed or purchase established plants from local garden centres/nurseries. The variety of plants in this selection will reward you with a vibrant bloom display from early spring until well into fall. To determine quantities to plant, consider the size of your garden. All plants listed will thrive in a sunny location.

Common Name (Cultivar)	Botanical/Scientific Name	Blooming Season	OPALS Ranking
Black-eyed Susan	*Rudbeckia hirta*	Late Summer to Fall	5
Blazing star	*Liatris spicata*	Summer	4
Butterfly weed	*Asclepias tuberosa*	Summer	3
Columbine	*Aquilegia canadensis*	Late Spring	1
Monarda bee balm	*Monarda didyma*	Summer	3
Purple coneflower	*Echinacea purpurea*	Summer	5
Sunflower	*Helianthus annuus*	Summer	1
Sweet William	*Dianthus barbatus*	Summer to Fall	1 – 3, varies
Yarrow	*Achillea millefolium*	Summer to Fall	4

Legend:

According to OPALS ranking: 1 = low and 10 = high, very allergenic

The following poppy selection is perfect to grow in containers or gardens. Consider growing from seed or direct seedling in the spring, after the last frost. Excellent drainage is necessary for poppies, as they tend to get root rot. Poppies can be planted in fertile soil in full sun, and can be grown in large containers on your balcony, deck or porch.

Common Name (Cultivar)	Botanical/ Scientific Name	Description	OPALS Ranking
Ladybird	*Papaver commutatum*	Displays fire engine red petals	3
Danish flag	*Papaver somniferum*	Bright red fringed flowers	3
Oriental choice mix	*Papaver orientale*	Provides a mixture of long stem, single blooming flowers	3
Corn	*Papaver rhoeas*	Brilliant red flowers seen in the fields in Europe	3
Iceland	*Papaver nudicaule*	Large pastel shades with crepe-paper-like petals	3

Legend:
According to OPALS ranking: 1 = low and 10 = high, very allergenic

Canada's 150th Anniversary

As I sit here writing the *Veterans Gardening Guide*, Canada is preparing to celebrate its 150th anniversary of Confederation on July 1, 2017. I immigrated to Canada in 1962 from Eibergen, the Netherlands, as a young lad of twenty-six. I am filled with much gratitude for my adopted country.

As a gift for our 150th anniversary, the Netherlands bred a special tulip. The flower was created to look like the Canadian maple leaf flag, and it's the official flower of Canada's anniversary.

It was the Canadian Forces who led the liberation of the Netherlands, and we even provided sanctuary for the Dutch royal family when their country was under Nazi occupation.

The first tulip beds in Ottawa, the national capital of Canada, were planted in 1945 when the Netherlands sent 100,000 tulip bulbs as a postwar gift of gratitude for the role that Canadian soldiers played in the liberation of the Netherlands. The year after that, they sent another 20,000 and promised to send another 10,000 bulbs every year. Since 1953, Canada has been hosting the largest tulip festival in the world to commemorate the event.

"The tulip represents gratitude and the long-standing friendship between Canada and the Netherlands. Blooming in the colours of Canada's flag, *Canada 150* tulips will bring both pride and joy to gardens and

communities from coast to coast to coast," said His Excellency Cees Kole, Ambassador of the Kingdom of the Netherlands.

There were numerous sesquicentennial birthday celebrations across Canada in 2017 with Canadians standing proudly to show off this remarkable country to the world.

Rules of Life

These are wise words from a veteran who is housebound. With his permission, he asked me to share with others.

I am a child of God

I am — I can — I will

I can do my best at all times, because God has given me four things

A body to work with

A mind to think with

A soul to love with

A will to choose with

I'll, with God's grace, always try to do what He wants me to do.

TEN SECOND REMINDERS

- ✓ Nothing is worth more than this day.
- ✓ If you go in the wrong direction, God allows U-turns.
- ✓ You'll never find peace of mind until you listen to your heart.
- ✓ Always choose tasteful words — you might have to eat them later.
- ✓ Our goal is to be good ancestors.

In Flanders Fields

This famous poem was composed at the battlefront on May 3, 1915, during the second battle of Ypres, Belgium, by Lieutenant Colonel John McCrae. The poem and the poppy are the recognized symbols of remembrance for Canadian and United States soldiers. In Canada, we celebrate Remembrance Day on November 11. The United States honour its soldiers on Memorial Day, held on the last Monday in May.

In Flanders fields the poppies blow
Between the crosses, row on row,
That mark our place; and in the sky
The larks, still bravely singing fly
Scarce heard amid the guns below.

We are the Dead. Short days ago
We lived, felt dawn, saw sunset glow,
Loved, and were loved, and now we lie
In Flanders fields.

Take up our quarrel with the foe:
To you from failing hands we throw
The torch; be yours to hold it high.
If ye break faith with us who die
We shall not sleep, though poppies grow
In Flanders fields.

TWENTY-TWO
HELPFUL VETERANS ORGANIZATIONS

Organizations

There are many organizations that do phenomenal work to support our honoured veterans and first responders. I am pleased to include a few of these that provide information, services and other supports.

Recently I found out about an organization that helps personnel of the military, EMS and firefighters deal with PTSD. It's called Mission Butterfly. It is another admirable organization devoted to helping our soldiers and frontline workers heal. Their non-drug healing techniques are very effective, and healing is measured in months not years.

Mission Butterfly
http://missionbutterfly.ca

Legion Magazine
www.legionmagazine.com
Offers a blend of military heritage and Canadian history with articles by noted historians and journalists.

National Service Dogs
www.nsd.on.ca
A Canadian organization offering service dogs for veterans and first responders who are suffering from PTSD in Ontario, British Columbia and Alberta.

Patriot PAWS

www.patriotpaws.org

Patriot PAWS trains and provides service dogs to American veterans with mobile disabilities and PTSD at no cost.

Telephone: 972-772-3282

Veterans Transition Network

https://vtncanada.org

A charity that delivers programs to struggling veterans across Canada, helping them lead healthy, productive lives reunited with those who care about them.

Wounded Warriors

http://woundedwarriors.ca

www.woundedwarriorproject.org

Delivers programs to veterans across the Canada and the United States.

TWENTY-THREE

LAST THOUGHTS

Glossary of Terms

ALLERGIES A medical condition that causes someone to become sick after eating, touching or breathing something (pollen) that is harmless to most people. When a person comes in contact with the allergen, their immune system's reaction can inflame the skin, sinuses, airways or digestive system.

ANNUAL Plants with a life cycle that last only one year. Annuals grow from seed, bloom, produce seeds and die in one growing season. The plants must be replanted each spring. Think of it as "yearly" planting that is needed by the gardener.

BROADLEAF Any deciduous tree (such as the maple or oak) or certain evergreen trees that have broad, flat leaves instead of needles. Most broadleaf trees shed their leaves in autumn.

CANOPY Refers to the above-ground portion of a plant, formed by the collection of individual plant crowns. Sometimes the term refers to the extent of the outer layer of leaves of an individual tree or group of trees. Common canopy trees include ashes, birches, crepe myrtles, horse chestnuts, maples, oaks and others.

CONIFER Mostly evergreen trees and shrubs having needle-shaped or scale-like leaves and include forms (such as pines) with true cones and others (such as yews) with an arillate fruit. Most coniferous trees keep their foliage year-round.

CROSS-REACTIVITY Some people with pollen allergies can develop respiratory symptoms after eating raw fresh fruit, vegetables, nuts or seeds that contain proteins cross-reactive to the pollens. For example, an individual with a birch pollen allergy may experience accelerated symptoms after eating certain trigger foods and then breathing in the pollen from a birch tree during allergy season.

CROWN The crown of a plant refers to the totality of an individual plant's above-ground parts, including stems, leaves and reproductive structures. The size and shape are also used to determine the overall health and vigour of the tree.

CULTIVAR Commonly refers to an assemblage of plants selected for desirable characteristics that are maintained during propagation (plant breeding). When the botanical (scientific) name for a particular plant cultivar is given, the part of the name that indicates the cultivar follows the genus and species names.

DECIDUOUS Are trees that drop their leaves for part of the year. Deciduous trees have broad, flat leaves. Common examples of deciduous trees include oak, maple and hickory.

DIOECIOUS Refers to plant reproduction, as in two separate plants (male and female) needed for reproduction. You must have one male plant growing in or around your landscape for the pollination of a fruit-bearing female plant. Examples of dioecious plants include juniper shrub, aspen tree, pussy willow bush, white ash tree, holly and yew shrubs.

DORMANT Also referred to as dormancy of a plant or bud, means the plant is alive but not actively growing. The outer leaves and above-ground foliage may die back. During dormancy, plants will stop growing and conserve the energy needed until better weather conditions are present. This process happens naturally during the climate and weather seasons within a respective plant zone.

EVERGREEN Is a plant (shrub, tree) that has green leaves throughout the year. They lose their leaves eventually, as the leaf grows old, dies and is replaced. Each species differs as to when needles drop, adding to the confusion. Evergreens don't lose their leaves all at once (in autumn/fall) as do deciduous trees.

HARDWOOD Trees with broad, flat leaves compared to coniferous or needled trees. They produce a fruit or nut, and generally go dormant in the winter. The most common species are beech, birch, cherry, hickory, magnolia and maple.

NATIVE PLANTS Grasses, flowers, trees and other plants that are indigenous to a given area in geologic time. This includes plants that have developed, occurred naturally or existed for many years in an area. Some native plants have adapted to environments with very harsh climates or exceptional soil conditions.

OPALS˚ Abbreviation of Ogren Plant Allergy Scale developed by Thomas Ogren to rank plants for the potential to cause allergy. More than 130 possible factors were used to develop the allergy rankings for plants. One set is positive and one is negative. Examples of negative criteria are tiny flowers, exerted stamens, small (less than 25 microns in diameter) size pollen grains and an extended bloom period. Examples of positive criteria are complete flowered, sticky, heavy pollen grains, presence of nectaries and a brief blooming period. Based on these factors, plants are ranked on a scale from 1 being less allergenic to 10 most allergenic. OPALS ranks each plant against other plants of the same type (e.g., perennials are ranked only against other perennials).

PERENNIAL Plants don't need to be replanted each year as they come back year after year. Think of it as "permanent" planting. There are some cases where the plant has reached maturity after two years and may needed replanting. Sometimes the plant dies over the winter due to extreme conditions or during the growing season from too much water or not enough, and less than ideal light conditions.

PLANT HARDINESS ZONES A geographically defined area in which a specific category of plant life is capable of growing, as defined by climatic conditions. First developed by the United States Department of Agriculture (USDA), the use of the zones has been adopted by other countries, including Canada and Europe. The plant hardiness zone for your area helps you understand how likely you will be to successfully grow a particular plant.

POISONOUS A plant that when touched or ingested in sufficient quantity can be harmful or fatal to the person. The most common problems associated with poisonous plants are from contact with the sap oil that may cause allergic skin reaction — poison ivy, poison oak and poison sumac.

POLLEN Is a fine to coarse powdery substance comprised of microscopic grains from the male part of a flower or a male cone. Typically, pollen is yellow in colour, but it can also be white, grey, green, brown, red and even purple. Male plants will produce pollen, although not year-round. Pollen is transported by the wind, insects or other animals. Pollen is a common trigger of seasonal allergies and asthma.

POLLINATOR Is an animal (primarily insect, but sometimes avian or mammalian) that moves pollen from the male anther of a flower to the female stigma of a flower. Only fertilized plants from the pollinator can make fruit/seeds, and without them the plants can't reproduce. Pollinators (bees, butterflies, hummingbirds) drink the sugary-sweet nectar that is made by flowers.

SOFTWOOD Trees have needles. Examples are cypress, hemlock, pine, redwood and spruce.

SPECIES (SPP.) There are over 300,000 known species of plants. Species also refers to part of a botanical/ scientific name. For example, there are over 12,000 species within the fern grouping or community.

TOXICITY The degree to which a substance (a toxin or poison) can harm an individual or animal. For example, a plant that when touched or ingested in sufficient quantity can be harmful (rash on contact) or fatal to a person.

VETERAN This is a person who has successfully undergone basic training and is honourably released from service. Men and women may serve their respective country in times of war and during peacekeeping missions. In Canada, a veteran is anyone who took an oath to be ordered to die for Canada — generally in the Forces or RCMP. Becoming a veteran takes place at the time of the oath. Veterans earn the greatest respect and honour for their contribution to represent their country.

Sources

During the writing of the *Veterans Gardening Guide*, a wide variety of helpful resources and research materials were used. It would be impossible to list all sources. I am filled with heartfelt gratitude to all those who share in my love of gardening with others, and take the time to write articles, blogs, books and conduct lectures.

Bailey, L.H. *Manual of Cultivated Plants.* New York: The Macmillan Company, 1924.

Blazek, Diane. Executive Director, National Gardening Bureau, who supplied gardening information.

Hewson, Mitchell L. *Horticulture as Therapy – A Practical Guide to Using Horticulture as a Therapeutic Tool.* Guelph: Greenmor Printing Company Limited, 1994.

Lawrence, Ed. *Gardening: Grief & Glory.* Tatlock Woods Publishing, Wakefield, QC, Canada. Printed and Bound in Canada by Friesens.

Ogren, Thomas L. *The Allergy-Fighting Garden*. Berkeley: Ten Speed Press, a division of Random House LLC, New York. 2015.

Rietman, Diny. Supplied gardening information and historic information.

Thornton, Robert John, and Bewick, Thomas. *A New Family Herbal: Or, Popular Account of the Natures and Properties of the Various Plants Used in Medicine, Diet, and the Arts.* Richard Taylor and Co, London, UK, 1810.

Killian, Sue C., with McMichael, John. *Allergy and Cross-Reactivity.* Xlibris Publishing. 2017.

WEBSITES

David Suzuki Foundation. *Can Indoor Plants Improve Air Quality?* 2016. http://davidsuzuki.org/ what-you-can-do/queen-of-green/faqs/cleaning/can-indoor-plants-improve-air-quality-inside-my-home.

Canadian Honey Council. http://honeycouncil.ca/bee_trivia.php.

Cole, Evan. Pollinator Partnership. San Francisco, USA. www.pollinator.org.

Go Botany – New England Wild Flower Society. https://gobotany.newenglandwild.org.

Government of Canada Agriculture and Agri-Food Canada. *Plant Hardiness Zones in Canada.* December 18, 2014. http://sis.agr.gc.ca/cansis/nsdb/climate/hardiness/index.html.

Government of Manitoba. Winter Sunscald and Frost Cracking: Tree Bark Damaged from Winter Bite. www.gov.mb.ca/agriculture/crops/plant-diseases/print,winter-sunscald-frost-cracking.html.

Johnny's Selected Seeds. Winslow, ME, USA. 2017. www.johnnyseeds.com.

Kids with Food Allergies, A Division of the Asthma and Allergy Foundation of America. www.kidswithfoodallergies.org/page/food-allergies-and-cross-reactivity.aspx.

Lady Bird Johnson Wildflower Centre. *Native Plants Listing*. 2017. www.wildflower.org/plants-main.

Landscape Ontario. *Pruning shrubs and evergreens.* https://landscapeontario.com/pruning-shrubs--evergreens.

Mayo Clinic. www.mayoclinic.org/diseases-conditions/allergies.

Missouri Botanical Garden. Plant Finder. www.missouribotanicalgarden.org.

National Food Institute, Technical University of Denmark. *Food Allery Information.* www.foodallergens.info/Facts/Pollen&Food/Which_Foods.html.

The National Capital Commission. *The official tulip for Canada's 150th anniversary is unveiled.* May 09, 2016. www.ncc-ccn.gc.ca/celebrate/tulips-capital/news/2016-05-09/official-tulip-canadas-150th-anniversary-unveiled.

United States Department of Agriculture. *USDA Plant Hardiness Zone Map.* 2012. http://planthardiness.ars.usda.gov/PHZMWeb.

West Coast Seeds. Organic seeds. www.westcoastseeds.com.

Wildflower Information.org. *Wildflower Plant Profiles.* 2006. http://wildflowerinformation.org.

William Dam Seeds. Untreated and organic seeds. www.damseeds.com.

PHOTOGRAPHS

Davy, Kelly. Photographer of Canada150 tulips.

Prakke, Gerard. Photographer of courtyard garden.

iStock by Getty Images. Stock photos. www.istockphoto.com.

Adobe Stock Images. stock.adobe.com.

ABOUT THE AUTHOR

Peter Prakke was born and educated in Eibergen (Gelderland), in the Netherlands. He graduated from agricultural college and since then has worked in agriculture, husbandry and horticulture in the Netherlands, England, Kuwait and Canada. Peter was the first manager of the State Experimental Farm of Kuwait in 1961. He has been a technical consultant on the Time/Life publication of the *Lawn & Garden* and turfgrass consultant at Queen's University, Kingston, Ontario.

Peter initiated the Plant a Tree — Create a Park© in Smiths Falls, Ontario, where he and his wife raised their two children. Most recently he created the Bravery Park™ to honour our veterans in allergy-friendly park settings.

A past recipient of Landscape Ontario's Garden Communicator Award, Peter organized horticultural therapy sessions with 6 – 10-year-old cancer patients at McMaster Children's Hospital in Hamilton, Ontario.

Author Photo: ©Larry Arnal

He works tirelessly to promote allergy-friendly schoolyards and writes for publications on the many gardening topics of importance to him. The *Veterans Gardening Guide* is his first book and is comprised of the many gardening articles he has written through the years.

You can contact Peter at one of the following websites that he is involved with: www.healthyschoolyards.org; www.safegardening.org; and www.veteransgardeningguide.com.

The information in the *Veterans Gardening Guide* is presented by the author based on his years of horticultural knowledge and experiences is not to be considered all-encompassing and is open to interpretation by the reader. The recommendations in the guide will not cure pollen-allergies, asthma or COPD but can greatly reduce many of the triggers and symptoms to make drug therapies more effective.

CPSIA information can be obtained
at www.ICGtesting.com
Printed in the USA
LVHW01s1109280418
575249LV00005B/7/P